THE BOOK OF
EXODUS

Also by Vivien Goldman

The Black Chord (with photographer David Corio)

Pearl's Delicious Jamaican Dishes: Recipes from Pearl Bell's Repertoire

Kid Creole and the Coconuts: Indiscreet

Bob Marley, Soul Rebel—Natural Mystic
(with photographer Adrian Boot)

The Making and Meaning of

Bob Marley and the Wailers'

Album of the Century

THE BOOK OF
EXODUS

VIVIEN GOLDMAN

Three Rivers Press
New York

Published in the United States by Three Rivers Press, an imprint of the
Crown Publishing Group, a division of Random House, Inc., New York.
www.crownpublishing.com

Three Rivers Press and the Tugboat design are registered trademarks
of Random House, Inc.

Library of Congress Cataloging-in-Publication Data

Goldman, Vivien.
The book of Exodus: the making and meaning of Bob Marley and the
Wailers' album of the century / Vivien Goldman.—1st ed.
Includes bibliographical references and index.
1. Marley, Bob—Criticism and interpretation. 2. Reggae music—
History and criticism. 3. Reggae musicians—United States—Biography.
I. Title: Exodus. II. Title.
ML420.M3313G65 2006
781.646092—dc22   2005030540

ISBN-13: 978-1-4000-5286-8
ISBN-10: 1-4000-5286-6

Design by Leonard Henderson

First Edition

CONTENTS

THE BOOK OF
EXODUS

Jah People keep on moving. The author on the road in Germany with the
Wailers during the *Exodus* tour, 1977. *Left to right*: Bob Marley, Family
Man Barrett, and the author.
© *Kate Simon*

Today we talk kind of personal, I don't come down on you really with blood and fire, earthquake and lightning, but you must know seh that within me all of that exists too.

—*Bob Marley to Vivien Goldman,*
April 30, 1977, Chelsea, London

OVERTURE

NATURAL MYSTIC

WINTER, 2004. NEW YORK'S LOWER EAST SIDE. I'm surprised to note my fingers tremble slightly as I pull the little yellow plastic box with its cheeky Mickey Mouse logo out of my underwear drawer and unclip the lid. The loony box itself evokes a distant day when cassettes were still quite new and appropriate storage scarce. The ferrous oxide tape within is black gold—audiocassettes of my 1970s interviews with Bob Marley, labeled in a hasty scrawl that suggests the reality of the time: if I'd missed something, I could always talk to Bob again. No chance of that now, except perhaps in dreams.

It seems like eons ago that I lent this box of cassettes to Island Records in London, which was interested in using them for a documentary. They were rejected thanks to the lousy audio, as my cassette players were always crummy. My fellow Bob Marley biographer and friend, Tim White, taped over his old Bob interviews; he needed the cassettes. We were all very broke then, just starting out. Someone at the documentary production company lost the originals and I only got back copies, rather annoyingly. It's actually miraculous I still have them, having changed countries various times on my own exodus and lost most other material things: the carved furniture my Jewish grandparents managed to take with them from Germany in the 1930s, with its carved roaring lion heads; the red brocade couch that new refugees crashed on as they arrived from whatever hell they'd fled in Germany; the albums from my wall of sound, with every Al Green and Johnny "Guitar" Watson album and everything by the Wailers, including a copy of *Burnin'* that Bob had autographed for me in his loopy, sloping scrawl: "Best of every love, Bob Marley." Yet somehow, I still have this Mickey Mouse box of memories. Over a quarter century has passed since I first transcribed these talks; I can only hope the tapes haven't rotted, and I wonder what they hold.

Finally listening to these interviews reminds me of the sad time in 1981 when Bob was making his last stand against the cancer at Dr. Josef Issels's clinic in Germany and I was sick in London with a very obscure disease called Bornholm's syndrome. From my mother's bedroom, where I was convalescing, I would phone Denise Mills, the lanky, languid, but efficient British blond assistant to Island Records' founder, Chris Blackwell, who was now in Germany as one of Bob's main liaisons to the world. "He's keeping it together," she would say in her reassuring, matter-of-fact way. I didn't know when Bob was sent home to Jamaica, making it only to Miami. On my first day back home, my friend arrived from Lagos with a gift from the revolutionary Nigerian musician Fela Anikulapo Kuti, who'd heard I was sick: a plastic film container full of their special "jam," a sticky dark brown paste of condensed marijuana. Warily, I took a small taste. Seconds later, I was propelled from my chair and began banging my head against my pride and joy—my wall full of albums—as a green bolt of lightning split me, seemingly rearranging my molecular structure. Soon after, though, I started to feel much better and even went out for dinner with my friend. When I opened the door to my room, every surface was covered with phone messages. While Fela's jam had been healing me, Bob had taken wing.

As I listen to the first tape, sitting in my Avenue C studio more than two decades later, I seem to feel that ganja jam tear through my gut again. Mixed with the splashes of children jumping into the Kingston Sheraton's swimming pool and the soft cocktail jazz of the hotel bar, tape warp makes Bob's laconic drawl hiccup horribly at regular intervals, rendering it unusable for a movie, perhaps, but sending me spinning back to 1976. Lurid bougainvillea bloomed behind the round white table with its blue and white awning, where I sat with Bob and a writer from *Ebony,* as Chris Blackwell and Bob's streetwise manager, Don Taylor, popped in and out of the conversation. My regular photographer and friend, Kate Simon, circled us, snapping away. Bob laughed a lot that day, particularly when Kate teased him for looking vexed. That was the radiant, award-winning cover shot of *Kaya,* the record that followed *Exodus.* The Wailers' art director, Neville Garrick, said he picked that shot because it was so rare to find one of Bob really laughing.

As the conversation progresses, it becomes clear that we're talking just days before the shooting: Bob talks about recording "Smile Jamaica," which was cut right before the attack, and says he'll play me the rhythm when I next come to visit him at his home, 56 Hope Road. It's hard to transcribe the interviews because Bob is so uncannily prophetic, it's disturbing. (Or awe-inspiring. It's just weird.) I shiver when he pauses, chuckles dryly, and says, "Jamaica great, mon, the greatest place on earth. But is a funny place, y'know. De people dem love you so much, they would kill you." At the time, of course, while all of us chatted by the swimming pool, I took it as a figure of speech; now I have to play it twice to believe my ears, as in some three days' time, that's exactly what would occur.

In examining the story of how the album *Exodus* was made, I discovered that this eighteen-month period—which had also been a significant time in my life—became more mysterious the closer I looked. On the most basic level, the given wisdom about the album's creation was that it had been written and recorded in London and that the songs had been written in a rush of creativity after the assassination attempt on Bob's life. But as I prodded both my interviewees' and my own memories of long-ago people and events, and pieced together the basic story of how *Exodus* was recorded, a very different picture emerged, one that was eloquent about Bob's creative process and his single-minded commitment to his music and message. The journey itself came to have its own bittersweet poignancy as, following in Bob's footsteps, I tracked the most turbulent period of his intense existence, when he moved like a fugitive between Kingston, London, Nassau, and Miami for two years from 1976 to 1978.

Sometimes information, repeated with only the smallest of changes, came in the dreams Bob confided to friends, who never forgot them—and in the sheer number of generally earthbound types I spoke to who had communicated with Bob in dreams. It is not impossible, but rather pointless, to try and examine Bob and his work without realistically acknowledging the existence of the spiritual and mystic dimension to his every day. In a literal, unpretentious way, Bob was quite consciously plugged into his prophetic skills. "Every song we sing come true, y'know," he said to me seriously in his Chelsea refuge in April 1977. Bob was looking at me closely as if to test my belief. "Some songs are too early, some happen immediately, but all of them happen. Burning and looting happen—so much time, it's a shame. The curfew. Yeeeeees, mon—everything happen."

The Kabbalists say that dreams constitute one-sixtieth of the potency of prophecy, and Bob's reality was well enmeshed with dream life. Several of his friends earnestly quote me dreams that he had vividly reenacted for them, and that he felt for a fact were a portent. They seemed as significant and real for him as a business contract and he relied on them for information.

But no matter how many people think that Bob Marley himself is the Natural Mystic he hymns on *Exodus*'s beguiling opening track, increasing celebrity and cash flow never insulated the man from human stress. In his own rich dream life, he confided to friends in 1976, he clearly foresaw trouble ahead.

Dreadlocked lawyer Diane Jobson, Bob's closest female friend, reminisces on a balcony in a chalet at Strawberry Hill, a hotel suspended high in the Blue Mountains above Kingston, where Bob took refuge after the attack. She is smartly dressed in a narrow knee-length skirt and funky, chunky high heels, her yards of dreadlocks wrapped in a silky scarf signifying over two decades of commitment to the Rastafarian ideals Bob taught her. As she speaks, lightning splits the sky and great booms of thunder crash round us, as if underlining the gravity of her recollections. Raindrops thud onto the balcony's canvas awning in an endless drumroll as she reenacts the dream Bob told her about, just before the invasion: " 'I had a vision last night, Diane, that Hope Road was full of gunmen in uniform shooting at me. But Jah just *my-st-ic-ally* make me skip the bullets.' " Her voice mimics Bob's own intonations; you could almost see the Skip dodge bullets as he would a soccer tackle, kicking the ball at a sharp angle and leaving a goalie in the dust, as I'd seen him do so many times in the yard of his Kingston house. Bob also told British reggae singer Delroy Washington of another dream set in the same place the shooting would occur. In it, a great shadow suddenly washed over a mango tree. The yard fell dark, as if someone had turned off the light switch, and Bob found himself shivering with fear.

Without wanting to further mythologize the man, it's a stone-cold fact that since leaving this planet, Bob Marley has become one of those mythic cultural figures who take up residence in the collective unconscious and flicker in the twilit mental movies of dreamers everywhere. He was a larger-than-life energy transmitter whose frequencies could fine-tune people's receivers on a mass level. In the days just after his passing, he was broadcasting on a very powerful frequency. I heard several stories from generally pragmatic people who'd all had their first psychic experiences triggered by Bob: very specific dreams—visions, even. I rarely dream, or remember them, anyway, and my first experience of dreamtime communication happened then, too, with Bob reassuring me, in the spirit of his song "Three Little Birds," not to worry 'bout a thing. More than one interviewee for this book had been jolted by dream encounters with Bob in which he acted as a kind of shamanic spirit guide, always appearing as a moral mentor, benignly reassuring and optimistic, or as a stern but caring father figure, firmly admonishing the dreamer to stick to what he or she knows is right and work hard. None of these everyday dreamers wanted their names used.

Call me shameless, because I'm going to brave telling you how, to my own amazement, when the going got hard in writing this book, I too had a dream. Bob, Wailers bass player Family Man Barrett, and I were in Bob's big bedroom in Knightsbridge, London's Oakley Street. As always, Fams was cheerily skanking round to reggae music blasting out of portable speakers he'd rigged up to his boom box, decorated with Rasta stickers of lions. We were all chuckling at something, and Bob said, "Come here. I want to give you a present."

From under the bed he pulled out a large trunk and flung back the lid. It was stacked high with two piles of papers. "Take something," Bob offered magnanimously. "I want you to have whatever you want." Hesitantly I studied the contents and pulled one out at random. It was a double-page spread of imagery, on heavy vellum. To the left was a massive head that radiated a universal antiquity, as if it would have been equally at home in ancient Bali or Zimbabwe. The original bright colors were now worn away to pockmarked bone. The face's broad forehead and stoic, seen-it-all wisdom, with its hint of defiant humor round the generous, sensuous lips, definitely suggested our profound joint ancestry, a common human root. The other, right-hand image seemed somehow to be a gypsy: a dangling girl, upside down, spinning from a sharp outcropping of land, suspended above what might have been a bottomless chasm, or possibly a conveniently located featherbed to drop onto. I showed Bob my selection. "Ya, mon, you tek that one," he said, and nodded approvingly. "That one is good."

And so, to write this book and attempt to plug into an ancestral knowledge we all have a right to, even then in my dream I knew I had to welcome letting go and allow myself to fall down, down, down, deep into the past.

Basing Street Studios, Ladbroke Grove, West London, February 1977

RINGS OF BLACK FABRIC BEAT like a heart in the center of the big speakers, pushing out a fat bass pulse through the studio's padded doors and out into the lounge, where a dramatic solo game of foosball was reaching a climax. In the black-and-white-linoleum-floored lounge area, with its coffee machine, Habitat couches, and rubber plants in plastic pots, a wiry Rasta in fatigues crouched intently over the table. A few other young Rastas, wearing khakis; red, green, and yellow knitted belts; and hats bulging with dreadlocks, stood and observed. Rapidly, the player's right elbow pulled back and up, and with an audible thwack, the tiny ball hurtled and rattled round the stiff plastic uni-legs of the competition, settling smartly into a goal. He shouted, *"Jah!"* and as if they'd scored a goal too, the youths chorused, *"Rastafari!"*

Inside the former church that housed a neutral-toned studio was a gathering of the West London division of the reggae family. Even the brown-carpeted walls of the split-level studio and the wide screen dividing the control room from the recording area gave the feel of being in a space capsule whose windows reveal another world. There was so much khaki worn that, at a glance, you'd have said it was an army. Some dreadlocked heads nodding in rhythm sported tall knitted hats or leather tams stuffed high with years of locks, a growth as impressive as that of baobab trees, while others sprouted baby twirls, signals of righteous intent.

Most musicians don't appreciate too many guests in the studio. But that and every night Basing Street hosted a party crowd of dreadlock devotees. Many of the notables of London's reggae scene loafed or listened, bred'ren such as Trevor Bow from Sons of Jah; Mikey "Dread" Campbell, manager of Ladbroke Grove's young lions, the band Aswad; Delroy Washington; representatives of the Twelve Tribes of Israel; and this writer, the features editor at *Sounds,* the punk rock weekly. At that time, I had known and worked with Bob for two years, first as his publicist for Island Records and then as the journalist most frequently assigned to report on the man and his music.

But everyone present at Basing Street Studios felt part of the Wailers' extended family, and we all watched intently as the high priests of this temple—executive producer Chris Blackwell, bandleader and bass player Family Man Barrett, producer Karl Pitterson, and tape ops Terry Barham and Dick Cuthell—moved as if participating in a sacred ritual. It's a quaint memory now, when mixes are made by one person hunched over a computer. But in the analog mid-1970s, a mix was a team sport, a many-hands-on affair that could look like a football pile-up but required immense concentration and sensitivity. Alert and focused, the sound men sat at the desk, ears straining, hands poised. Standing behind them, others darted forward to quickly change a sound, like back-line foosball men kicking the ball of the groove back to the main players. The flashing hands manipulated the music, slipping over and between one another across the mixing board with a coordination that was improvised but which looked like Alvin Ailey. Urgently pushing up and pulling down faders, twisting knobs with crisp control and a flying finger release technique, they made different instruments surge and drop dramatically. Forty fingers deftly sought the rhythm's pressure points and massaged a deep dynamic from the musicians' soulful lines. Finally, the bass and drums achieved a perfect positioning: a proud, commanding two-step that led the listener on an unknown but necessary path.

Relaxing back in his big chair at the desk, satisfied with the bass's primal thud, Blackwell said softly, "Hail the Skip."

The padded door swung heavily open, and someone called, "Come now."

Smiling his lopsided grin, the Dread at the foosball table straightened up and eagerly strode into the control room. Amid nods and approving greetings, Bob Marley—aka Robert Nesta Marley, Jah B, Robbie, the Tuff Gong, or the Skip—walked in like a winning warrior and accepted the acclaim quietly but without reserve. After all, he so nearly never made it to that blessed moment: hearing his hymn to reinvention, repatriation, and rebirth ring out from these top-range studio speakers in this hip West Indian enclave of London, surrounded by friends like family and by coworkers who gave him maximum respect.

So now Marley stood, a black survivor turned musical conqueror, in the capital city of the old colonizers who had once ruled his native island of Jamaica.

But as Marley's longtime bred'ren mused a quarter century later, leaning against a car outside the Miami recording studio where Bob's children Julian and Damian were recording, Jamaica was not really their island, nor was it Bob's. For sure, it was the beautiful, bountiful scrap of land where the winds of slavery and commerce had blown the sails of Bob's forefathers' ships. The lovely island was a designated breaking station for many slaves en route from Africa to America. They landed in Kingston, Jamaica, as if by happenstance—because there were many other colonies that would have found a use for stolen Africans. At home, the English kept their consciences at bay by keeping the slave trade offshore. So till it was stopped in 1837—a full twenty-nine years after it was actually banned—the sickness of the slave trade was the brutal way that the English, African, and Arab races met.

However random it may have been, it was rich, blood-drenched Jamaican soil that nurtured both Bob Marley and the lost souls who tried to kill him in his own home in 1976. It was a shattering realization, a level of betrayal different from any he'd experienced in a life that had already offered both opportunity and misadventure. A crime committed by people whose identities he now knew but still had to keep secret from almost everyone in this room, and from everyone he might meet. Because, right now, Bob Marley didn't know to what extent he was still a wanted, hunted man, watched by any number of entities, from the CIA to the warring downtown gangs of Kingston, themselves bloody puppets of bigger foreign interests. His very presence in London was under wraps. At that moment it seemed possible that he might never be able to return to live in Jamaica. One part of him yearned to be with his bred'ren, the footballer Allan "Skill" Cole and other Rastas who were exploring the *livity*, the way of living, in the eternal Rastafarian spiritual homeland, Ethiopia. The African land was to Rastas as Canaan was to the wandering Hebrews of the desert in the Book of Exodus. Following the dictum he'd also be singing soon in "Heathen," "He who fights and runs away / Lives to fight another day," Bob Marley was on his own exodus, destination unknown.

The producer looked at Bob. "Ready, Skip?"

Leaning in a corner of the hessian brown-carpeted walls, Marley knew that his movement had been guided to the right place. He nodded.

Broad-shouldered, bearded engineer Karl Pitterson unleashed the rhythm with a flourish and settled back. Topped with lyrics of gritty clarity, the stirring strut of the track marshaled many facets of Bob's present situation: his unexpected enforced exile, and that of his intimates; issues of trust and destiny. While speaking of the Rasta drive for repatriation to Africa, this tune is also a dynamic call to break out of whichever slavery you're in, your own special slavery, mental or physical, and seek your own Promised Land, wherever or whatever it may be. The song works on many levels. But clearly, based on the electrified reaction of those gathered at the studio that night, it functioned on the most basic and essential level of all. It felt natural to follow Bob's roared command on the chorus: *You gotta move!* The whole studio was dancing, stepping and skanking from the sofa to the stairs. In their wheely chairs, the high priests were grooving. Triumphant, Bob broke into his own step, locks flying like lightning, arms punching, stepping out of Babylon.

When the high of the chorus hit, Bob looked round and beamed to see that everyone was singing, like we'd always known the words: "Exodus! Movement of Jah people."

And on many levels, we all did.

At Hope Road before the Peace Concert, Bob wrestles with issues as old
as the Bible, 1978.
© *Dan Asher*

1

SEND US
ANOTHER BROTHER MOSES

"I WAS A STRANGER IN A STRANGE LAND," said Bob Marley to me softly. He quoted the biblical verse of Exodus 2:22 almost to himself, intimately, as if the verse had been a familiar friend during his London exile following the attempted assassination on his life that had happened three years before, just yards away.

The brand-new blond-wood studio we were sitting in for this interview for a 1979 cover story for the oldest British rock weekly, *Melody Maker,* indicated that Marley was at a height of his career, artistically and professionally. Personally, too—we could hear children shouting excitedly as they played outside his house at 56 Hope Road, Kingston. He was about to record *Survival,* the first album he would ever make in his own studio, and it had taken him more than three decades to get there. He had truly survived a dangerous passage, and now, looking back, it was Exodus's well-worn words that made sense of his experiences.

A chapter a day is the Rasta way, and Bob never went anywhere without his old King James Bible. Personalized with photos of Haile Selassie, it would lie open beside him, a ribbon marking the place, as he played his guitar by candlelight in whichever city he found himself. He had a way of isolating himself with the book, withdrawing from the other laughing musicians on the tour bus to ponder a particular passage, then challenging his bred'ren to debate it as vigorously as if they were playing soccer. Hurled into this unexpected journey, Exodus spoke to him now more than ever. Experiencing his own exile, accompanied by his old cohorts the Barrett brothers and Seeco, the grizzled Dread elder of the tribe, the ancestral narrative held a new meaning for Bob.

At the time it was recorded, Chris Blackwell recalls, it wasn't even a given that "Exodus" would actually be the album's title track. Only a very precise prophet could have determined that, a quarter century on, Bob and the Wailers' anthems would be hailed by *Time* magazine as the Album of the Century; but Bob knew its significance. In the coming years, the themes that summoned Bob—such as repatriation to a place where you really belong— would become increasingly relevant to us all as the global population grew more dislocated and deracinated, and as refugees in ever increasing numbers would surge around the world, often looking to the Americas and Europe in their restless search for a home. Fleeing for a better life, or simply a life, they all rise to the challenge Bob chants in "Exodus": "Are you satisfied with the life you're living?"

Exodus was a natural theme for Marley. Its issues of power, betrayal, hope, disillusionments, and the search for serenity were all uppermost in his mind as he created the *Exodus* album with the Wailers. The Book of Exodus deals with leaving familiar oppression behind, braving the unknown, and letting faith guide you to a brighter future. These ideas have increasing relevance as we are hit by a contemporary litany of troubles that can be read like the plagues at a Seder, the communal Passover meal at which, every spring for the last two thousand years, the escape from Egypt has been reenacted, sometimes at great peril, wherever there are Jews.

As each plague is named, you delicately dip a finger in your glass of wine and let a drop drip down for each disaster inflicted on the Egyptians. It's understood that the red wine symbolizes a drop of blood. Today's plagues, to which the ideas of Exodus very much apply, might read thus: wars; starvation; pestilences such as AIDS, malaria, and TB; genocide; ethnic cleansing; ecological collapse; greed; corruption; and disasters both natural and unnatural.

My intention in writing this book is to show the significance of Exodus both in Marley and the Wailers' musical canon and in the man's life. The light of the eternal themes of the Bible's Book of Exodus shines in the Wailers' work of that name, just as artists have reflected it throughout history. This work aims to show how the biblical narrative of the Hebrews' flight from Pharaoh, orchestrated by Moses in conjunction with God, interlinks with Marley's liberating message and the Rastas' dream of the African diaspora's return to the Motherland, inspired by their deity Haile Selassie.

Like the souls the Kabbalists describe as sparks of light, many artistic and cultural endeavors revolve around Exodus. By telling some of their stories, I hope to ignite those sparks into a steady flame that illuminates the universal meaning of both Exodus and the life and work of Bob Marley.

The narrative of the Hebrew Exodus from Egypt that comforted and strengthened Marley in his time of affliction is so graphic that it lends itself easily to a visual treatment. See the frames flash past: The organized slaughter of Hebrew male babies in the mean slave quarters, at Pharaoh's command. The Israelite baby bobbing in the basket on the river, hidden by reeds, watched from a distance by his concerned sister, Miriam. She leaves only when she's seen him discovered by Pharaoh's daughter. Once adopted, Moses the Hebrew foundling is thrust into a classic role-reversal situation—the slave turned ruler. Then comes the political awakening, when Moses sees an Israelite slave abused by an Egyptian, and slays the oppressor. Struggling to hide the heavy corpse out of town in the sand, he has to deal with the knowledge that he too can kill. Moses' rural retreat as a shepherd in Midian, and his first marriage, to Zipporah, the daughter of Jethro, who would become his mentor. The trippy encounter with a blazing bush that speaks for Hashem—it's all like something at a Burning Man festival. Afterward, anyone can see his intimate exposure to glory, burned right on his face; Moses never looks the same after being so close to the celestial fire. To hamper social ease further, Moses stammers and is hard to understand. He relies on his brother, Aaron, as his lieutenant.

Still, Moses has unbeatable access to God, and carries the whole road map to freedom in his head. An effective leader, he wheels, deals, and hustles his tribe out of four hundred years of familiar captivity, in the same quest for the Promised Land that Bob Marley sings about in *Exodus,* except that Bob calls his destination Africa, the land of his father, Jah Rastafari. Moses' tools include the plagues, which intensify from creepiness to cataclysm and whose grotesqueries, including insect swarms and infanticide, are still the stuff of horror flicks. There are the great Exodus set pieces that Cecil B. DeMille's Cinemascope movie *The Ten Commandments* visualized so vividly in 1956: the Red Sea rearing into froth-topped liquid cliffs, and the tables turning when the freed captives see their old slave drivers drown.

With Moses leading the great trek, there is much dissension in the ranks, as the Hebrews dissed their deity, Hashem, with raves around the golden calf, exactly the sort of pagan idolatry that the patriarch, Abraham's One God, had warned them about. With classic timing, the tribe unleashed their debauch while Moses was descending the mountain carrying the tablets with the Ten Commandments, the template for most of the world's belief systems. Making matters worse, Aaron had apparently colluded in their defection from the new idea of the One God. It was when Moses, mad as only he could be, confronted the wrongdoers and smashed the sacred stone tablets before them that the transgressors finally felt the sting of their betrayal. Perhaps a defining moment in the history of guilt, it was only then that the ragtag Hebrews became the Jewish people.

Then, Moses' final frustration, the last time God shows Moses his place. At his final face-to-face meeting with his Creator, Moses learns that he will not be allowed entry into Canaan, the Promised Land. He will have to find satisfaction in a glimpse from a mountaintop and the bittersweet realization that though he has hauled his tribe of fractious Hebrews out of slavery, Moses still won't get to taste that milk and honey he's been craving through forty years of false starts and wandering in the wilderness.

And the movement has never stopped. For refugees from Cambodia, Rwanda, Bosnia, all the world's dispossessed populations shifting and scuffling restlessly round alien territories in search of shelter, the Bible's Exodus suggests a possibility of finally finding a safe dwelling. In the trajectory of Moses' tale—the man who makes it all happen, but ultimately only gets to glimpse the home he'd dreamed of—we learn that even being part of the survival process can be a privilege, its own reward. For those in rage, turmoil, or despair, Exodus and its echoes in the Psalms offer a sense of a solution, or at least the encouragement of inspiration.

Moses' drastic reinvention as a reluctant, ambivalent leader demonstrates and represents all human potential for resurrection, change, and spiritual growth. The lessons Moses learned and delivered as the Ten Commandments serve as a fundamental moral yardstick for the dominant religious expressions that are collectively called Mosaic—Christianity, Islam, and Judaism.

The transformation implicit in the Exodus saga is reflected in our frontiers and cities. Both pleasure and conflict come from these new meshings and confrontations. Cultures collide and repel, or commingle and integrate, and new tribes take shape. Fresh strata of society shift, sift, and settle down as restlessly as grinding tectonic plates. Just when everything seems calm on the surface, communities seething with newness can suddenly convulse in a volcanic jolt of shock. That's when bombs blow and blood flows. But after the pain and rage, always, is the hope for a smoother tomorrow. It is a magnet, the hope embodied in Exodus's saga of a wandering tribe persistently following its faith to arrive at a place where it can live freely. And if you only get to glimpse the Promised Land from afar, isn't there some achievement in just having got that far, and having helped to bring about that change?

There is an exhilarating promise of emerging into a new and better life on the other side, but even the bravest can feel frightened at leaping off the sharp edge of their bad reality into the dense cloud of the unknown. Yet none of the potential downsides of leaving the life you know can ultimately deter children of Exodus. Not the threat of living outside the law as refugee or illegal immigrant, the loneliness and longing for family and the familiar, or the strong possibility of confronting new obstacles.

The word *exodus* is now routinely used to describe any mass departure, whether it's stars from a Hollywood agency, Israelis pulling out of Gaza, or New Orleans residents begging for a bus out of the Superdome to get somewhere, anywhere, away from the horror. Then, now, and always, Exodus suggests a grueling trek for survival.

Some follow the idea of Exodus but never even get to see their Promised Land from afar. Roasted in a truck left in the sun at a border, drowned as a homemade raft sinks, or shot just yards away from freedom, every fallen refugee who dies chasing freedom is an Exodus martyr.

Yet within every belief system that identifies with Exodus, including Jews, Christians, Muslims, and Rastas, the dominant narrative of Exodus has a profound subplot: that great forty-year trek through the wilderness can also be a journey within oneself.

The drama of Exodus has a special meaning and offers a seductive sense of wish fulfillment for Bob Marley, and indeed any socially conscious artist's primary constituency: the sufferers, the second-class citizens, denied a passport, whose movements or potential development are restricted; or anyone locked in a life-or-death struggle with a dictator, or just with a discouraging system.

By plugging into the ancestral sacred escape depicted in the Bible's Book of Exodus, Marley was well aware of participating in a pre-Christian tradition: using Exodus's dynamic saga of Moses leading the Israelite slaves' escape from Egypt as a shorthand, or template, for rebel music. Marley's *Exodus* has provoked reflection and an artistic response from all manner of artistic and political folk as well as religious people, and is a common thread linking seemingly very different lives. Enslaved Africans on the plantations of the American South turned to the story of Exodus and called on Moses to lead them in spirituals such as "Let My People Go." Modern-day refugees and rebels in the front-line states of southern Africa (especially Zimbabwe), in Nicaragua and Poland, in Palestine and Israel all turned to Marley to articulate their existence. When Marley himself turned to Exodus for the same reason, the world embraced him as never before.

All these Exodus avatars were tuning in to the same fundamental frequency—the inspirational idea of Moses and his ragtag crew of recently freed Israelites. In his song "Exodus," Bob Marley related that ancestral movement to the travels and travails of his own tribe, Jah People. They actually make it out of slavery and start life anew, in freedom, self-determined in their own place, led by Moses under the direction of their one deity. Also known as "Hashem," "He who was, is, and will be," and "the One whose name must not be uttered," the One God is exultantly hailed by Rastafarians as Jah!

Having been privileged to share Bob Marley and the Wailers' *Exodus* cycle in Kingston, London, and Europe, I originally wanted simply to tell the record's story in this book. But as I researched, I found that the social, political, cultural, and spiritual implications of the album went much further than could be conveyed in a conventional musical story. The Wailers' popularity had spread steadily beyond their original West Indian and student constituency since the band began in the early 1960s. But the vision, passion, and clarity of *Exodus,* and the band's adept absorption of new textures, rhythms, and technologies into its reggae, turned *Exodus* into a truly important artistic statement and a pivotal release that consolidated Bob Marley and the Wailers' career.

In an astonishing discussion with the Wailers' bass player, Family Man Barrett, he explained to me how specifically he and Bob had chosen to build a new link in a conceptual chain of creation as old as the Bible when they recorded their Rasta anthem, "Exodus." Discovering the connections between the members of the tribe of Exodus, from whatever century or country, and seeing their progress somehow refracted in Bob's and the Wailers' own experiences showed how often relationships and situations that seem specific and very much of their time are actually eternal.

Ironically, the immense publicity surrounding Bob's narrow escape from death, and the sensational media scrutiny over his romance with the Miss World of the time, Cindy Breakspeare, catapulted Marley from the entertainment pages to the front-page headlines in virtually every international publication. So in trying to silence the Tuff Gong, his enemies just turned up his volume.

The crucial sixteen months that began with the assassination attempt, spanned the band's exile and the making of their *Exodus* album, and culminated in the glorious optimism of the Peace Concert was one of the most significant times of Bob's life, and has never been sufficiently considered. My hope is to convey that brief period's intensity in this book. In that short time, just as his message was being universally seized like manna in the wilderness, the Rasta who did not believe in death was forced to consider anew the meaning of mortality.

Jamming for a journalist's microphone, Peter Tosh, Bunny Wailer, Rita Marley, and Bob Marley (seated l. to r.) help develop Jamaican music in 1960s Kingston.

Urbanimage.tv/Trax on Wax/Astley Chin

2

DON'T WORRY 'BOUT A THING

WHILE GOATS GRAZED AND FIRES BLAZED in the scrubby acres of downtown Kingston's no-man's-land, there was a moment when a visiting music journalist could partake of a fruit cocktail by the swimming pool of the Sheraton Hotel and see a galaxy of reggae stars parade across the hotel's quaint neo-Oriental bridge by a waterfall. Notorious for its rum punch, the outdoor bar by the pool was populated by hustling and dealing reggae stars in 1978: U Roy, I Roy, Burning Spear, Dennis Brown, Jimmy Cliff, Sly and Robbie, Jacob Miller and Inner Circle, Tappa Zukie, the Mighty Diamonds, Big Youth, and more. Sporting their most ranking (coolest) threads, Clarks shoes, slim-legged slacks worn with Italian argyle sweaters, and big-brimmed, jewel-colored felt hats, they all came to do the uptown hustle in neutral, cosmopolitan territory, less than ten miles from the political ghetto conflicts, but superficially, at least, a world away. The youthful independent sector of the British music industry, basically Richard Branson's Virgin Records and its former distributor and current rival, Chris Blackwell's Island, was competing to sign the front line of Jamaica's militant artists.

As a writer, then features editor, and resident reggae nut of a weekly British rock music rag called *Sounds* between 1975 and 1979, I was ludicrously lucky to have that swimming pool as my second home when the record industry was staggering into its affluent postadolescence, particularly as it was soon to be balanced by an even longer stay in the ghettoes of Trench Town and other parts of the capital. My first "lig," as music-biz jaunts were called, was in 1976 to cover Bunny Wailer's beautiful album *Blackheart Man,* his first solo release after leaving the Wailers. On frequent assignments over the next two years, I saw the Sheraton's poolside population change from the families of visiting businessmen and the odd intrepid tourist to the serious music industry schmoozers described above.

This sudden upswing in the Jamaican music industry was good news for me. I was on a mission to turn on the readers and convert the paper's "rockist" lads, who assumed the readers were all air-guitar heads just like them. If we could all just tune in to reggae's aspirational, informational words, its subtle, sinuous harmonies, and the pulverizing power of its great rhythm sections, I hoped, a more inclusionary and positive atmosphere might arise.

Of course, the improvement was due in no small part to the kudos Bob won for Eric Clapton's 1974 "I Shot the Sheriff" cover, and the band's own success with "Rastaman Vibration," which had even made an impact in America. The great public love for the live version of "No Woman, No Cry," from the Wailers' 1975 London Lyceum show, synchronized with British punks' enthusiasm for reggae, had made the music all the more commercial.

But there was another business backstory to this surge of interest in Jamaican music. Rather than feeling threatened, Island's Chris Blackwell appreciated the way another label, Virgin, was also investing in the island. Having competition made his patriotic love for Jamaican music a more valid global business and confirmed his commercial instincts. Virgin's interest in Jamaican music began as a personal campaign of one A&R man, a white South African political exile called D. A. "Jumbo" Vanrenen. "Virgin first got involved in 1974. Sales in Europe had been slow but suddenly our export division, Caroline Exports, was selling huge amounts of U Roy to the Nigerians, who were flush with oil money at the time," Vanrenen explains. "One Nigerian businessman actually came into the London office of Virgin's founder, Richard Branson, and opened an entire suitcase full of cash on his desk. Then a couple of years later, the Nigerian generals clamped down on imports and everything slowed down again."

But by that time, with Bob Marley as its figurehead, Jamaican music was officially a global pop genre. Writing for *Sounds* enabled me to track the whole process. My perspective was unusual, as my initiation into Jamaican music came in part from selling it to the press, as the reggae publicist for Island Records, promoting Bob Marley and the Wailers, Aswad, and the righteous rootsman Burning Spear. Right after the release of the Wailers' *Live!* in 1975, I left both Island and PR to write full time. The team I joined at *Sounds* was so aware of our underdog status compared to the big boys, *Melody Maker* and *New Musical Express,* that we had nothing to lose by throwing ourselves behind the new underground punk and reggae scenes. "Music is the message," our slogan said, with no hint of irony. The strategy worked and was pursued, and thus Jamaica became my second home.

For a reggae fan, the island was intoxicating in 1976. The scene was always right there. All the reggae icons still revered now were very visible at scenes such as music entrepreneurs Tommy and Valerie Cowan's office on Oxford Road, where musical legends regularly dropped by for juices and banana bread under the straw-shaded outdoor tables: Sly and Robbie, and any variety of trios, such as the Heptones, Abyssinians, or Mighty Diamonds. Memorably, Gregory Isaacs would roar right into the yard on his motorbike, looking "well hard" (hip) in his leather waistcoat and those popular welder's shades whose perforated side flaps hid your eyes, thus preserving the inscrutability so crucial to cool. In a navy blue tracksuit and militant black beret, the original Wailers singer, Peter Tosh, would yell as he practiced high-flying karate kicks in the car park. There were even rare urban sightings of Peter and Bob's old cohort, Bunny Wailer, rolling in from the bush in his dusty Range Rover. It was literally a small world, packed with talent, and as I became a convert to street dances in mountaintop villages and ghetto blocks, I was glad to become a reggae expert.

Many of the musicians helped with my immersion into Jamaica. With the *New Musical Express*'s Neil Spencer, I went to eat fried fish, dumplings, and boiled bananas at the home of the celebrated bass player Robbie Shakespeare. Before he moved uptown, the great Shakespeare's shack on Jaques Lane was as basic a wooden shelter as any other on the unpaved, unlit alley. The Wailers' bass player, Aston "Family Man" Barrett, escorted me and Kate Simon to Skateland to see local bands such as Jacob Miller's Inner Circle make the roller-skating rink shake with their thunderous bass. Lounging on a tree trunk jutting over the aqua Caribbean, Burning Spear reasoned about Rasta and rebellion on the beach at his Culture Yard at St. Ann's Bay, edged with rickety wooden fences. There were no tourists or film crews around. In the fields of Clarendon, while Joseph Hill of the group Culture was showing me how to split an aloe vera leaf to squeeze its sap as a natural shampoo, I remember a Dread shouting as he roared past on a big motorcycle and hurled a whole bale of ganja into the field for the musicians' pleasure, his long locks floating behind him like a flag as he zoomed past.

While brightly painted buses whizzed past inches away, I bought every single I could find on the Abyssinians' Clinch label, with its hand-drawn logo of brotherly clasped hands, at the harmony trio's own tiny kiosk situated bang in the middle of the lanes at the bus station. Pushing through the bustle of Coronation Market downtown, weaving through the shouting higglers (market tradeswomen) and squawking chickens, my heart would pound with excitement at getting to hear the Top Ten singles at the city's famous musical hub, Randy's Records. At the Channel One pressing plant, I saw old singles being melted down into a gluey black soup and then poured by hand, like pancake batter, onto an unwieldy presser to be reborn as a new single. In those days, the vinyl of Jamaican 45 records had bubbles that would make a stereo's needle skip even on a new tune, and people rolled spliffs in brown paper bread bags, as regular rolling papers were a luxury.

In retrospect, this previously unknown job description of reggae writer that I shared in London with writers like *Black Music*'s Carl Gayle, who pioneered journalistic patois, and *Black Echoes*'s Penny Reel, who channeled Damon Runyon, seems to have been miraculously well timed. The music of mid-1970s Jamaica hit a creative peak that the island has never topped. The sounds created in studios such as Studio One are still currency for twenty-first-century Jamaican superstars such as Shaggy, Sean Paul, and Beenie Man, who regularly reference that era in their dancehall music. Since Jamaicans are a wandering tribe, the island's many styles of pop have subsequently been absorbed and repurposed by the children of expats, including rappers Biggie Smalls, KRS-One, and Busta Rhymes. Reggae and its sister sound, dub, whence came the remix, and its successor, dancehall, went on to spawn new styles for decades to come, including American rap, British jungle, and Puerto Rico's reggaeton. But the spark was truly lit in that mo-

his youth. "You grow everything. You don't really have to kill yourself to get a place or have money, you can eat and bathe and make clothes and build your own house." He was always nostalgic for the comforting cluck of feeding chickens, his childhood chore that he evokes on "Who the Cap Fit." "Some nice rivers and trees . . . ," he said, a faraway look in his eyes, "and de country people inna Jamaica, dem true people. Real country people, a so dem stay, dem seh, 'Good mornin' ' and 'God bless you.' Town make people think away from their roots." Among these civil, God-fearing country folk, Bob was marked as special from birth. He read palms with uncanny accuracy, liked to entertain grown-ups by singing calypso, and absorbed gospel and spirituals in church. But even in that seemingly secure childhood, Bob experienced wrenching divisions.

Bob's father, Norval Marley, was a white Jamaican land surveyor who'd been disinherited because of what his family saw as the folly of his middle-aged marriage to Cedella Malcolm, a teenage bush girl. When Bob was six, Norval sent for Bob to join him in Kingston. But very soon, his father dropped Bob off at the house of an old lady and left him there to care for her. Cedella might have lost her son permanently had a friend visiting Kingston not seen the youth in the street and half remembered the address he'd given her. Cedella took the bus to town and tracked down her son, knocking on doors house by house. There was a joyous reunion, but Bob was left with a fear of abandonment and sensitivity to betrayal that lasted a lifetime. He never read palms again. The only times Bob got physically harsh was when he felt abused or betrayed, professionally or personally. Those feelings he could not abide.

But soon, it was Cedella who went to Kingston to try to make a future for them both. Cedella had forged a relationship with a local man named Thaddeus O'Riley in 1957, and was sharing his cramped quarters on First Street, a block away from the sea. Small, slight, and light, Bob stood out in his new ghetto area of Trench Town when he went to join her. In Jamaica, color consciousness is so encoded that it's a virtual rule that the fairer your complexion, the higher you live on the slope up to the Blue Mountains. Down in the sweltering yards with their open gutters, where the sea wind blows sweet relief through the tenements, pretty much everyone but Bob Marley was as dark as their African ancestors when they were disgorged from the slave ships onto the beach not far from Trench Town.

At first, as the outsider, Bob had to prove his position in the tenement yard hierarchy. Thaddeus had a son, nicknamed Bunny, who, friends recall, claimed the top-dog slot by virtue of seniority and genes. If a few kids had to share a bed, you could be sure it would be skinny little Bob who'd wind up sleeping on the floor.

But Bob was already accustomed to fending for himself as best he could. Any resentment he might have felt about his mother's inability to consistently provide a home for the two of them together was tempered by the love she showed, such as the way she brewed him drinks from herbs, preferably grown in her own garden, even if it was just a corner of a drab tenement yard. As she prepared food, Cedella would sing hymns in her low, soothing voice, and Bob loved to listen.

After Cedella and Thaddeus split, Cedella inherited a nearby apartment from an emigrating cousin, where Bob could stay with her. But according to her biography of her son, *Bob Marley: An Intimate Portrait by His Mother,* coauthored with the fine Jamaican writer Anthony Winkler, Thaddeus's violent behavior was a factor in Cedella's decision to move to Wilmington, Delaware, effectively abandoning Bob—again. Cedella told writer Stephen Davis that Bob was being harassed in the yard for having a white father, and she wanted to create a better environment for him.

Still, the end result was that Bob was on his own again. By then, though, he had his music, his bred'ren Bunny, and the other youths in the yard. They were intent on absorbing all the music they could get. Wily ghetto youths were almost unstoppable when they wanted to squeeze into a show to see visiting American artists such as Ben E. King and the Drifters, Mahalia Jackson, Fats Domino, or Curtis Mayfield and the Impressions. Bob had begun working as a welder, but after a spark got in his eye, he was keener than ever to drop the manual labor for music.

He was not alone. Trench Town was a musical environment, full of harmony trios refining their own special techniques. Progressive musicians Joe Higgs, of the Higgs and Wilson duo, and burru drummer Alvin "Seeco" Patterson would take the time to coach the youths and develop their talent. At night, after eating the food cooked over a lovingly tended open fire in the communal pot, the youths would take turns playing their community's old guitar, owned by Vincent "Tata" Forde, an elder of the community. Bob spent hours under the verandah of a corner of the yard, hunched over Tata's old guitar manual. He soon released his first singles with producer Leslie Kong, but brotherhood beckoned. Bunny realized that Bob was too good to waste, and they co-opted a tall, skinny guitarist called Peter McIntosh, or Tosh (born Winston Hubert McIntosh) for short, who was fond of wearing bobble hats and cool shades. Together they became the Wailers. In their earliest years and during Bob's absence in America, singers such as Junior Braithwaite, Beverly Kelso, and Cherry Smith also passed through the ranks. But Marley, Bunny, and Tosh were always the core trinity.

Not a great one for discussing his past or anything personal, in a rare moment Bob reminisced, "When we were starting out, we didn't play a lot of shows, just like Christmas and Easter morning. We'd be up there at the Carib Theatre [one of Kingston's main venues], but we was always the underground, always the rebels," and here he growled with satisfaction, "We come from *Trench Town*. So you'd hear about Byron Lee [the hugely popular middle-of-the-road bandleader] and all that society business, but we came from down so, named *Wailers,* from *Trench Town,*" he affirmed. "So we stay, and we're glad of it. You've got to be someone."

After Cedella left for America, Bob found shelter with his mentors, the musical hit maker Clement "Coxsone" Dodd of the Studio One label and Tata of the First Street yard. There he also learned about love, as he romanced a young backing singer who worked as a nurse, Rita Anderson. Through some stormy times, she was to be his companion and coworker, as well as his wife, for life. Bob was loyal in his partnerships. On his final recordings he was still dealing with many of his longtime crew, particularly the Barrett brothers, and he still had a relationship, if sometimes prickly, with those he'd moved away from, including Peter and Bunny.

THE BIGGEST REVOLUTION in Jamaican music came round the time that Dodd was scratching labels off his new R&B singles so no one at his dances would know what they were, thus maintaining his exclusive edge. The arrival of the transistor radio effected an almost greater transformation in musical consumption than the iPod fifty years later. Now you could sit under a tree in a tenement yard and hear what was grooving New Orleans or London. Prior to its innovation, music delivery systems were fairly static. Much of rural Jamaica only heard the radio at some public space such as the local rum bar, with its rented Bakelite "rediffusion box" placed on a high wooden shelf. To hear the latest sounds in the 1950s, teenagers clustered round the wooden booths at Stanley Motta's electrical store on King Street.

But with the same skill and imagination that somehow cobbled together decrepit cars with bullet holes in the window and gaps in the floor so they could zip through traffic, Jamaicans constructed sound systems to travel the island.

Sound systems were more than just entertainment. They were portable culture, the musical lifeblood of the island, circulating through towns and villages. Their towering speakers, like hand-painted wooden standing stones, required teams to transport and work. Commerce and excitement buzzed around sound system dances, much as they do around big sports events. Flamboyant eccentrics abounded among the great sound system men, most notably a tough but colorful ex-cop named Duke Reid and his Trojan sound, named after his trusty British Bedford Trojan van. Wearing a crown and draped in ermine, Reid was known to rev up the crowd by firing two pistols over their heads. Dodd, his main rival, was a gentler, cooler figure; "Sir Coxsone" was keen on pushing a jazzier, more melodic feel. One of Dodd's key protégés and talent scouts was an impish youth named Lee "Scratch" Perry, also nicknamed Little. A keen, quick talent spotter, it was Perry who insisted that Dodd sign a young Pocomania practitioner named Toots Hibbert and his trio, the Maytals. Hibbert started out with a high-energy stomp, "The Six and Seven Books of Moses," brimming with "heartical" revivalist energy. Along with tunes like Desmond Dekker's "Israelites" and the Melodians' "By the Rivers of Babylon," it's part of reggae's Exodus theme.

Between Duke Reid and other sounds, such as that of downtown favorite Prince Buster, wars would frequently break out. The main ringleader was Reid, the former cop who never lost contact with the thugs he used to arrest. His "dancehall crasher" goons would storm into a rival DJ's dance and terrorize the crowd, stabbing people or pelting them with rocks. The dancers would inevitably rush out and seek entertainment elsewhere—generally at an adjacent Duke Reid dance.

Still, sound systems were a laboratory for the music. Many of Jamaica's innovations began at the dance, notably the art of DJing, or toasting, freestyling over a record in a way that would give it another life and an extra spark from the personality of "toasters" such as King Stitt, U Roy, I Roy, and the inimitable Big Youth. Sound systems proved to be a significant unifying force in the Jamaican diaspora as well as an international industry. Jamaican "toasters" also begat the freestylers rocking the mike in the 1970s in Manhattan's "Rock Steady Park," many of whom came from Jamaican families.

All these innovations and the sheer strength of the musicians' talent made Jamaica into a musical crucible whose heat still scorches contemporary music.

The island's motto is "Out of many, one people," and the same principle applies to Jamaica's music. Every tribe that stayed on the island left something of its swing, and that starts with the original inhabitants, the indigenous Taino or Arawak Indians (whose language contributed the words *hammock* and *barbecue* to English). Apparently the Taino enjoyed the music of a violinlike instrument they made out of bamboo and reeds. So when the Irish overseers arrived with their fiddles, it was not a completely new technology on the island. Lurking in the soul of mento and other Jamaican musics, too, are those jigs and quadrilles. Captive musicians' "quadrille bands" played for their masters. But Jamaican country people loved the quadrille square dance, and the Wailers captured why in their catchy chorus "Ska quadrille," on "Rude Boy," a 1965 Studio One single.

Abiding faith is one reason why the drum survived, despite being banned in Jamaica, as it was in all the British colonies. Late at night on the plantations the captives would vanish into the bush to conduct their African worship ceremonies. At these literally taboo gatherings, ancestral belief systems were remolded as new generations replaced the old and Africa became a more distant memory. As they did in Cuba and Brazil, the ancient motherland spirits shifted their shape and were reborn, spawning multiple religions: Candomble in Brazil, Santería in Cuba, Vodoun in Haiti, Shango in Trinidad, and Pocomania Revival and Kumina in Jamaica. Rastas adopted the burru drumming style that descends from Ghana, as Jamaican master drummer Junior Wedderburn explains. Often described as a heartbeat, the distinctive burru Rasta Nyabinghi drum pattern literally mimics the pumping beat of a healthy heart; which is why, some say, classic Rasta-based reggae is one of the most satisfying genres of music. The taller repeater drum is usually covered with the skin of a female goat, which creates a higher pitch, while the lower bass funde, known as the thunder, is tuned more deeply and is traditionally made from the skin of a ram. Thus the essence of male and female meet mystically in the heartbeat drums of Jamaica.

The Africans who found themselves in Jamaica were already a muticultural crew, coming from as far down Africa's west coast as Angola. The captives might never have met in Africa, but united in their shackles, a pan-African community in exile took shape. Ibo and Yoruba people from Nigeria, Mandingos from Sierra Leone, and Coromantees from Ghana's Gold Coast all had to overcome language differences as they struggled to deal with their loss of liberty. The Coromantees became known as the toughest, often leading the island's frequent slave uprisings and breakouts. Escaped Coromantees founded the legendary Maroon tribe, so fierce that the British were forced to sign a treaty with them that ironically depended on the Africans capturing other escaped slaves and turning them over to the British authorities.

But wherever they were in the world, the displaced and scattered Africans retained certain elements of prayer. Worshippers reach for a transcendental union with the metaphysical world, and if they make a connection, become a vessel for mystical forces to manifest among humans. Once seized by the spirit, communicants may writhe and seem possessed of an abnormal energy and speak in tongues that sound like babble but could be a cosmic language. Their eyes may roll back in their head, and inside their skulls the believers see something far from the place of worship in which their physical body lies shaking. The Pocomania rituals may strike fear and even disgust or anger in the hearts of unbelievers, but every drop of fresh blood sprinkled in the corners of a new building for good luck, an everyday occurrence in Jamaica, represents an unbroken bond between far-flung African descendants.

In so-called polite white 1960s society, the African drum had no place. However, they were beating hard down among the tracts of shantytowns around West Kingston, crowded with an exodus of new arrivals from the country, all in search of the good times independence offered. Government censuses of the time indicated that right before independence, half of the island's unemployed were already crammed into Kingston. The restless, frustrated youths were ripe for the communal consciousness of Rasta and the nights-long grounation Nyabinghi drum and chant sessions that channeled Africa.

Coming from Nine Miles, Bob understood all these forms of devotion as innately as he did the hymns, gospel, and spirituals he occasionally sang in church. Like 1960s teenagers round the world, he dug the Beatles, who started releasing music around the same time as the Wailers, and American black music. But much of the island's generally accessible musical fare was bland. Before the Wailers and their independence generation came of age, the island establishment's musical mind-set was stuck in the colonial groove. The top-selling record, as Chris Blackwell recalls, was Hoffman's light operetta *The Student Prince*. Party music meant American soul, jazz, and R&B, or Trinidad's calypso, and Caribbean music was the gentle folk shuffle of mento, with its raunchy "Big Bamboo" innuendo, performed by small groups of men in straw hats playing brightly painted bamboo percussion and square-bodied guitars called rhythm boxes.

The span of the Wailers' career is the story of Jamaican pop. Boogying in its bones is jazz, which is umbilically bonded with the island. Mento musicians, too, were steeped in jazz and often played alongside local big bands, such as Eric Dean's, at the hotels that provided a circuit and a living for many local musicians. Boogie-woogie piano from masters such as Willie "The Lion" Smith, along with Fats Domino's New Orleans joie de vivre, lope through the earliest ska 45's, like producer Chris Blackwell's first hit, 1962's bouncy "Boogie in My Bones," by Laurel Aitken. Rasta drummers such as Count Ossie and the Mystic Revelation of Rastafari have always united jazz improvisation with the hypnosis of the drums. The lateral complexity of American jazz was many ska musicians' aspiration, as you can hear in Don Drummond's haunting trombone solos, whose jazzy timbre embraces the African-inspired minor keys beloved by John Coltrane.

"The musicians were hip to what was happening in America, like John Coltrane," explained Coxsone Dodd in a rare interview in 1995. "Ska was a sprawling sound, but when Don Drummond would play, it was so neat and mellow, he carried the ska sound forward. Then when the American R&B came in, it hit us hard, because it was very danceable."

Dodd's access to America made him perhaps the island's predominant importer of American R&B. Dodd was focused on giving the right American tracks the Jamaican ska treatment in his own studio. Every phase of African American jazz resonated in Jamaica, as well as the crooning doo-wop harmonies of groups such as the Moonglows. Perhaps most important was the consciousness and melody of Curtis Mayfield and the Impressions, whom the Wailers referenced on *Exodus*'s closing track, "One Love."

Often referred to by its many illustrious alumni as "a reggae university," Studio One's troupe of singers and players went into work every day, absorbing one another's creativity. As ska evolved into reggae, and the Wailers grew with it, Dodd the hit maker noticed that Bob was a keen talent. He could coach and arrange backing singers, including Rita. In his efforts to keep Jamaica bopping, Dodd soon grew to rely on Bob as an arranger, musical director, and A&R man, as he once had relied on Lee "Scratch" Perry. Nostalgically, Dodd grinned as he described how, on trips to Chicago, New York, and New Orleans, he would rummage through attics and basements to discover rare sounds. It was then Bob's job to listen to every 45 and tell Dodd which he thought would work as a reggae cover version. In that way, Bob deconstructed, analyzed, and grew to understand many significant American soul and R&B singles, a learning process that informed his own scrupulous songwriting.

Although little used, the legendary studio was a time capsule of the 1960s when Clement Dodd granted me that rare interview in 1995. Studio One was never modernized. Square wooden mento boxes, with round sounding holes and metal keys like giant Zimbabwean kalimbas, still sat on the top shelf; the roots of reggae music were still there, ready to go. Red, green, and gold pegboard insulated the walls, the wooden vocal booth had an agreeably hand-hewn look, and a mural of a tropical beach beckoned in the still air. The same vision of indolence might have tempted the hardworking musicians back when Don Drummond, Roland Alphonso, Tommy McCook, and others who, as the Skatalites, made ska happen in that very room, back in 1962.

Sitting at a vintage wooden office desk, the venerable producer smiled proudly as he gestured toward a side area that had been Bob's "kotch" when he was young and hustling.

It was clear that Dodd's feelings toward Bob were paternal, despite any business problems. In that dawn of an industry, evidently feeling that by providing the tools of production and sometimes their vision they were creative partners with the artists, virtually every Jamaican producer either added his name to the musicians' publishing credits or simply claimed songs as his own. The cowboy character of the Jamaican music business in those early days meant that a flat session fee was a one-time buyout (as in no more cash was due), though extra money might be handed over for a hit on an informal, ad hoc basis. Producers felt quite justified; in their minds, they were artists, too, plus they carried the risk. Vocalists and musicians were, if not disposable, at least generally available. It took years for the industry's vision to be adjusted. The Wailers virtually never got paid proper royalties for their early work, and it always rankled.

In the first years after independence from Britain in 1962, Jamaican ghetto youths weren't dominated and obsessed by political parties. But before the decade was out, guns started to arrive on the island, reputedly smuggled in by politicians investing in their own power for the 1967 elections. Curfews were imposed, tanks and jeeps filled the streets, schoolchildren ran the daily gauntlet of army searches, and the island was virtually a military regime. This decline of Jamaican civilization was accompanied by a phenomenal sound-track commentary of "rude boy" music from artists such as the Wailers.

Sometimes a song sums up a moment, and that happened to the Wailers' "Simmer Down," an uncut cry to a torn generation from one of their own. Played with panache by the classic Skatalites team, including Don Drummond, the single had the faintly moralistic, admonishing tone that characterized many rudie records, while its sheer adrenaline rush suggested wicked fun. Released in the summer of 1964, "Simmer Down" stayed at the top of the Jamaica Broadcasting Corporation radio charts for two months at the beginning of the next year. Bob's reedy tenor urged the rudies to "control your temper," with documentary urgency, and this caution showed a very different Wailers from the slick trio who in just a couple of years would dress for stage in gold lamé Beatles jackets and covered Tom Jones's "What's New Pussycat" and, as Bob reminded me with a twinkle, the Beatles' "And I Love Her." The Wailers had been anointed as the voice of the sufferers and rudies. Neville Garrick recalls an encounter in a bar with an infamous ghetto badman named Zacky the High Priest, when the feared enforcer was so delighted by the Wailers' attitude that he made the DJ put on their new single, the aptly named "Put It On," over and over again.

Ska was the sound track to independence, and it fizzes with optimism and excitement, as if every bar was a new adventure. Many Jamaican rural folk had taken that fateful exodus journey on a careening, crowded bus with chickens squawking in cages strapped to the roof, to seek a new life in Kingston.

The rude-boy genre became a permanent template for rebellious youth attitude. The music hit the frequency of militant youth, and to those in the know, it was an incendiary sound track to ideas of Black Power filtering into Jamaica from America. First, Afros became the defining 'do, to be superseded by dreadlocks a decade later. The attitude and style of rude-boy music continued to echo down the years, inspiring punks such as the Clash and the Sex Pistols and producing the jaunty Two Tone movement in Britain in the 1980s, with bands including Madness, Selecter, and the Specials. Even the high-spirited Los Angeles punk/ska scene of the 1990s, spearheaded by No Doubt, is a descendant of rude-boy ska. Some of the band's greatest success came with a 2003 release recorded in Jamaica, called *Rock Steady*. To be sure, many of No Doubt's listeners had no clue that rock steady was a Jamaican rhythm of the 1960s—but then, as the young Wailers sang, quoting an old country proverb: "Who feels it, knows it." But with the same intuition that tells a DJ when to touch a record to make a drum break keep on rolling, musical tastemakers sensed that the time had come to cool down the groove. All the young rudies began to get ready to do rock steady, as instructed by the suave Studio One crooner Alton Ellis on his single of that name. In the face of mounting heat in the streets, cool was everything, and after a couple of years, the frenetic bounce of ska started to seem too upfront and uncontrolled. With rock steady, couples could also cut straight to the primal hip-to-hip synchronization that DJs call wind 'n' grind.

"We just felt the music needed to slow down. It was time for a change," Dodd says about why ska mellowed into rock steady. As ever, Dodd's acute antennae had picked up a social shift. The dream was rapidly becoming tarnished. Frustration and discontent erupted in the riots of 1963, and ska's exuberance cooled down into rock steady three years on.

After three scorching singles, the Wailin' Wailers, as they were then known, released a more spiritual streak of music, including a version of "The Ten Commandments of Love," written by New Orleans maestro Aaron Neville. Their trajectory had slowed, and, unhappy with their business situation, the Wailers feared they were getting nowhere. Then Cedella managed to get Bob American work papers. Bob tried sticking with Coxsone for another year, but the sense of stagnation grew.

"We expect to get some money [from Dodd], for this is Christmas. Then the guy give me sixty pounds after we make so much hits," Bob explained to Dread journalist Carl Gayle in 1975. "So me just leggo and go live with me mother in America."

BOB FLEW TO JOIN his mother in Delaware on the day after he married Rita, in February 1966. After being a ska star in Kingston, though, working entry-level jobs in Delaware was something of a culture shock, but Bob adjusted. "As a youth, I was always active, never lazy," he told me, looking back on the time. "I learnt a trade, welding, so dealing with those things is part of my thing. I enjoy dealing with parts, and I never really mind 'cos I just did it as much as I wanted to do it. Anytime I felt fed up, I didn't really look for a job." Still, work had to be done. Bob had plans with his bred'ren to make more music in Jamaica, "And besides," he added wryly, "my mother wanted me to have a regular paycheck."

In Delaware, Bob informed Cedella that he'd married Rita. Perhaps more disturbing to Cedella was also Bob's drift toward Rasta: Rita was an adherent, while Cedella was a churchgoer. To practice in peace, he used to play guitar and compose alone in the basement. "Over there now, me find the music still in me. Singing and writing some good tunes like 'Bend Down Low.' " But working in isolation, Bob missed the Kingston music scene. His fellow Wailers continued to release well-received singles such as "Let Him Go," piercingly led by Bunny and well into the new rock steady feeling. While Bob's core constituency, the downtown rude boys, were terrifying the town, they were also on some level becoming emblematic of rebellious disaffected youth, the underdog biting back. News from home made him itch even more for his true life's direction. "That rude-boy business was bad, bad music," Bob said to me with some pride, adding, "But them shouldn't have said 'rude boy,' dem shoud have said 'Rasta,' you dig me? But in them times me didn't know Rasta."

Indeed, in tedious hours spent working factory jobs, in hotels and warehouses, Bob was experiencing a shift in his relationship to the life he'd left behind. At that distance from home, there was a new perspective on life, and its reverse. Thoughtful, Bob began to feel like he was wasting precious time. He told friends that he knew he was not going to live to grow old, and even prophesied the age he would leave the planet. One specific moment of consciousness definitely hit Bob when he was in Delaware. Over the phone, Rita told Bob how she went to see Haile Selassie drive through town. Bubbling, his young wife told Bob that His Imperial Majesty had smiled directly at her and waved. In the palm of the regal hand, she swore she'd seen the imprint of a nail. More than ever, Rita felt committed to Rasta. But Bob was also to experience a visitation from H.I.M.—only his was not of the flesh.

"When I was leaving Jamaica in 1966, Rasta philosophy was going round," Bob recalled. "In America now I say, 'Wait, I wonder if this is my future.' Jah—God—came to me in a vision and gave me a gold ring. He was an ordinary man with a felt hat and a brown jacket—an ordinary brown jacket, and a coat, not a raincoat, like the Jamaican people wear," he described to me enthusiastically. Jah gave Bob a ring, and when Bob told his mother about the visitation, she in turn gave him a golden ring that had belonged to his father. He wore it for a few days but gave it back. "I never want to get involved with no gold ring, gold watch. I want to remain the person I am. Once I start love gold, something might happen," he concluded earnestly.

The sighting of Jah—the first of many—prompted Bob to explore Rasta. After seven months in Delaware, Bob returned to Jamaica with a clear mission.

The first part of Bob's task in Jamaica was spiritual. He grew increasingly involved with the Rasta group, the Twelve Tribes of Israel. With its hipper, more inclusionary attitude, Bob was one of many reggae artists who flocked to the Twelve Tribes in the 1970s. A visionary Rasta mystic and ice-cream vendor named Vernon Carrington developed the organization in 1968. He viewed Rasta through the prism of the Bible's wily Jacob, whose father was Isaac, Abraham's son. A righteous hustler, Jacob scored his elder twin brother Esau's inheritance in exchange for a bowl of lentil soup and even manipulated their father into giving him the special blessing he'd planned for Esau. As he lay dying, Jacob summoned his twelve sons to his deathbed and assigned to each a different character.

Carrington made the conceptual leap of linking each calendar month to the personality of one of Jacob's sons, as a fundamental template for Rasta *livity*. In his alternative cosmic horoscope, every living soul is understood to be a reincarnation of the tribal Patriarchs. Thus, within the Twelve Tribes of Israel each member is assigned his own tribe depending on his birth month. Born on February 6, 1945, Marley manifested Joseph. Definitely a biblical rock star, Joseph had one big problem: the enemies ready to attack whom Bob sings about on "Exodus." Joseph's siblings were so jealous of the many-colored coat Isaac gave him that they sold their own brother into Egyptian slavery, where he was only saved by his skill at interpreting dreams. But Joseph was a survivor, with a full and blessed *livity*. In Genesis 49:22–24, Joseph is described as "a fruitful bough . . . archers shoot at him . . . but the arms of his hands are made strong by the hands of the mighty God of Jacob." The looks, gifts, and charisma that made Joseph a target for the plots of scorned women also empowered him, years later, to save the lives of his brothers, even though they'd betrayed him. Bob was to find the lessons of Joseph particularly relevant.

The other aspect of Bob's plans when coming home from America related to music and business. He was tired of being ripped off by every producer. With Bob's seven-hundred-dollar savings, the Wailers started their own hole-in-the-wall independent label and record store, Wail'N Soul'M, in 1966. A true mom 'n' pop organization, it was valuable experience and lasted for more than two years. Though Bob never stopped working with his core team of the Wailers, he also began collaborating with American soul man Johnny Nash, whom he'd met at a Rasta grounation, and signed a publishing deal with Nash's manager, Danny Sims's JAD. Over the next four years the Wailers recorded dozens of sides for JAD. But as their Rasta faith deepened, the singers were all drawn to the apocalyptic thunder of the Nyabinghi drums and a more revolutionary form of expression than Sims envisaged, and began instead to work with Lee "Scratch" Perry. Besides a wicked new militant posture and sound, Scratch would also bring Marley another crucial component of the *Exodus* team: the rhythmic powerhouse of brothers Aston "Family Man" and Carlton "Carly" Barrett, the anchors of Scratch's musicians, known as the Upsetters.

As youths, Family Man and Carly, whose father was a blacksmith, built their own instruments. Carly played drums, his brother bass. Family Man's bass was made from a wooden two-by-four for the neck, with a body made of plywood and curtain wire for strings. He'd lean the contraption on the floor, "to get that real bass sound," Family Man recalls, chuckling. The Barrett brothers went on to become the spine of Jamaica's sound as the leading session combo, working under different names for each producer.

Fams finally got his own instrument when one of his main clients, a jovial producer called Bunny "Striker" Lee, brought a short-necked, violin-shaped Hofner bass back from the U.K. He'd purchased it from one Lee Gopthal, boss of the reggae label Trojan, who'd bought it from the Beatles' manager, Brian Epstein. So the previous owner of the bass on which Fams played those catchy Upsetters instrumental hits that both mods and skinheads partied to in England, such as "Return of Django," was once Paul McCartney.

While the musical explorations of the Wailers, Scratch, and the Barrett brothers were progressing, Bob signed a publishing and recording deal with JAD. Sims invited him to work in Sweden on a film sound track with Nash. When nothing emerged from that project, Sims signed Bob to CBS, where he'd contracted Nash. There were some flurries of attention as Nash recorded Bob's sexy song "Guava Jelly" and CBS released Bob's single "Reggae on

Broadway," but Bob's career still seemed stuck. To salvage the situation, Sims invited Peter and Bunny to join Bob in London. Marley and Nash did play a mini-tour of local high schools, but the Wailers felt they were going nowhere. Then urgent Nash business called the JAD team back to America, and the Wailers found themselves stranded in London, broke and without their passports, which had been held by the Home Office.

"When the right time comes," the Rastas say, and just in time a Trinidadian entrepreneur, Brent Clarke, informed Family Man that Chris Blackwell was interested in investing in a combination of Jamaica's key vocal trio and rhythm section: the Wailers and the Barrett brothers. Shortly thereafter, Bob found himself with Brent Clarke in the white brick lobby of a trendily converted church on the West Indian Carnival route. The Island office was commonly known by its address, Basing Street.

"They held a tape out to me," remembers Suzette Newman, then a lowly tape archivist barely out of school, who later became a chairman director of Island's offshoot company, then rose to become chairman of Blackwell's U.K. operations. "As I took it, I saw that the tape box said 'CBS' on it. I asked them, 'Are you sure it's all right if we listen to this?' I remember Bob shook his head and said, 'Yes, mon, there won't be no problem.' " Newman, from northwest London, switches into a natural Jamaican patois, catches herself, and laughs. "I somehow knew right then I was going to have to learn to speak their language."

She was not alone. The Wailers spread the language of reggae over three albums: *Catch a Fire* (1973), *Burnin'* (1973), then *Natty Dread* (1974), all on Chris Blackwell's Island Records.

Blackwell was one of those golden colonial boys who always seemed so glamorous to their pasty cousins in England. A British paper voted him one of the country's handsomest men in the early 1970s. His Irish military father was stationed on the island when he married Blanche Lindo, of the celebrated clan of Sephardic Jews whose own exodus from the Spanish Inquisition in the fifteenth century led them to Jamaica.

But his parents divorced, which led to money troubles, and one of young Blackwell's formative moments was sitting on the steps of their grand house on Hope Road (later to become the Terra Nova Hotel), watching bailiffs remove the family's belongings. This financial catastrophe gave him an edge, a hunger, that separated him from others of his class. He was also unusual for his social milieu in relating to Rastas, at the time generally held to be machete-wielding madmen.

Pretty soon the record business won him over, and Blackwell produced a local jazz pianist on *Lance Hayward at the Half Moon Hotel,* and Cuban-born Laurel Aitken's *Boogie in My Bones,* a swinging uptempo shuffle that became a local monster in 1959. He called his new label Island after the movie of Alec Waugh's novel *Island in the Sun.*

Thus encouraged, Blackwell decided to try his luck selling Jamaican music in England after independence in 1962, selling 45's from the back of his Mini Cooper. Remarkably quickly, he scored a hit with the quirky ska tune "My Boy Lollipop." The singer was a skinny girl named Millie Small with a sky-high beehive and a piercing falsetto, and her disc became the first Jamaican record to enter the U.K. Top Twenty when it hit number two on the U.K. charts in March 1964.

Swinging London rocked with style and sounds in the late 1960s, and Blackwell's Island gathered some eclectic and impeccable talent, both on its own label and via distribution deals with new, young independent labels such as Virgin, Chrysalis, and Joe Boyd's Witchseason and the glittering glam of Roxy Music. The extended family included folk rockers Fairport Convention; the stomping blues rock of Free; Traffic, featuring teenager Stevie Winwood's Brummie sharecropper rasp; the fragile confessional singer-songwriter Nick Drake; and a pretty half-Greek youth with luxuriant dark curls named Cat Stevens, who became the definitive bed-sit bard.

But although he'd drifted off, Blackwell had never intended to abandon Jamaican music, and when sexy, impassively cool Bob Marley sauntered into his Basing Street office, he recognized his opportunity to help develop an authentic Jamaican reggae/rock star. Going on his gut, and against everyone's advice, Blackwell gambled the unprecedented sum of £4,000 for Bob, Family Man, and Carlton to make an album, *Catch a Fire,* in 1972. Adding touches of blues-rock guitar by Wayne Perkins, an American musician who happened to be recording in the room next door, *Catch a Fire* caught the ears of a new audience for the Wailers. The lyrics evoked a heightened world of zinc alleys and iron shackles, of churches ablaze and provocative sex. Bob, Peter, and Bunny traded leads and backed one another with the familiarity of years.

"Harmony is one of the best vibrations ever," as Bob put it. " 'Specially when you go through a certain period of time, so you don't have to go too hard to find the right harmony, then it nice."

However, the demands of the international marketplace soon clashed with the band members' temperaments. During the uncomfortable *Catch a Fire* promo tour, Bunny tired of their diet of fish and chips (pretty much the only edible thing available in England that wouldn't violate Rasta dietary restrictions) and low-grade ganja, and made his position clear by splitting in November 1973.

"*Burnin'* was the breakup record, where Bob broke up with his friends from boyhood," Blackwell says. "Though it had good songs on it, it's not a good record—its cohesiveness, its sound, even the playing. It would have been a big disappointment, but the songs on it were so good, particularly 'I Shot the Sheriff'—though the recorded version is too slick, nothing like as good as the live version [from *Live at the Lyceum!*]. That song was one of the most important things for Bob."

Part of Blackwell's promotional strategy was to make rock stars aware of the Wailers. "You've got to remember that at that time, when people were always discussing solos and how musicianship was important, these reggae guys were novelty music. But I wanted people to view the Wailers as being really great music." They struck gold when British blues guitar hero Eric Clapton's version of "I Shot the Sheriff" became an international success in 1974. Blackwell recalls, "At that time, Eric was God, right? So people looked to see where God was going for his material, and it led back to Bob."

But after *Burnin'*, when it was clear that there was no more mileage left in the original Wailers trio, Peter also withdrew, miffed at the promotion of Bob to leader. The future of the band was in obvious doubt.

Speed in regrouping was essential. Family Man in particular was insistent that they could carry on. Together, the Barrett brothers and Bob holed up at Blackwell's Hope Road home and constructed a studio round the back. With the threat of losing their record deal with Island looming, the nexus of Marley and the Barrett brothers created a landmark album, *Natty Dread* (1974). Traffic's Chris Wood introduced them to American guitarist Al Anderson. But the making of the album was so random that they eventually met a player by stopping a guy walking down Chelsea's Kings Road carrying a guitar case, to ask where they could find some weed. And when the three Rasta divas Judy Mowatt, Marcia Griffiths, and Rita Marley joined the outfit as the I-Three, fairly late in the process, the shape of the future Wailers began to emerge.

The new Wailers chart a different course. Bob Marley, Family Man Barrett, and Junior Marvin concentrate on their guitar tuning before a show in 1977.
© *Kate Simon*

3

WALKING CREATION ROAD

"WHAT I LIKE ABOUT OUR MUSIC is the way it progress," Bob said of the Wailers' lengthy evolution, and *Natty Dread* was a crucial moment of change for the band. Minus Peter and Bunny, Bob and the Barrett brothers were determined to reinvent the Wailers and Jamaican music.

"The first two records, *Catch a Fire* and *Burnin'*, didn't do well in Jamaica, but *Natty Dread* was a hit there and outside. *Natty Dread* was a killer record. It really delivered the goods," says Blackwell. "But it was a very different sound from the first two, with Peter and Bunny's [prominent] harmonies; it was now solo voice with vocal harmonies. *Natty Dread* stands on its own."

Certainly, Bob's evocation of Rasta and sufferers' ghetto runnings had never been clearer than on this record. The everyday petty harassment he chronicled on *Natty Dread*'s "Rebel Music (3 O'Clock Road Block)," with its heartfelt cry for revolution, showed Bob as a passionate militant who still felt the urge to express tenderness and sensuality. On the title track he hymned Trench Town, lovingly tracing the territory of his youth, walking through the embattled area from First Street to Seventh Street. The moving positivity of "No Woman, No Cry" makes the song sound like a psalm. Bob very literally describes both the poverty and the true wealth of his old tenement yard *livity:* "And we will cook cornmeal porridge / Of which I'll share with you . . ."

Despite their evident brilliance, the departure of the temperamental Peter and the rather grumpy Bunny freed Blackwell to steer Bob and the Wailers into the mainstream. "We were projecting Bob as a black rock artist, not R&B. Unless I could get Bob on the road, there was no way that we could break him. Radio wasn't playing it, and we weren't making records for radio, we were making records as milestones in his career, to push the career along, not just to have a hit with the first record. It was all about building an artist. So when *Natty Dread* was a breakaway hit in Jamaica, it gave them a lot of credibility. It was great because before it was a Jamaican hit, I felt that the stuff I'd added to the records could well have damaged his credibility at home. I was very concerned about that, because for him to be happening overseas and not at home would not be doing him justice. Reggae suddenly jumped into the middle class; suddenly all these people who thought it wasn't cool before were raving about the groove of 'Lively Up Yourself.' "

With that development, Bob's circumstances changed. Prior to this period, Bob had no settled home of his own. His wife, Rita, and their four—soon five—children were out in rural Bull Bay, and Bob was often there. But Scratch remembers that at the time when Bob moved uptown, he was frequently crashing in the producer's house.

Before the release of *Natty Dread,* Blackwell, Bob, and his recent manager, Don Taylor, struck an unusual deal. The first album had been recorded on an advance of £4,000, and advances had grown on subsequent records. But now Taylor confidently demanded £1 million for the next three albums. A seasoned gambler, Blackwell was in his element cutting a deal, and countered by agreeing to that sum—but for ten albums. It was Bob who cut off any further bargaining and accepted the arrangement, including Blackwell's curious sweetener: the £125,000 price of the house that Blackwell owned and Bob already stayed in—56 Hope Road would only have to be paid for if and when he ever left Island Records.

Bob had great hopes for Hope Road. He was as eloquent as I ever saw him when he enthused about what the move meant for him and his tribe. "[It's] not the people me a talk about, but the ghetto is a prison. When the law comes out, they send them into the ghetto first, not uptown. So how long does it take you to realize— bwaoy, well they don't send them uptown, y'know! So we'll make a ghetto uptown. *Every day* I jumped fences from the police, for *years,* not a week, for *years.* You either stay there and let bad people shoot you down, or you make a move and show people some improvement. Or else I would take up a gun and start shoot [my attackers] off, and then a lot of youths would follow me, and they'd be dead the same way. I want some improvement. It doesn't have to be materially, but in freedom of thinking."

The gracious old building is a central player in Marley's story. With its drive curving up to a colonnaded front door, the Hope Road place was a small-scale urban Great House with a yard dominated by a sturdy, stately mango tree. By the time Bob moved in, the neighborhood had changed, reflecting the island's new social mobility. The big old single-family houses were being split up into apartments or pulled down to make way for modern condominiums and swimming pools. Jamaican prime minister Michael Manley moved onto the street. Though the building's structure remained intact, change came to 56 Hope Road, too. "When Mrs. Gough moved out," Family Man reminisces dreamily, referring to the old lady who was the last remnant of the house's previous colonial life, "we took over."

The house quickly became a bohemian enclave amid the avenue's posh sobriety. Its early transient residents included the jeunesse dorée of Kingston, rebel scions of successful old families, such as actor Winston Stoner (the chief of police in Perry Henzell's movie, *The Harder They Come*); actress Esther Anderson, an early love of Bob's who shot the *Burnin'* sleeve and starred alongside Sidney Poitier in a film called *Warm December;* and a lively, vivacious beauty named Cindy Breakspeare, manager of a nightclub called Dizzy's in Northside Plaza in Liguanea, farther up Hope Road. They were a new kind of independent Jamaican crew.

"When Bob got to Hope Road, it was a different vibe," Tony "Gilly" Gilbert, one of Bob's key "spars" and fellow footballer, says nostalgically. "Moving up to higher heights and another level to greatness. Bob was thinking about a transition. I loved him for doing that."

As I quickly learned, in its Rasta incarnation the house was a bustling commune, free-living, free-loving, constantly alive with activity, from the never-ending game of soccer playing out on the front lawn to the endless preparation of salt-free Rasta food in the kitchen, usually manned by Gilly. "Bob would get up early, then we would exercise," says the strapping Gilly, who was one of Bob's main athletic companions. "We were soccer players in the club league and Bob was a hard worker, so he would train to have that breath control. We would go to the beach in Bull Bay and run along the hard sand, then run a seven-mile journey up continuous hills to the Cane River, go under the waterfalls, and get rejuvenated. Then we'd go back to the beach and have roast fish with the Dreads, go back to Hope Road, and Bob would write songs on his guitar. It's a pity a lot of the songs he didn't get to record before he went on to another journey."

The floating population of young people hanging at Hope Road seemed huge, with a special concentration of friendly, giggling girls grooming their hair in the general area of Family Man's quarters.

During the early days at Hope Road, Bob's friendship with a housemate developed into a romance. His new consort and his partner through the *Exodus* era and beyond was the glamorous club manager and fitness instructor Cindy Breakspeare, an uptown girl.

It was well known that Bob led a quite separate romantic life outside of his marriage, and that whatever her personal feelings, Rita, no fool, had evidently made her own accommodation with the facts—or else they'd have been in the divorce courts already. "Everybody knew that before me, there was Esther Anderson and any number of others," Cindy says matter-of-factly. At that time the growing Rasta movement was also engaged in exploring different ways of relating, and variations on African polygamy.

Another son, actor and singer Ky-mani Marley, was born in 1976 to Bob and Anita Belnavis, the Jamaican table tennis champion.

But the love affair between Bob and Cindy, thrown together as Hope Road housemates of a very different background and social standing, was slow in growing. On his nighttime rounds, Bob had shown his interest from quite early on, often stopping in at the club she ran to check on his stunning young friend. Even before they really got together, Bob would send his close bred'ren footballer Allan "Skill" Cole round to keep an eye on her while he was on the road.

Cindy tapped into an intimacy with Bob that enabled him to show her a special tenderness. She fondly remembers the day Bob found her at home, examining a piece of driftwood she'd just found on Hellshire Beach. Her boutique, Ital Crafts, had just opened, and Cindy planned to get the driftwood turned into a glass coffee table. To her surprise and pleasure, Bob promptly offered to do it. "Me is a tradesman, you know," he reminded her with a smile. Bob did a beautiful job, and the piece sold soon, and for a good price, with no mention of who made it.

As their relationship progressed through the early part of 1976, recalls Cindy, a pattern developed. During the day, Bob would be occupied with his responsibilities to the band, his family, and the community. But some nights he would secretly spirit her away, without letting anyone know. Cindy's face lights up at the mention of stolen moments in their hut at Strawberry Hill, with its creaking steps leading up to a mosquito-screened verandah, and inside, two spartan single iron beds. "But as his career took off even more, those nights became fewer and fewer," Cindy recalls ruefully. With Marley, lover though he was, the music always came first.

THE INTENSITY OF *Natty Dread* was starting to convert even those rock diehards who usually felt reggae was somehow inferior. When I arrived to work as a junior press officer at Island Records in mid-1975, still fresh from studying at Warwick University and already freelancing for *New Musical Express,* my American boss, Brian Blevins, was very insistent: "Bob Marley is the most important artist for the company right now—and the big boss, Blackwell, is very personally involved."

Selling Bob Marley was easy, as I was personally on fire about his work. In long hash-hazed evenings huddled around the gas fire, listening to records on a little stereo in our communal student digs in Coventry and Leamington Spa, my friends and I would listen to Miles Davis, Janis Joplin, David Bowie, and the Wailers' *Catch a Fire.* I had the luxury of being a publicist who didn't have to fake it. Though it may seem astonishing now, in 1975 Bob Marley was not an easy sell. I particularly remember the tussle with the then music editor of *Time Out* magazine, John Collis, who simply didn't want to know—quite rudely, too. Breaking all the protocol, I managed to get Tony Elliott, the publisher, to listen to the album. As it did every time it reached enlightened ears, the music did the work; Dennis Morris's jubilant shot of Bob wound up on *Time Out*'s front cover in time for the big Lyceum show that was coming up on July 19, 1975.

Such great news earned me my first meeting with Chris Blackwell, a private session in his surprisingly small, bright, plant-filled room at the back of the building. By now, Island's success meant a move from the office on Basing Street into a grand, rambling building, a former laundry in Chiswick's St. Peters Square. I ran through the list of reviews and articles, and Blackwell was impressed. Neither of the previous albums had received such a reception. "It's great you're so enthusiastic," he said, "and you realize that Bob is quite special. He deserves all the hard work."

Crucially, there was a creative respect that underpinned their professional connection. Bob entrusted Blackwell with the overall sound of his music, a rare rapport between artist and record company executive. Indeed, Blackwell's passion for Bob's artistry only deepened his acute commercial instincts. One night as the Wailers played at the Roxy in Los Angeles, Blackwell was moved to hear a full chorus of voices from the audience sing along with Bob on "No Woman, No Cry." Right then, he decided to record the next appropriate show. His hunch was confirmed at the two nights the band played at the London Lyceum, which introduced American guitarist Al Anderson's rich blues-rock-reggae guitar solos. Despite a rash of lawless youths steaming the audience, the gig was an epochal outpouring of feeling toward Bob, the Wailers, and all they stood for. Marley's appearance that night sparked a brushfire of ideas—Rasta, black identity, and universal higher consciousness— that can never be put out. For some audience members, including dreadlocked filmmaker Don Letts, the show was a personal epiphany. "There was a duality to being black and British at the time that Bob's lyrics bridged. That gig was the nearest to a religious experience I've ever had," he says.

For Blackwell, too, it was triumphant to absorb the scene he'd dreamed of for so long—all young London ecstatically reaching for the light that Bob Marley embodied as he stepped, skanked, and swung onstage. The singer used the entire performance area. Bob would drop back to sync up with Carlton Barrett's drums, then sidle and skip across the stage, knees flying high as if he were juggling a soccer ball, to huddle with the newly ensconced I-Three—just Judy and Rita, as Marcia was pregnant—archetypes of Rasta womanhood with their headwraps and stately step. Bob controlled the stage, everything on it, and the whole crowd.

"This gig was special for us. It was at the *Lyceum,* in *London,*" reminisces Family Man, emphasizing the location's big-time significance. "The show was sold out and we heard there were two and a half thousand people inside, and the same amount outside trying to get in."

The unruly crowd prompted the venue to summon the police's Special Patrol Group for crowd control, as the show's promoter, Mick Cater, remembers. "They actually ripped the fire doors off the wall, so another fifteen hundred people got in like that. But that was the night the rest of the world caught up to Bob Marley."

"It was like a hippie event. The crowd was half black and half white, with a lot of people sitting on the floor, passing round spliffs," recalls writer and Marley biographer Chris Salewicz. "The smell of hash was very strong. It was boiling hot, so halfway through the set, the theater was able to open its roof to let in some air, which got everyone excited. It was the first time we saw Bob shout, '*Jah!* Rastafari!' and his shamanic persona. It's still the greatest gig I've been to."

The crowd was unusually receptive, as Marley tapped into its hunger for music with meaning. "We knew that night was different, because the people start the applause at the beginning of every song, as soon as they heard the one drop from the drums, as well as at the end," chuckles Fams. "It was very unusual. Everyone on-stage get high from the feedback from the people. That's what made 'No Woman, No Cry' such a great, great moment and spirit."

Soon after, the *Live at the Lyceum!* album of the concert came out. "The record had a killer version of 'No Woman, No Cry' that really elevated everything," Blackwell remembers. "It was their biggest hit yet." The buzz around Bob Marley's new-style Wailers had become a roar. Although intended for U.K.-only release, popular demand meant it soon came out in America.

After all my passionate pushing of Bob Marley, I missed that Lyceum show. The day I was to collect the Wailers at Heathrow, I was woken very early by a call saying my father, Max Goldman, had died.

My grandmother had had a small kosher restaurant for students near the famous Alexanderplatz, and my father, like many of his family, started out as a classically trained, Gypsy-inflected violinist. He was a prewar Berlin raver who used to climb into nightclubs by a back window if he didn't have money to get in. His Exodus experience began when he was arrested in the street and taken to Nazi headquarters in Berlin. An official came into the waiting room full of nervous Jews and asked if anyone wanted to go to the toilet. My father was sitting there, lost in self-recrimination—why hadn't he already left Germany, like so many of his friends? By the time he realized he might as well use the facilities, they'd already left the waiting room. Granted permission by the guard to follow them, it was only when he was out in the hallway that he realized his fellow prisoners were nowhere to be seen—and that here was a precious possibility of escape. Ever so casually, my father strolled through the bureaucratic building's labyrinthine corridors till he reached the street. Macky, as he was called, always liked to say the hand of God led him out. He jumped in a cab and went to his mother's, where he'd already stashed a forged passport. Taking only her few jewels and his beloved violin, he set out on his own exodus. He got to know the refugee discipline of staying cool while the guard on the train slowly scrutinizes the fake papers. But everywhere he fled, the Nazis soon invaded, often sending those who helped him to concentration camps. Macky planned to go to Palestine, but his ticket was stolen in Paris. In the end, though, he survived, went into the garment business, pampered three daughters, and enjoyed a full life in northwest London, dying in his sleep in his own bed, with his loving wife beside him—a blessing that had seemed unlikely when he was on the run.

So I met Bob Marley for the first time after sitting the mourning week of shiva. The small, laconic figure glanced at me, then absently gazed through the window at the trees of St. Peters Square while I explained why I'd missed the big show. Used to at least a reflex condolence, I paused for a moment—but it didn't come. Then I remembered that Rastas didn't deal in death, so I quickly made a mental adjustment and explained his promotional day. There were journalists from the regular music press, but also, strangely, a man from the *Financial Times*. Bob nodded and said nothing—obviously a man of few words. My heart sank. It seemed as if Bob might not be the ideal candidate for me to be offering to a writer from the "straight" press.

After two days of steering Marley through a series of journalists, I was vastly amused by the way he played some of them with patois, pushing them to the point of frustration by deepening his accent, then suddenly slipping into a more familiar speech just when they'd all but given up. Many were baffled by his discursive, scattered retorts and arcane expositions of Rasta theology, but my fears were misplaced. Regardless of any communication problems, all the writers left even more fascinated by Bob Marley.

Both Family Man and Scratch were very involved in the production of the next record, *Rastaman Vibration*—in particular, Scratch's sizzling dynamic is clear on "Crazy Baldhead," summed up by Blackwell as "a wicked kind of strident rhythm." The I-Three were now smoothly integrated into the group, and the Wailers' exploration of rock/reggae fusion was furthered by the addition of two American guitarists, Donald Kinsey and Al Anderson, alongside the Wailers' longtime Jamaican stalwart, Earl "Chinna" Smith, whose subtle approach to rhythm was impeccable.

"You can't go on repeating yourself all the while," Bob insisted. "When I pick up a record and give my advice, I don't really come back the next time and advise the same thing. *Natty Dread* come through and people say, 'What is a Rastaman?' Rastaman vibration is positive," he quoted the song's lyrics, "so we can't really go back and say, 'Cold ground was my bed last night,' " a reference to *Natty Dread*'s "Talking Blues."

"*Rastaman Vibration* was very much more geared to America. *Live at the Lyceum!* had already done very well in England, I was more in America at the time, and Bob was happy there because it was starting to wake up, there was a vibe happening," recalls Blackwell. "We did a great marketing job and took a big advertisement out in the *New York Times*." The album became Marley's only top ten record in America, reaching number eight.

Getting through to America, particularly black America, was very important to Bob, who hoped to help bind the split of slavery. As in England, the first people to tune in to the Wailers, after their roots constituency, were hippies and students. A sleeve was once again designed by the British team of Eckford and Stimpson, and as reggae titles of the day used to say, it was "straight to students' heads." With insider jocularity, a note announced that the waffle of its corrugated, hessian-look brown sleeve was made to clean weed. The theme of the campaign was suitably rugged, all earth tones flashed with the Rasta colors.

To firmly brand the disc's Rasta identity, Marley took a suggestion from his close friend, the ruggedly handsome footballer Allan "Skill" Cole. Skill was a Rasta and suggested making a song out of an impassioned speech calling for disarmament, abolition of nuclear devices, and racial equality that Haile Selassie gave to the United Nations on October 4, 1963. The powerful incantatory effect of Selassie's repetition, reminiscent of a gospel preacher, became "War," a martial cry for peace. Disillusion with the system marked songs such as "Rat Race" and "Night Shift," which evoked Bob's dreary work experiences while staying with his mother in Wilmington, Delaware, in 1966. But most significantly, the apocalyptic mistrust that infuses "Want More" and "Who the Cap Fit" foreshadows the imminent events that would change Bob's life forever.

Rastaman Vibration went on to earn Bob America's ultimate youth culture accolade of the time—an exuberant *Rolling Stone* cover shot of Bob with his guitar, wearing black leather trousers, his big concession to rock star chic.

"*Rastaman Vibration* really did pretty well," Blackwell concludes. "It didn't sell millions of copies in today's terms, but it did well in that it might have sold eighty thousand copies.

"After that, everything was shifted back to Europe because of the thing that happened in Jamaica."

4

JAH PEOPLE

"MONEY IS LIKE WATER IN THE SEA," Bob Marley insisted earnestly on that late 1976 afternoon as our conversation by the Sheraton pool turned to business and politics. "People work for money, den dem don't want to split it. It's that kind of attitude," he continued scornfully. "So much guys have so much—too much— while so many have nothing at all. We don't feel like that is right, because it don't take a guy a hundred million dollars to keep him satisfied. Everybody have to live. Michael Manley say 'im wan' help poor people. . . . They feel something good is gonna happen," he said reflectively, then continued, "We need a change from what it was. It couldn't get worse than that." Sounding more sure, he concluded fiercely, almost defiantly, "You *have* to share. I don't care if it sounds political or whatever it is, but people have to *share*."

Bob's last comment might sound odd; why should the outspoken revolutionary poet Bob Marley be so concerned about anyone's political misinterpretation? But we were speaking in 1976, just days before the free Smile Jamaica concert he was due to play for the people, and large crowds are always volatile. Bob was conscious of the heightened tension that always surrounded the buildup to a Jamaican election. His generous humanist statement

Bob spreads the word of Jah with his bred'ren the Wailers on the *Exodus* tour in 1977, with Neville Garrick's image of Haile Selassie looking
on. Frequent Wailers collaborator Earl "Chinna" Smith plays guitar (l.).
© *Dennis Morris/Bob Marley Music.*

could be labeled as socialism. People might say he was definitively backing Michael Manley's socialist People's National Party (PNP), with its affiliation to Castro and Russia, and rejecting the Jamaican Labour Party (JLP), headed by Edward Seaga, dubbed in widespread graffiti as "CIA-ga" because of the American secret service's overt support of his team. That could mean trouble.

Times had changed since Bob and Rita had backed Manley in the 1972 election. The island seemed to be full of guns. People were more desperate and violent, and Bob was a far more public figure. Now he had to screen every word and be extra careful not to be misunderstood.

For an effectively fatherless mixed-race child of the rural areas and stifling ghettoes to be receiving more acclaim than any Jamaican ever was a wake-up call that, like it or not, a new society had actually arrived. Bob's international success made him a symbol of a troubled island's hopes. He now found himself in the unenviable position of being the prize of a tug-of-war between the island's two political parties. As the material for *Exodus* began to brew in 1976, the island was convulsed with lethal political agitation, and Bob's star status did not confer immunity—rather, it was the reverse. "People see him as a big man now, gone international," as his boyhood friend Mikey Smith explains. "Everyone want Bob Marley deh 'pon their team."

Less than two decades after Jamaican independence, the system left behind by the British had frayed, and the infrastructure was crumbling. I remember arriving in Jamaica from Los Angeles once, having been shopping earlier that day, and how obscene it was to compare LA supermarkets' towering stacks of produce with the island supermarkets, with shelves so empty they seemed to sell air. There was music, style, and creativity in abundance, but shortages of everything else from rice to rolling papers.

Driving anywhere was an adventure, as the ancient taxis seemed to be held together with rubber bands and hope, and the roads all over the island had potholes like craters. Power cuts were as regular as police roadblocks. What was Jamaica to do? In a sense, Jamaica had functioned as a satellite farm for invaders and colonizers ever since the Spanish killed off all the indigenous Tainos within fifty years of landing in 1690, and gave the town of Montego Bay its name because the whole area was a giant pig farm for *manteca*— Spanish for "lard." The island's abundant fertility produced globally desired commodities like coffee, sugar, spices, and rum, as well as the human fruits of slavery.

But in the new postcolonial world in which ska and the Wailers began, the island's international role and how it was going to earn its living was uncertain. Spearheaded by John Pringle, the father of the Jamaican tourist industry, the island was repositioning itself to welcome the vacationers who, it was hoped, would replace the waning demand for local bauxite, previously the island's primary export. However, outside of jobs in hotels, comparatively little cash trickled down to reach the sufferers, as the tourists didn't stray much beyond the hotel compounds. The island was in the middle of an identity crisis, and the worldwide acclaim that Bob, a member of the traditional underclass, received only emphasized how greatly things were changing. It was a battle for the soul of the island. Each political party was set on running things its way, and it was generally understood that blood would inevitably run in the process.

Deadly tribal wars, the seeds of which had been planted centuries before, were being fought between the opposing JLP and PNP areas. Families turned against one another from block to block. People risked death to cross Kingston's disputed areas, such as the area between Fifth and Seventh Streets, or the several desolate areas where soldiers camped out and extracted rough justice from any passerby.

But Jamaica has always been a fighting island. Racked with conflict ever since the genocide of the Taino, Jamaican people are traditionally ready to rise in revolt when necessary. The "soul rebel"
that Marley declared himself to be is a very Jamaican archetype.
The rebel spirit was present during the innumerable slave riots on
plantations; the defeat of the British in 1739 by the Maroons;
among the Africans who escaped and flourished in the impenetra-
ble jagged hills called the Cockpit Country; the surges of worker
unrest and unionization that swept the island in the 1930s as the
PNP and JLP founders began to divide the island's allegiance; the
rambunctious rude boys who terrified timorous citizens after independence in 1962; and the Rastafarians, whose revolutionary influence first burned in the 1930s but glowed much brighter when Bob
Marley's flashing dreadlocks raised Rasta awareness globally, four
decades on.

" 'Brown man rule' is the way regular Jamaicans express their
combination of derision, resentment, or resignation towards their
everyday reality," explains Trinidadian journalist Isaac Fergusson,
a friend of both Marley and Tosh. "The masters had the guns, they
had the food, and they chose what women they wanted to breed.
Before emancipation, these men bred mulatto children selectively
for sale, knowing that the beautiful females fetched the highest
price. After emancipation, these brown-skinned children of rape,
selective breeding, and of natural human attraction, too, were put
into power by the old masters to control their darker-skinned relatives in the underclass. That happened not just in Jamaica but all
across the Caribbean."

So during Bob Marley's childhood, the ruling class were the
privileged descendants mostly of mixed Spanish, French, British,
and Portuguese blood, who over the centuries merged with a Se-
mitic merchant class of Jews and Arabs. One light-skinned Ja-

maican girl who otherwise looked just like my German Jewish auntie Judy explained to me that her grandfather was a European Jew, and wittily called the genetic cavalcade "browning out."

One might have thought that Bob, light-skinned mix that he was, would benefit from this phenomenon. But here was a brown child lost in the ghetto without the expected money and power of his class. He had to learn to defend himself. Caught in the crossfire of the resentment, he was constantly tested by both black and white. Despite his global acclaim, Bob was never fully accepted by the privileged class.

Effectively ruled by the famous "21 Families" clique of the wealthiest and most powerful brown Jamaicans, colonial Jamaica was an almost feudal banana-republic backwater, and the gap between classes and colors was a chasm. Given the size of the island, it's perhaps no surprise that its politicians have always seemed a rather incestuous crowd. Universal suffrage came to Jamaica as late as 1945, but the island's two parties, the Jamaica Labour Party and the People's National Party, were created in the tempestuous 1930s by two cousins who effectively split the island between them: the bluff, assertive William Alexander Clarke Bustamante of the JLP, fond of brandishing a pistol, who largely represented the interests of the elite, and the PNP's more intellectual, socially minded populist, Norman Washington Manley. The men were linked by a shared maternal grandmother, Elsie Clarke Shearer. They both orchestrated and exploited the conflicts between organized labor and management that swept from the banana plantations and sugar cane fields to the ports, and strikes all but closed down the island, building in intensity as the decade drew to a close. The extreme unrest was used by Bustamante in particular to agitate in London for the island's independence, which was eventually granted in 1962.

JLP leadership seemed a high-risk assignment. After the resignation of the party founder, Bustamante, in 1967, his successor, Donald Sangster, soon died under mysterious circumstances, just a few weeks after becoming prime minister.

Succeeding him as JLP leader was a leading trade union man, Hugh Shearer, a somewhat darker-skinned cousin of both Bustamante and Manley. On the streets, Shearer's nickname was "Pharaoh," and many found his judgment to be less than Solomonic. All Jamaica's sufferers were angered by his inflammatory response to the rise in murder, robbery, and mayhem fueled by the increasing availability of handguns. Shearer's directive to the Jamaican Constabulary Force was a curt "Shoot first; ask questions later."

Opposing Shearer in the 1972 elections was his relative Michael Manley, Norman Manley's son. Quick, sophisticated, and cosmopolitan, Michael Manley graduated from the London School of Economics in the 1960s, when it was a perceived hotbed of radicalism. With his movie-star wavy hair and chiseled jaw—rumors swirled about his love life—and his safari suits expressing solidarity with emerging Africa's leaders, Manley had the common touch. His connection with the people was enhanced by his alignment with the Rastas and Ethiopia. He aligned himself with powerful Dreads like Bob's Rasta mentor and former producer and manager, Mortimo Planno.

Planno was part of a Jamaican Rasta delegation that traveled to Ethiopia and encouraged Haile Selassie to visit the island, which Selassie did in 1966. On this trip, which changed Rita Marley's life, His Imperial Majesty was so overwhelmed by the massed Rastas hailing him at the airport that he took a while to leave the plane. During this visit, Selassie gave Manley a staff that was promptly dubbed the Rod of Correction. Over a decade later, Manley still used it to great advantage, flourishing the rod at meetings around the island to adoring crowds hailing him with shouts of "Joshua! Joshua!"—the name of Moses' biblical protégé and successor, which Manley had claimed for himself.

Rita and Bob were among the many musicians who supported Manley's program in 1972, particularly intrigued, perhaps, by the suggestion that he would legalize the sacred herb that hovered, whispered but unwritten, around the campaign. The couple joined artists including boy wonder Dennis Brown and the smooth crooner Alton "Mr. Rock Steady" Ellis, two of Jamaica's finest singers, on the traveling PNP Musical Bandwagon. The result of this musical activism was a radio ban of all the PNP musicians' records, including those of the Wailers. The ban was lifted, however, when Manley swept into power with an unprecedented majority of thirty-seven seats to the JLP's sixteen.

IN HIS CANNY DEPLOYMENT OF Rasta ritual and symbols, Manley was tapping into a primal aspect of Jamaica. With every successive wave of clampdowns by the police of either party, starting in the mid-1930s, and continuing through each decade, the first victims of harassment were always Jamaica's Rastafarians, often referred to as "blackheart men" for their fearsome aspect. Not many islands can boast their own belief system; particularly not one that has gone on to sweep the world, as has Rasta. But Jamaica has always had a love affair with religion and spirituality. In common with enslaved Africans in America, Jamaicans perfected a way of making Christianity, which operated on one level as a tool of the slavers' control systems, into their own cosmic discourse.

Though slave owners, pastors, and missionaries in Jamaica pushed Christianity via a cluster of Christian groups like the

Pentecostals, Nazarenes, and Seventh-Day Adventists, the stolen Africans managed to cling to their beliefs and practices and transmit them to their children against all odds. So the spirit of African worship never was suppressed, despite all the British efforts, and the drums remained in the Pocomania, Revivalist, and Kumina faiths, to inspire every generation of Jamaican artists.

However, for many, the relationship between Jamaica's religions was something of an open marriage. Thus, in the countryside it has always been common for Pocomania worshippers who spoke in frenzied, foaming tongues at a tent revival meeting on Friday to double as dignified, devout Christian churchgoers on Sunday. In case of any of life's little upsets, it was also common to then consult an Obeah man or woman.

These concurrent streams of spirituality were joined by a new cosmology, Rasta, channeled to the believers by Jamaican visionaries like Joseph Hibbert. Though he was born in Jamaica in 1894, Hibbert grew up in Costa Rica, where he joined an occult Masonic group known as the Ancient Mystic Order of Ethiopia. Returning to Jamaica in the early 1930s, which was a decade of fierce social upheaval and rioting on the island, Hibbert began to preach the divinity of Ethiopian ruler Haile Selassie to people hungry for a new system. He was soon joined in his mission by a sailor called H. Archibald Dunkley, who helped Hibbert launch the Jamaican branch of Selassie's Ethiopian World Federation in 1938.

But the man who really focused what eventually became the Rastafarian movement was the charismatic Leonard P. Howell, who, like both Hibbert and Dunkley, was repeatedly harassed by the police. Howell was incarcerated in both prison and a mental hospital for firing up Jamaicans with his faith. After his release from prison on a sedition charge (he'd been selling postcards of Selassie, claiming they were passports to Ethiopia, which they were on a metaphorical level), in 1940 he founded Pinnacle, the first Rasta commune. Pinnacle was an independent Rasta republic that served as a base for Howell's Ethiopian Salvation Society. Though raided incessantly, Pinnacle was a fully functioning community with its own industries, such as shoemaking. A model of an alternative, self-contained community, Pinnacle was a focus for the Rasta musicians.

As an example of what Burning Spear calls "social living," Pinnacle was run according to the Bible, which is the template for Rasta patterns of life. That belief was so fundamental that it's enshrined in doctrine of the original Rastafarian preachers in 1930s Jamaica, who taught that Rastas are the original Israelites; as Rasta lawyer Diane Jobson told me, "You call yourself Jewish; I am a Jew." Exhortations to smoke weed are culled from Genesis 9:3, Psalms 18, and Revelations 22, and the imperative of not cutting one's hair is taken from Numbers 6, just as it is by Jews who sport payis, the long side curls that are effectively Yiddish dreadlocks. Vigorous and uninhibited debate about the Bible is a crucial part of a good grounation, just as it is in a yeshiva's spirited Talmudic shi'urim debates. Naturally, preparation of salt- and scavenger-free ital food—Rasta's kashrut—by demurely dressed Rasta daw'tas was a constant ongoing process at Pinnacle, where simply getting water was a daily chore.

The original Nyabinghi was a warrior princess from what became Rwanda, who died fighting the Europeans in the battle for Africa. A cult developed around her that was revived among Ethiopian fighters in the 1930s during the Italian invasion, and was soon adopted by the Rastas in Jamaica to identify the strictest, purest, most orthodox group within the Rasta movement.

The pulse of Pinnacle was those Nyabinghi grounation sessions that sometimes lasted for days, with Rastas beating the funde, kete, and repeater drums in round-the-clock relays, chanting down

Babylon by firelight and the midday sun. Such prolonged drumming and chanting leads to a trancelike state of abandon fueled by giant chalice pipes full of weed, an experience that Chasidic reggae singer Matisyahu compares to Bible students at a *fahrbreng* gathering, their reasoning enhanced by the preferred tipple, *mashkeh*.

Hip uptown Kingstonians would drive out to the wild Rockfort Hills to experience a session; it was at such a grounation that Bob first met Johnny Nash in 1966, for example, when the visiting American singer was curious to explore Rasta. The more spirited sisters, like Drummond's flame Margarita, would dance by the firelight. However, few, if any, females drummed or drew on the chalice.

Heading the whole metaphysical, numerological cosmology of Rastafari, and frequently acknowledged in an exultant shout that bursts from the gut, is Jah Rastafari: the Rasta God, Haile Selassie, emperor of Ethiopia, often affectionately yet respectfully called H.I.M., the acronym for his full, resounding title: His Imperial Majesty Haile Selassie I, King of Kings, Lord of Lords, Conquering Lion of the Tribe of Judah. Selassie's divinity was based in part on the understanding of his 1930 coronation as the fulfillment of biblical prophecy: "And a black king shall arise in Ethiopia." Selassie's flamboyant style certainly had a majesty all its own. Enhancing his mystique, he was frequently flanked by lions, the king of beasts, who had the run of his palace. As he feasted, scraps would be flung to starving crowds outside the kitchen door, and Selassie would drive in pomp through the streets of the capital, Addis Ababa, dispersing random largesse to his illiterate, impoverished people by flinging money to the crowd.

The Haile Selassie phenomenon is rich in contradictions. The unconverted find it hard to understand why Rastas believe that God is a man whom many nonbelievers regard as a vicious, greedy dictator, while to the Rastas, Selassie is a progressive, benignly paternal deity, the essence of justice and goodness, as befits a direct descendant of wise King Solomon and the adventurous Queen of Sheba. Selassie is a complex puzzle. H.I.M. really was committed to progress, sometimes almost appearing to fetishize Western-style technical development at the expense of social growth. Yet at the same time he followed aspects of an ancient order he barely questioned—though according to the courtiers interviewed by writer Ryszard Kapuściński for his revealing book *The Emperor,* Selassie delighted in promoting trusted leaders from among the ranks of the poorest, following his instinct instead of the established order.

From airplanes to hospitals, banks, and a standing army, Selassie introduced many elements of the modern world to Ethiopia. While not a great reader himself and mistrustful of the written word, he nonetheless built a university in Addis Ababa—which was later to prove the scene of much of the student unrest that led to his overthrow by Colonel Mengistu Haile Mariam's Marxists in 1974 and to the forced exile of H.I.M.'s own family.

Haile Selassie's rise to power was not a given. A quick-witted rural chief, Selassie was a small, slight outsider to the court, who surprised many when he was picked to rule the country instead of his more physically imposing, Communist-learning cousin Lij Yasu. Particularly at a time when international black heroes were all too few, Selassie was a supreme and incomparable black king, whose speeches are as noble and uplifting as those of Martin Luther King Jr. Bob Marley's adaptation of a speech by Selassie on *Rastaman Vibration*'s "War" indicates the force of his oratory: "Until the philosophy that holds one man superior and another inferior is finally and permanently discredited and abandoned—everywhere is war." In Selassie's speeches reside his aspirational self and higher consciousness. He was heavily criticized for neglecting mass deaths from the famines that regularly ravaged Ethiopia's northern regions; however, H.I.M. evidently regarded a certain amount of human wastage as both natural and inevitable. Selassie sincerely felt his power was absolutely divine and that any perceived harshness was utterly justified to keep control of a nation he was sure would be lost without him.

For oppressed, displaced Africans looking on from afar, there seemed to be very good reasons to attribute godlike qualities to H.I.M. A repeated refrain in the Passover Seder is *dayenu*, meaning "enough"; that is, any of the many divine blessings the fleeing Hebrews received might have sufficed to make them believers. In the same way, surely it was enough that Haile Selassie had fended off invasions from within and without, including one by Mussolini, and was the strong black ruler of a nation that had preserved its integrity for two thousand years. For Rastas, of course, Selassie *is* divine. His Majesty with no apology. Bob had been utterly committed ever since first receiving a vision of H.I.M. wearing a brown raincoat, while he was living in Delaware with his mother in 1966. He then took on the new Twelve Tribes name, Joseph, which the Bible describes as meaning "a fruitful bough."

When I quizzed Bob about the wisdom and propriety of worshipping Haile Selassie, who by then had become typified as a ruthless dictator, he snapped incredulously, "So you want me to worship a *white* god?" But I wasn't the only one asking. Bob sometimes found himself having to defend his deity to some surprising infidels. As old friend Nancy Burke—Jamaican artist, elegant model, and Air Jamaica stewardess—remembers, "We were sitting in the kitchen in Chelsea with one of Selassie's granddaughters, and Bob seemed very taken with her. She didn't share his views on Selassie being God. Not at all! She kept saying that he was her grandfather, just a man, and that his regime had forced so many people to flee the country. Bob got quite upset—he kept saying, 'Is so you talk about His Majesty?'"

Rastas love to study the *Kebra Nagast,* a mysterious sacred text over a thousand years old, which mixes Jesus Christ with the Old Testament. Based on the prophecies in this work, Rastas consider Selassie the 225th regal descendant of Sheba and Solomon, and hence a direct relation of Jesus Christ. Another aspect of Haile Selassie's appeal to Rastas is that he represents a pure African royal bloodline; anyone who doesn't believe that the Bible's characters weren't well equipped with melanin is delusional. For many centuries, Ethiopian culture was so undiluted by outside influences that it wasn't until after Selassie's passing in 1975 that the country adopted the same calendar as the rest of the world. Thus, Ethiopia represented a pure essence of Africa that most of the rest of the continent, divided and distorted by the foreign intervention of colonialism, could only strive to remember. Much of the work of Nigerian rebel musician and father of Afrobeat, Fela Anikulapo Kuti, for example, was motivated by rediscovering and redefining what it means to be African in the postcolonial era.

Ethiopia endured two invasions by the Italians, first in 1896, then again during the period 1935–1941, when Benito Mussolini's Fascists overtook the country, slaughtering some five hundred thousand Ethiopians and renaming the country Abyssinia as part of their attempt at cultural genocide and the erasure of Ethiopia's ancient identity. The massacre galvanized descendants of Africans in the diaspora, particularly in Jamaica, where news of the horrors encouraged many people to become Rastas in solidarity with their beleaguered roots.

Like Bob Marley years later, Haile Selassie himself became a refugee in 1936, fleeing to London on his own exodus and attempting to wake the world to the threat of Fascism. When *Time* named H.I.M. its Man of the Year in 1936, the magazine wrote, revealingly, "If [Selassie's work] ends in the fall of Mussolini and the collapse of Fascism, His Majesty can plume himself on one of the greatest feats ever credited to blackamoors. Above all, Haile Selassie has created a general, warm and blind sympathy for uncivilized Ethiopia throughout civilized Christendom." Ironically, Ethiopia had one of the oldest undiluted Christian churches in the world, the Ethiopian Orthodox Coptic Church.

However, it appeared to some observers that for whatever reason, Selassie was at that point interested in distancing himself from the black community. Whatever the truth of that claim, its mere suggestion enraged one of his greatest supporters, Marcus Garvey, a patron saint of Rasta and Jamaica, who was also a refugee in London, having been deported from America. "When the facts of history are written Haile Selassie of Abyssinia will go down as a great coward who ran away from his country," Garvey thundered in the pages of his monthly magazine, the *Black Man*, in 1937.

HE MAY HAVE BEEN MISLED, but Garvey's fury at what he perceived as the emperor's betrayal of the black race is understandable. He was deeply invested in the idea—the ideal—of Ethiopia. Even the anthem of the Universal Negro Improvement Association (UNIA), founded by Garvey, hailed the nation: "Land of Our Fathers" was written by UNIA's official composer, a black rabbi from Barbados named Arnold J. Ford, whose congregation, Beth B'nai Abraham, was the spiritual home for Harlem's growing Afro-Jewish population. Frequently, Garvey invoked Psalms 68:31: "Ethiopia lifts up her hands toward God." A descendant of the Maroons, and the youngest of eleven children, Garvey was born in 1887 in St. Ann's Bay. The lovely cove was later to be the birthplace of both Bob Marley and his contemporary, Winston Rodney, aka Burning Spear, another Studio One alumnus who often sings of Garvey.

Garvey's parents were a well-educated couple (though his father was to die in the poorhouse) who had spirited debates about their baby's name. Somewhat prophetically, as Garvey did indeed grow up to be a leader of his people, his mother wanted to name him Moses. However, his father felt uncomfortable with the child being so closely identified with the Bible and organized religion. They finally compromised, by giving him the middle name Mosiah.

They could scarcely have predicted how Marcus Mosiah Garvey's accomplishments, travels, and travails really would bring Moses to mind. On his often reluctant quest, the biblical prophet Moses also roamed: from Egypt to Midian, then to Ethiopia and back, all before leading the Hebrews across the desert to the Promised Land. Garvey was absolutely tuned in to the ideas of the Book of Exodus, and specifically referred to the flight from Egypt in his rolling, preacherly exhortations: "In the one age or period the one race rule or triumph, while the other stalks under the heel of oppression . . . the Jews in Egypt . . . the Negroes in America."

After shuttling between Panama, Ecuador, Nicaragua, Honduras, Colombia, and Venezuela, like many Jamaican economic migrants, Garvey moved to London in 1912, and founded the *Black Man.* As he wrote, "I had not much difficulty in finding and holding a place for myself, because I was aggressive." He was consistently striving to make his vision of black economic independence, equality, and repatriation to Africa a reality by any means possible, principally the United Negro Improvement Association, which he founded in Jamaica in 1914.

From then on, Garvey continued to travel wherever necessary to spread his mission. Two months after a UNIA chapter was founded in Harlem, it had a membership of two thousand. Among his most potent projects was the 1919 launch of the Black Star Line, a fleet of ships to transport black Americans to Liberia, a country established by America specifically to provide a homeland for slaves' descendants. A mighty initiative whose impact rings down the ages, this ultimately proved to be Garvey's undoing. As the magnetic force of the UNIA swelled its ranks of international sympathizers into the millions, hatred of Garvey was growing among the political elites, including black establishment leaders such as W. E. B. Du Bois. Convicted on trumped-up charges of mail fraud relating to the line, he was deported to Jamaica amid solemn crowds weeping to see his departure in 1927. Nonetheless, popular imagination continued to be captured by the Black Star Line, which inspired many reggae songs by roots artists such as Fred Locks and Freddie McGregor, and an ongoing discussion about the ideas of both repatriation and reparations for slavery.

Garvey was a showman with substance who in a very modern way understood the importance of projecting a strong visual identity. A master of image in his plumed helmet and imposing gold-braided uniform, Garvey's majestic ritual and display shocked the unaware into realizing that blacks were not automatically second-class citizens, as they'd been so neatly categorized by a separatist society. He was the most prominent pan-Africanist to date, and his charisma and vision helped weld the African diaspora into a more cohesive community.

Through all his times in the wilderness, Garvey was always regarded as a great leader, and hailed as the Black Moses. Yet even that accolade was used against him. In his appeal for pardon, written from federal prison in Atlanta, Georgia, on June 5, 1925, while incarcerated for mail fraud, Garvey wrote: "The following statement of the learned Judges of the Circuit Court of Appeals shows an unreasonable prejudice toward me in their opinion: 'It may be true that Garvey fancied himself a Moses, if not a Messiah.' There is no evidence in the record to show that I at any time ever asserted the belief of being a Messiah; the records will show to the contrary that

I have always been a Christian. . . . The reference to my being a Moses is based upon the colorful and prejudiced newspaper exaggeration and the undercurrent of whispered and propagated enemy movements."

This pan-African world citizen died without ever seeing Africa for himself, in a poignant echo of Moses' story. During Garvey's final stay in Jamaica, children jeered and threw stones at him in the street until, brokenhearted, he made his way back to England, where he died in poverty in 1940.

Eight years later, Haile Selassie dedicated a fertile Ethiopian valley, Shashamane, to the black people of the West as a site for African descendants' right of return to the Motherland. Much of Bob Marley's *Exodus* time in London was spent helping the Jamaican Rasta body, the Twelve Tribes of Israel, fulfill Marcus Garvey's vision by developing homes and farms there, and Shashamane was a refuge for Bob's bred'ren, star footballer Allan "Skill" Cole, when he joined its expat Jamaican community after the 1976 shooting at Hope Road.

In much the same way as the popularity of Marley's oeuvre has increased every year since his passing, Garvey's influence keeps on growing. Acknowledging the wrongs done to one of the country's most significant sons, Edward Seaga ordered that Garvey be disinterred from Kensal Green Cemetery in West London—not far from Basing Street, where the Wailers recorded *Exodus*—and buried him in Jamaica's National Heroes Park in 1964. Garvey's impact is incalculable, as he influenced every black political thinker of the modern age, including Martin Luther King Jr., Malcolm X, and Bob Marley.

FOR THE MOSTLY DREAD INHABITANTS of Trench Town ghetto set by the scrubby seaside, Garvey's words rank up there alongside those of Haile Selassie and the Bible. Their guidance was very necessary as the relationship between Jamaica's two ruling parties and their followers became more toxic after 1972. Up to that point, political opponents lived in the same yard and didn't automatically reach for their guns if they disputed one another's loyalties. But as gas prices got higher, jobs fewer, and money scarcer, the toxicity of the intertribal venom grew more lethal in the four years running up to the election of 1976.

When the zoning of the area changed in that year, it split what had previously been a majority JLP area into two: First to Seventh Streets, known as Rema, remained Labourite, and was now separated from its northern side, Arnett Gardens, which became a PNP section of South St. Andrew. As surely as when the border was drawn in 1945 between Pakistan and India, a new set of hostilities was born among former neighbors. Because people possessed so little materially, the success of "your" party meant everything—food, homes, jobs, success with women—to the people caught up in downtown's civil wars.

PNP rhetoric boasted of eliminating the Labourite community whose territory separated their area from the Caribbean, because they wanted "to see the sea." To prove their point, they dispatched bulldozers that razed two whole blocks of homes between Fifth and Seventh Streets. The rubble then became a dangerous no-man's-land with a sea view, onto which bold youths would sneak out at night to tap into the public phone wires and call friends in America—a reckless "bandooloo" move that could easily result in death.

Michael Manley's opponent was now the complex Edward Seaga, whose offbeat route into politics was via academia and music. These two men would engage in a battle for Bob Marley's soul. Manley could work Rasta, but Seaga knew something too about marshaling spiritual forces. While a student at Harvard he wrote about Pocomania, and adding to his credentials as an Obeah expert, if not practitioner, he also coproduced a 1955 field recording of Jamaican spiritual drums.

Unsurprisingly, it was widely held that Seaga could call on some sinister supernatural backup, and Obeah accusations hovered round his campaign, as did the belief that Seaga had been a covert CIA man since his Harvard days.

As two equally weighted opponents squared off in 1976, Kingston was a town on fire, a lawless police state. Police road checks were common. On the way home from a show by the drum troupe Ras Michael and the Sons of Negus, we were stopped and made to get out of the car three times within a few miles. Occasionally, these encounters had some slight amusement potential, as in the one among very many in 1978 that saw Johnny Rotten, Nancy Burke, and myself being lengthily frisked on the side of a winding Blue Mountain road until the cops got the punk singer's identity. Then it was all "Is him a mek 'God Save the Queen'! You safe, mon!" while nonetheless extracting a "white tax" of a couple of hundred Jamaican dollars, anyway. Such moments of levity aside, the endless harassment was brutal. Almost all street fatalities occurred as "ghetto runnings" down below the belt of Kingston, Half Way Tree, and in 1977 alone, over two thousand people were murdered.

Tension crackled everywhere. Though they were some years younger, Michael Smith and Doyley of the First Street harmony group Knowledge grew up on the block with Bob, alongside the DJ Massive Dread. "Things changed starting 1974, and it end up we don't go nowhere," Mikey recalls fervently. "We couldn't go to Wareika Hills, because the PNP control those areas; we couldn't go even up to Half Way Tree, and we certainly couldn't reach up to 56 Hope Road no more. When you cross a borderline in those days, dem look over the fence at you, some men would approach you and ask you where you come from. You can't say you come from Rema or you *dead*. You know you could be shot or lynched. When you cross a borderline in those days, there was no turning back."

Bob had his own way of dealing with it. On a visit to Hope Road, when he paused from taking energetic puffs on a communal "chalice" and passed it on, I asked if he was bothered much by the police. "I hardly ever on the streets to get stopped. I is a man who don't really travel up and down too much," he replied laconically. Effectively, the stress on the streets was keeping Bob at home, just like his bred'ren in the ghetto. But as always, wherever he was, he had to play soccer, and he liked a sports field in the downtown neighborhood called Boystown, right by Trench Town. Accompanied by his friend Devon Lewis, a footballer from a PNP area, Bob drove down via First Street and checked his old mentor in the yard, Vincent "Tata" Forde, then headed toward the football pitch. But even before they reached it, they could see a shoot-out start up ahead between people from Rema and Arnett Gardens hanging around outside the field. There would be no match that day. As Bob watched the sudden gunfire blaze, the frown line between his eyes deepened and he shook his head. "Bwaoy," he said slowly, "look how t'ings change and de people dem a live now." At that moment, as Michael Smith says, "Bob knew he never have the power to stop it. It had gone out of his hands. And Bob was the only one who could stop politics dem time."

Throughout, it was Bob's job to somehow remain an apolitical neutral zone, while both parties pushed to co-opt him. Never was his nickname the Skipper more relevant than in this necessity to steer safely through the opposing camps, ideally alienating no one while retaining his integrity.

The task was not easy. At one stage, Bob even had a confrontation with his Trench Town bred'ren from the group Knowledge in the yard at Hope Road, for reasons they're unsure of. That day, the members of Knowledge were feeling somewhat outnumbered in the yard by members of the rival political party, Seaga's

JLP, also called Labourites or Junglists, since they come from the area called Concrete Jungle. Suddenly Bob burst out of the house where he'd been reasoning with some JLP dons, and for the first time spoke so harshly to the Knowledge Dreads that they left Hope Road for good. Was Bob trying to protect them from their enemies? Had the Junglists been spreading false rumors to Bob about his childhood bred'ren? The members of Knowledge didn't know, but the row was symptomatic of the knife-edge "heavy manners" of that time, which required discipline to overcome.

Bob was all too familiar with the grim, shabby corridors of a prison that was newly constructed to cope with those who fell afoul of the authorities at the time, during the declared state of emergency; he was often called on to bail people out or plead their case to the governor. Architecturally inspired by concentration camps, the forbidding Gun Court was the automatic destination of everyone found with a gun; no trial was necessary under the state-of-emergency laws. Known by its inhabitants as "Red Fort," the prison also functioned as Jamaica's answer to Robben Island, the South African jail where Mandela was incarcerated under apartheid. Opposition JLP leaders were routinely incarcerated there. Prisoners included Babsy Grange, later to become minister of culture under Seaga. Also among its incarcerated while I was merrily exploring Jamaican music in 1976 was Bob's childhood friend Claudius "Claudie" Massop, the JLP area leader.

While Massop and his like did time, the real players in Jamaica's downtown wars were oceans away, in America and Russia. It had been a big buildup to this mess. Playing the jilted lover, America cold-shouldered Cuba even before Batista's unabashedly self-serving ruling class was overthrown by Castro in 1959. This high school prom tactic ensured that Castro waltzed off with America's archenemy, Russia. Regardless of his other policies—Castro is as complex and contradictory a national leader as Haile Selassie—the bearded revolutionary befriended Jamaica in the 1970s, building durable schools and roads. He offered help when the IMF was only offering slave-driver deals on loans that were evidently not designed to help the island, which had been independent for less than two decades.

Manley's idealistic policies pumped money into the social sector. Like Gandhi, he pushed for self-sufficiency in areas such as agriculture, and limited imports of oil and automobiles. He outraged America by raising Jamaica's tariff rate on the island's sole asset, bauxite. Fearing a seizure of their property as Castro had done in Cuba, many better-off Jamaicans sold up and left for Miami, leaving a vacuum of professionals.

Tourism took a blow, recalls film producer Maxine Walters, who was then running the Jamaica Tourist Board. "The international hotel chains pulled out and the government bought everything. But the people really got behind it and even the big hotels were full," she concludes with satisfaction. Nonetheless, under the open-trade agreements demanded by the IMF and the World Bank, imported government-subsidized American powdered milk and chicken, below market price but often past its prime, was dumped on the island. Astonishingly soon, the island's cotton, dairy, and poultry industries were virtually killed.

As Michael Manley explains in Stephanie Black's searing documentary, *Life and Debt,* rather than trying to help boost a newly independent democracy, as he'd hoped, the IMF's terms were so brutally punitive that they brought tears to his eyes. But desperation made him sign in 1977, even knowing that they virtually guaranteed Jamaica would be trapped in an impossible cycle of increasing debt that would amount to another form of colonial subjugation.

All Manley's bold populist measures, even if they seemed extreme, were designed to make Jamaica more self-sufficient and independent. But his urge to adjust the balance of power, at least to some extent, and give Jamaica some autonomy and an existence outside being an offshore resource or satellite for its neighboring superpower, brought the hell of systematic destabilization down on his head from the Nixon government in America. Comparatively mildly, Manley called it "putting the squeeze on the economy," but the retaliation for Jamaica's headstrong impertinence in seeking some measure of self-determination was brutal.

Writer and filmmaker Saul Landau was shooting PNP campaign films for Manley in 1976 when, he wrote, "I witnessed Seaga's thugs use arson and gun terror as tactics to scare and alienate voters from Manley. . . . The world financial elite retaliated against (Manley's) 'radical' polices. Jamaica's ability to get loans and credit suffered as Jamaica's business elite simultaneously withdrew their money from Jamaican banks and refused to invest."

So even those who appear all-powerful must serve their own masters. In the sometimes claustrophobic confines of the island, however, where the real blood was shed, politicians seemed the kings, and the poor, the pawns.

The borderline and balance between "gunman," "area leader," "thug," and "brother" tends to shift according to who's talking. While some simply enjoyed the warrior life and its rewards, many young men evidently failed to get through their youth without being co-opted and used as muscle by the political party whose area they happened to live in. The killing of so many of the brightest area leaders together with the forced exile of so many others left the urban areas in the uncontested grasp of the island's desperadoes.

Bob Marley was an advocate of marijuana, the sacred healing

herb, but discouraged the use of drugs such as cocaine. Yet as co-caine was eroding more than the nasal membranes of America's R&B elite whose acceptance was part of Bob's strategy, it also blew money into Jamaica's outlaw gangs. Once again, Jamaica's lo-cation was making it an ideal entrepot. But now, instead of export-ing sugar and importing captured people, like the infamous "slave triangle" between England, Africa, and the Caribbean or America, the island was functioning as a transshipment point for a new type of trade triangle. Guns came from America to Jamaica; some stayed on the island, and the rest were sent on to Colombia in exchange for cocaine destined for America, via Jamaica, where a cut was ob-viously retained for domestic consumption. Nearby Panama was controlled by CIA favorite General Noriega, and JLP gunmen in Kingston were also enjoying American largesse for their collusion in the coke trade.

A warped tribute to the organization and efficacy of these down-town dons' private armies was the ease with which they morphed into the dreaded Yardie gangs, like the Shower Posse, that menaced New York and London in the 1980s. These gangs were famously headed by Vivian Blake and Jim Brown, each raised in Kingston and well known to Bob. Blake and Brown were both local community benefactors and gangster overachievers, whose extreme, gruesome killing techniques scored headlines for ruthlessness. Eventually, the top-ranking dons became warlords in the style of Colombia, with which they increasingly traded as Jamaica became a more important cocaine smuggling point. Once directly plugged into that big, bad cocaine cash, the politicians could no longer control their formerly contracted killers. In a sense, the ghetto dons had outmaneuvered their old Pharaohs.

However, as events around the making of Bob's *Exodus* indi-cate, certain threats to the status quo could arise to prompt Ja-

5

SMILE JAMAICA

Kingston, December, 1976. It was my time to go home to London. The many dramas of a Jamaican day, with its interminable army roadblocks and curfews, were about to be exchanged for a more familiar sort of stress. Leaving my packing at the hotel, I decided to visit 56 Hope Road to say goodbye to Bob and Fams; regretfully, I had to leave the island and return to the winter gray of London and the growing power struggles of the *Sounds* office in Covent Garden. Already identified with the brand-new Rock Against Racism movement, punk and reggae were being pitted against skinhead bands like Skrewdriver, associates of the white supremacist National Front, who were then gaining Parliamentary seats at an unprecedented rate. There were almost two million people unemployed in Great Britain, and they were wondering how great Britain really was. The social turbulence in London, which was at that time pretty gun-free, was less bloody and brutal than Jamaica's, but felt almost as wrenching for those on its front line. Power games were everywhere and I thought I was a player; but I was about to learn I didn't even understand the real rules.

Just as I arrived at Hope Road's old stone gateposts to find no one home, one of Bob's bred'ren miraculously appeared and shouted, "What! You still here?" Roaring with laughter, he threw

This cheery single from 1976 with its smiling sun label was meant to pro-
mote peace—but it helped ignite an exodus.
*Logo design: Neville Garrick. Used courtesy of Roger Steffens Reggae
Archive.*

open the door of his beat-up, patched-up sedan with such vigor I feared it would drop off. "Jump in!" the Dread said cheerfully. It was not till months later that I caused a scandal in downtown Kingston music circles, when producer Joe Gibbs punched me out in the yard of his studio; I got that black eye by quoting his artists complaining about payments. But evidently news of foreign journalists' misadventures at road blocks and street dance shoot-outs were already circulating, and I was teased all the way to what turned out to be a Wailers session at Harry J's.

It was a posh drive, taking us past a variety of Kingston's contrasting neighborhoods. Zigzagging down shortcuts off Hope Road, we cruised through tree-lined suburban avenues, past Kingston's stately homes: Jimmy Cliff's ample bungalow, the governor general's ornate pile, and the delicate confection of Devon House's pretty moldings. Eras switched as we turned left into New Kingston's Knutsford Boulevard, the 1960s futurism of the big hotels a symbol of postcolonial aspirations. Past my old hangout, the Kingston Sheraton, we struck east and up, as if we were going to the wild Wareika Hills where Rasta *livity* began in the early 1950s in encampments like Leonard Howell's Pinnacle. But instead we took a turn that led us to the lower reaches of Beverley Hills, so named because the streets bend and curve through low rolling peaks and crests, like the area's LA namesake. Inspired by the parallels, similar postmodern bungalows nestle in the Kingston mountain's folds.

Indeed, Harry J's at Roosevelt Avenue was like a little piece of California transplanted incongruously to Kingston's dusty streets. The most up-to-date facility on the island, Harry J's boasted a Siemens board identical to the one used by the Rolling Stones, which Chris Blackwell had bought for Harry J. Its cosmopolitan interior was a far cry from Bob's earliest recording environments, in rackety downtown concrete jungle environments like Leslie Kong's Beverley's, and Coxsone Dodd's crucial hit-maker, Studio One.

The session, engineered as usual by quiet, competent Sylvan Morris, was typically professional. "Work first, play later" was always Bob's motto. After all, the Wailers in combination with Bob Marley were not the island's supergroup by accident.

"My program now is to get really fit, but me a (do some) songs," Bob had mentioned to me a few days before, sitting by the Sheraton pool with a writer from *Ebony*. "If I have to do an album, I have to do an album, but me no really plan it out yet."

So, with the new Wailers' progress on track, the band was enjoying the leisurely amassing of material with no particular outcome in mind.

When we arrive the session is well under way and Bob is about to lay down a take. Turns out it's a session for a song Bob had mentioned he was working on a couple of days before, at the Sheraton. "It name 'Smile Jamaica,' and it deal with what's happening now—what should be happening now," he corrected. "Trench Town have to change. Long time, plenty people grown up there, and it have fe change . . . the political thing. But me never see myself, I never really call myself, political. Me only want to talk about the truth."

Here is what happened at that Harry J's session, as I wrote it just days later, for *Sounds*.

> Certain people in Kingston denounce Bob Marley for being a commercial Rasta (i.e., having sold out), but he certainly doesn't see himself that way. The night before, in the yard at Hope Road, he'd snarled contemptuously about some hapless individual, "'Im don' wanna smoke 'erb, mon, 'im just wanna get high."
>
> Bob in the studio is a serious t'ing indeed. He records at Harry J's, probably the most luxurious studio on the island.

Tonight Bob's laying down the vocals for his new single, "Smile Jamaica."

Wearing a yellow Spartan Health Club T-shirt, cut-off jeans, and the usual broken leather sandals, Bob's tucked away in a sound booth. By this stage of his career, Bob's a total master-singer. He spends three hours or more getting the phrasing perfect, adding a minute inflection here, changing the phrasing of a line there. Concentration is absolute.

There's quite a few brothers and sisters in the studio tonight—including two of Bob's backup singers, the I-Three, Rita Marley, Judy Mowatt, and Marcia Griffiths, wearing ankle-length denim. We all sit round on the shag-carpeted stairs, talking of this and that. Family Man, the bass player, is sitting at the board, rolling an endless series of perfect conical spliffs.

"Too much raas claat noise out there!" Bob shouts through. Family swivels round to us. "Bob say to be more quiet," he calls to us, "bred'ren be of one itation!" Pleased with his delivery, he carries on rolling.

In a break, Bob sits down next to me on a bench by the board. Drinking from a bottle of fruit juice, he explains in a low voice, " 'Smile Jamaica' is supposed to be what's happening now . . . because Jamaica's a place where—when you hear 'Rasta,' you hear 'Jamaica.' The outside world people think dat people in Jamaica is Rasta, but only some of de people is Rasta. So now that people start to accept Rasta, to deal with Rastaman as a human being instead of somebody you just curse every day, that's different."

Bob pauses, takes a hit off the juice.

"Jamaica need to smile, because in Jamaica everyone really vex too much." With that, he walked frowning to the board and asked Family Man to play the tape back. He listens to his *voice, leaning against the board, the line between his brows even deeper—his face is in a permanent screw. He might have written the song for himself.*

"Dat alright?" he enquires anxiously.

Not half, Bob. "Smile Jamaica" is probably the most instantly adorable single Bob's ever released. Funky horns punctuate. He pokes gentle fun at the outside world's conception of the island—"soulful town, soulful people, seems like you're having fun dancing to the reggae riddum—O island in the sun . . ."

It's a message of joy and unadulterated positive vibrations— Rastaman vibrations.

"Feeling up, feeling down, this feeling wouldn't leave me alone, then there came one that said, Hey Dread—fly Natty Dread, and smile, you're in Jamaica. . . !"

By this stage of the recording, Bob has deepened the quality of his singing. Every syllable rings out with meaning and love. As usual, Bob has a new message for his people, one that will be received with rejoicing. "Smile Jamaica" is one of the best singles I've ever heard; it's laughably catchy and impossible not to dance to. A palpable hit.

When Bob finishes, a Rasta mutters, "Strictly curfew, dis— under heavy manners." The hippest praise on the island.

It's poignant yet life-affirming, that nameless Rasta flipping into a compliment the pestilence of endless curfews that covered the land. Yet its very banality was to cause problems for Bob. At the end of "Smile Jamaica," Bob drawled that same expression, almost as an aside, "Under heavy manners, y'all." A shortened version of the current street expression "Heavy Manners and Discipline," it was a common catchphrase just then, also deployed by other artists, such as Big Youth. So Bob was showing that despite having "gone international," he was still hip to the streets, where the line referred to the rigors it was necessary to undergo to survive in those hazardous days.

At the time, the phrase really seemed quite normal, as curfews and roadblocks were indeed constant. Everyone was under "heavy manners," meaning that people knew what was necessary; and "discipline" truly was required to make it through the everyday conflict and frustration. But for conspiracy theorists, Bob's aside was a boost for the PNP, who had used the expression as a rallying cry on the campaign trail.

Yet despite, or because of, the heavy army and police presence, the violence just seemed to get worse. The sheer prettiness of Bob's song ignored the nightmarish ghetto violence that seemed to be the island's real story. Its cute strains were as tourist-ready as the white pinafores, red tartan skirts, and headwraps of the barefoot folk dancers performing for Independence Day. However, the Wailers' art director, Neville Garrick, sees the song working another way. We talk two decades later, by the swimming pool in the Ocho Rios garden of the late Denise Mills, Marley and Blackwell's trusted associate. Garrick cautions, "Don't forget, the lyrics also say, 'Cast away this evil spell, Throw some water in the well.' He was talking about politics. Even though the song was pretty, Bob was still sending a message, a warning." Garrick's opinion has to be valued; after all, he was the one Bob relied on to write down the words of his songs as he worked them out with his guitar. But despite the touch of manicured militancy in "Smile Jamaica," something about the track—which was originally released only as a single in Jamaica—must have grated on Bob, too.

Evidently Bob was not entirely convinced by the Harry J cut of "Smile Jamaica," or he felt he could get more mileage from the tune. Soon thereafter, he drove down to Scratch's Black Ark Studios with Rita, Judy, and Marcia Griffiths. There, a more staccato, percussion-driven take of the song was laid down, using Scratch's Upsetters. Far faster and rougher around the edges, it sounds like Bob's attempt to get some street roughness into the mix and dispel any possible MOR aura that might dull the song's sweet words. Island released the Harry J versions, while Scratch's was put out in various combinations of vocal and dub on the Tuff Gong label, which, as Scratch's biographer David Katz recalls with a chuckle, had wildly varying matrix numbers (possibly suggestive of the label's somewhat haphazard approach in that tumultuous time). The Jamaican cut of "Smile" bore a Neville Garrick illustration of a rising sun—a logo suggesting innocence that was to have sinister consequences.

"We put it to one side and there was some discussion about not having the record come out at all," Sylvan Morris remembers with a chuckle. "But in the end, it did. There was the Smile Jamaica concert coming up."

Definitively, Neville Garrick states, "It was Bob's idea to do a free concert." Inspiration had come from previous benefit gigs, such as the time in 1973 that the Wailers supported Marvin Gaye in aid of the Trench Town Sports Center. More recently, the island's media had bigged up a benefit that the Wailers played with Stevie Wonder for the Salvation Army School for the Blind, on October 4, 1975, during which Wonder jammed with Bob on "I Shot the Sheriff."

When Bob's benefit plan became known in 1976, he was approached separately by the JLP and the PNP, both eager for his support, but he chose to do a nonaligned event, albeit inevitably with government approval. "Michael jumped on it with full endorsement," says Garrick. "He said, 'All you guys have to do is rehearse.' " At first Manley proposed that the show be held on the lawns at Jamaica House, the prime minister's official residence.

"No, mek it somewhere central that don't have no political affiliation," Bob insisted.

"He knew that if we do it there, only PNP people gonna come, 'cos they were the ruling party, y'understand. So Bob was wise to that," says Garrick emphatically.

The situation was of sufficient concern that Bob sought counsel from Chris Blackwell. "Bob rang me up about the fact he'd been asked by Manley to do a show. There was some talk about an election coming up, and I said, 'It depends when the election is. Are you doing it for the party in government, or are you doing it for the country? Because if you play at election time, it could look as if you're doing it for the party. Check out when the election is,' " Blackwell remembers saying.

"Anyway, Bob couldn't get one response or the other. He announced he was doing the show, then almost right after that, Prime Minister Manley announced the election. So it really looked like he was doing a show for the PNP, and he'd always tried very hard to stay clear of politics, even though he was probably closer to the PNP, as most musicians are on the left. But he was not really into either of the parties."

Finally, the show was billed as a collaboration between the Wailers and the government's cultural office. So Bob was righteously angered when it was sprung on him that the election date had been brought forward to coincide with the Smile Jamaica show. Despite his best intentions, the Wailers' noble offering to the people had effectively been co-opted by Manley's PNP. The populist project now appeared to be little more than a promotional gig in the very territorial spirit Bob was trying to discourage. It was a cynical move on the PNP's part, which took a lot of the joy out of the idea.

The lightly sardonic voice of Bob's lawyer, Diane Jobson, drops uncannily into Bob's rasping snarl as she recalls how he said, "Diane, dem want to use me to draw crowd fe dem politricks."

No wonder Bob seemed extra thoughtful as he sang in the studio that afternoon, wringing every ounce of meaning from his optimistic vision of a happy island in the sun where everyone just got along.

After the "Smile Jamaica" session at Harry J's, the band split the studio quickly. The tune was cheerful, but as my article noted, Bob nonetheless had appeared distracted, anxious, despite his civility. A quarter century on, Sylvan Morris is still surprised at the speed of their exit. "Normally the Wailers would come into the studio so well rehearsed, they didn't even need a guide vocal to play the rhythm, and they would lay down two, maybe three tracks in a day," he recalls. "But that day they left after they'd laid down just one track."

As I was on my way out, Bob was sitting thoughtfully alone behind the mixing desk, so I went over to say goodbye and explain that the record company that had sent me over to interview bands was cutting off my hotel room, meaning I had to leave the island. "You no must leave 'cos of dat, man," he insisted genially. "You must come stay at Hope Road, long as you want."

So now I was to be a brief addition to that flexible, communal household.

Bob had encouraged Hope Road to become a "safe house," a neutral zone, in which youths caught up in the turmoil of the warring political factions could hang out and reason away from the old violent mind-set. He intended Hope Road to be a sort of uptown Pinnacle, the Rastas' uptown outpost. Some expressed surprise that Bob would reach out equally and try to show another way forward to youths from both parties, that he would sustain and deepen his involvement with feuding warlords. But as he said, "These are my bred'ren, who fed me when I had nothing. Without them I would have starved long time."

Although Bob and his bred'ren may have been involved in some of their own bad-boy business when they started out, it was nothing like what was seething now, in the buildup to the 1976 elections. It seemed as if the rival parties' respective alignments with the superpowers of America and Russia were two beams of white heat glaring down to focus on the lens of downtown Kingston, ready to ignite and burn its sufferers. At a certain point, Bob's utopian vision of the yard as sanctuary was bound to collide with street conflicts. He was in a delicate position, and to add to the irony, the enemies Bob was constantly trying to reconcile were often relations, old neighbors, and schoolmates.

Yet Bob's empathy with the downtown posses was endless. After all, he was no different, on many levels. He knew the psychology of these volatile youths all too well. "Is like dis youth grow up and him want to be fe real, and 'im don't want nothing stopping him being fe real," he said. "That means he'll kill for it if 'im supposed to, [because] 'im a strive fe reach somewhere, someone to be true to."

Taking up Bob's kind invitation, I found myself in a small property behind the main house, crashing on a mattress on the floor in the rehearsal room. Around five-thirty one morning I woke, restless, and looked out. Bob was standing in the otherwise quiet yard under the big mango tree, talking angrily to two men whom I couldn't see clearly. There was something ominous in their exchange. Even at a distance, Bob's body language was different from anything I'd seen before; tense and taut, he was brusquely intent on making his point. It was unsettling—and clearly a very private moment. I turned away and went back to bed. But sleep wasn't easy. For me, this brief and somehow troubling glimpse suggested a new side to this complex man, the rough one that gave him the name Tuff Gong—even tougher, perhaps, than the original Gong, the redoubtable First Rasta, Leonard Howell, who founded Pinnacle.

Among those who've reasoned about Bob's *Exodus*, it's usually held that the album is wholly a product of the traumatic event that was about to take place. But in reality, Bob already sensed that he was living in a time where imminent horror colored everyday beauty. Proof positive: relaxing in the rehearsal room late one night, I heard music floating up from below, so I drifted down the stairs that ran outside the building. The moonlit yard under the mango tree was crowded with around fifteen people sitting on the ground, the downtown kids who found refuge there and the Dreads who made it home. Tucked under the verandah of the little house was a bedroom with nothing but some hooks on the wall, a chair, and Bob, in dusty sandals and shorts, sitting on the edge of a narrow iron bed. It was just the kind that comes to mind when Bob lilts through the lines "We'll share the shelter / Of my single bed" on "Is This Love." Bob was playing his guitar, trying on chords for size.

A young girl sat at the other end of the bed, her eyes fixed on Bob. He sang to her and to all of us as he strummed wrath and reality on his twelve-string acoustic. His picking provided rhythm and hints of harmony as he sang: "Guiltiness, rest on their conscience, oh yeah . . ."

Everyone there was absorbed by the unaffected anger that stalked his crisp delivery. The words hit home to anyone who'd ever been aware of injustice in their lives—which meant everyone present, and many who would eventually hear the song in its majestic cut on the *Exodus* album. In that rapt crowd, hearing the fledgling sketch of a song that would soon seem prophetic, it appeared likely Bob was referring to our global controllers and their dependents whose very long spoon stirred the pot of ghetto conflict. Cynical as only politicians can be, powers in Jamaica and round the world callously pitted undereducated youths against one another in wave after wave of cannon fodder. Straight to their selfish heads went Bob's rolling, biblical words numbering the corrupt, those ultimately responsible for Kingston's bloody state.

Buoyed by Bob's proud melody and the words' righteous wrath, I slept better that night. I still had to go back to work in London—but now I felt recharged, ready to deal with my own set of politics, which Bob's song had clarified.

Feeling bouncy in my red tracksuit and silver trench coat, I raced into the office on my first morning back in London, ready to deal with anything. But I wasn't prepared for the serious look on the face of my editor, Allen Lewis. "Here, you'd better see this." He showed me a telex printout from Reuters: "Reggae Star Shot."

My heart thudded, not just for my narrow escape, but for the savage invasion of Bob's fragile utopia, and his very life. Before I sat at the sturdy IBM manual typewriter to write up the story, I grabbed the phone and sent a telegram to 56 Hope Road, sensing even then that by the time my words reached Jamaica, Bob and his tribe would be gone.

Bob contemplates at his Hope Road home, where he "brought the ghetto uptown." Frequent table tennis and football kept the communal energy high.

© *Adrian Boot/Bob Marley Music. Kingston, 1978.*

6

NEVER FORGET, NO WAY

FOR EVERYONE INVOLVED, the day gunmen tried to kill Bob Marley is etched in memory as if the invasion, as Family Man calls it, was acid flung right in the brain.

While not exactly open, the Wailers' rehearsals usually attracted a crowd of appreciative intimates. Those regulars who somehow avoided the attack tell their stories in hushed voices, with a frisson of survivor's guilt mixed with relief.

For many round town, December 3, 1976, was proving a difficult day, anyway. Chris Blackwell was on his way to Hope Road when he stopped off at Lee Perry's Black Ark to check out some new tracks. Sitting in the small, womblike control room, covered with red, green, and black fake fur and stills from kung fu flicks and Westerns of the spaghetti and Hollywood varieties, Blackwell was entranced by the neon towers and canyons of Lee Perry's spacey new track, "Dreadlocks in Moonlight," topped with the producer's own warbling vocals. "Me waan the Gong to voice dis ya one," explained Scratch. Blackwell said, "No. You can't improve on your own version. This is great. Make me a tape to carry."

So he sat down to watch Scratch work. No one mixed like Scratch. The skinny little man in a peak cap, undershirt, and shorts danced with the four-track TEAC from which he coaxed such shattering sounds. Darting in toward the knobs and faders, he'd flick them as if flame flashed from his fingertips, then twirl and pirouette, dipping back just in time to catch the beat. Blackwell was unsurprised when technical hitches made the promised few minutes stretch into over an hour. He resigned himself to being late for the Wailers' rehearsal.

For the Wailers' art director, Neville Garrick, the day was also not going as planned. Heading for rehearsal, he was stopped by a policeman and arrested for weed. Neville was already somewhat edgy, still shaken by the reaction he'd got when handing out his newly designed stickers for the Smile Jamaica concert to some Dread friends. One man retorted, "Me no put no political label deh pon my vehicle, Rasta." Garrick was confused, thinking everyone should know that Bob was performing an apolitical event. But then he looked at his own design again, and realized that the rising sun he'd blithely drawn to symbolize the dawning of a new, more loving island bore an uncomfortably close resemblance to the PNP logo.

Over at the villa of Dermot Hussey, the island's most noted broadcaster of reggae, the Wailers' keyboard player, Tyrone Downey, was lying on the floor trying to relax from the stress that had been going down at Hope Road. Sensitive and imaginative, Downey had been the baby of the Wailers, a protégé of Family Man, who'd first used him on sessions when Downey was twelve. He'd been nicknamed Jumpy when he first went on the road because of his wariness. Now Downey was legitimately nervous. Ever since the change of the election date that had so alarmed Bob, men had been bearing down on Hope Road, dropping heavy warnings to the singer. "Me hope you know what you a do, Dread," they would say, looking grim.

Hussey offered to drop off Downey and his girlfriend at Hope

Road for the rehearsal on his way to do *Progressions,* his eight
o'clock radio show. "I'll be back," Hussey announced as he pulled
away from Hope Road. He was in the habit of stopping by number
56 when Bob was readying for a tour, and as the rehearsals went
on from nine at night until two in the morning, Dermot had no intention of missing out on that night's session, bad vibes or not.

Hussey didn't know about the two plainclothes cops who had
been stationed outside the house during rehearsals, due to the gravity of the political situation, and thus didn't notice their absence.

Bob's friend and lawyer, Diane Jobson, had arrived at Hope
Road in good spirits, bearing especially sweet grapefruit and some
herb from Bob's favorite grower. But soon a profound nausea she'd
never experienced before washed over her. "Is you hold de nice
spliff, Diane?" Bob called out as she was leaving the kitchen.
Chuckling, she handed over some luscious buds and went to relax
and play with some of the yard children in Neville Garrick's little
house in the compound.

In the newly built narrow galley kitchen by the rehearsal room,
breezy and bright with a door at each end, Gilly the cook's blender
was whirring as he sliced and diced fruit with quick precision. He
could hear the Wailers' rehearsal perfectly. They had already polished "Baby We've Got a Date," "Trench Town Rock," "Midnight
Ravers," and "Rastaman Chant." Gilly remembers that when they
finished the I-Three's parts, Bob called a break, saying, "Fams, you
tek over rehearsin' the horns." So Family Man led David Madden
and the Zap Pow Horns into "Rastaman Vibration," a big favorite
in Jamaica. Now that the Smile Jamaica show was almost upon
them, everyone was looking forward to it, despite the tension in the
town. Bob was lighthearted, joking around with Fams and Carly
Barrett, who was sitting on a stool. Juggling the fat grapefruit
Diane had brought, Bob asked Neville to drive Judy Mowatt to her
Bull Bay home, a couple of hours away. She, too, had had bad

dreams the previous night and was still shaken. Neville protested; not only did he want to see the rest of the rehearsal, but the best herbsman on the island was due to pass through with his wares. It was getting dangerously near Christmas, when good weed is hard to come by, and Neville planned to lay in a store—particularly as his own was doubtless already being smoked by the cop who'd arrested him earlier. "Neville, you gwan like you love herb more than the rest of we," teased Bob. "Don't worry, we gwan hold some for you."

Thus reassured, and seeing fatigue in Judy's kindly eyes, Neville took the keys to Bob's new silver BMW and they set off. Now, this was a famous set of wheels, chosen because the initials suggested Bob Marley and the Wailers, and Bob didn't let many people drive it. Everyone started moving. Rita headed to her Volkswagen. Bob's friend and neighbor Nancy Burke was asked by Seeco to move her car so the girls could leave.

Nancy was feeling buoyant that night; she'd just got back from chaperoning Cindy Breakspeare as she won the Miss World contest in London. It was a great coup. In fact, even entering the contest had been daring of Breakspeare, as although Jamaican Miss World entrants had traditionally supplied wives for many local politicians, including Edward Seaga, Michael Manley's socialist Jamaica had dropped its Miss World membership, along with Cuba. Because of the tension in town, lately guards had been posted at the entry to Hope Road's circular drive, but no one was there and the gate was closed. Still, even that inconvenience couldn't dent Nancy's good mood.

She was dragged away from the kitchen by a little girl, one of Cindy's protégées, to join Diane Jobson and the other kids in Neville's cottage. Out on the road, Neville, Judy, and the Hope Road doorman, a Trench Town youth named Sticko, were already way off in the distance. Before steering her car through the gateposts, Rita paused to let another vehicle drive in—then screamed and jammed on the brakes as pain seared her scalp.

The other car's unseen passenger had shot her through her window and scorched on into the yard.

"Give me a juice, nah!" A booming cry in the kitchen made Bob and Gilly look up as Bob's manager, a swaggering, sharp-witted hustler called Don Taylor, strode in. But Taylor was followed almost immediately by three intruders—gunmen, charging in through the doors at either end of the kitchen. One brandished two automatics like he was Johnny Too Bad from *The Harder They Come*. They fired round after round, the sound deafening as the kitchen became a battlefield. The Wailers and their militant Dread posse were caught off guard. Indeed, even though this was the moment Bob had been dreading, when the shock came, he froze. Everything went into slow motion. He felt something push him, and he fell down; only later did he realize it was streetwise Don Taylor, raised working the volatile bars and brothels of the Kingston waterfront. The bullet aimed at Bob's heart instead smashed into his upper arm. Later, Bob was advised that an operation to remove it carried the risk of loss of control of his fingers, so the lead would stay there till he was in his coffin.

The noise of four automatics belching bullets suddenly silenced.

"I recognize one guy," mutters Gilly tersely. He won't name names. "They came in with two guns blazing and I ran out thanks to the power of the Most High." With an expertise learned in his childhood flights from the Trench Town cops, Gilly raced through the yard and over the wall. In the rehearsal room, bullets smashed into Carly's drum stool, and he fell to the floor. The next shots hit the wall, right where his head had been. Fams was trying to run for it but got caught up in the leads trapped under Carly's stool. The brothers disentangled themselves and sprinted for the bathroom, where they hid in the bathtub behind the shower curtain, hearts pounding. The Wailers' newest American guitarist, Donald Kinsey, was so freaked he left the island and the band the next day, never to return.

Tucked away in Neville's little house, Diane Jobson and Nancy Burke had no idea what was happening. Silently, both women prayed as gunfire spasmed as if it would never stop. Terrified, the children cowered under the bed. When the shooting stopped, all their hearts convulsed. In the silence, unthinkable questions shouted inside their heads. Had anybody—everybody—been killed? And was Brother Bob still alive?

The eerie quiet was broken when Nancy heard Seeco's wrenching shout outside their window. "Blood claat! Is Seaga men! Dem come fe kill Bob!" That view was instantly endorsed by word in the street, as passers-by said that before the ambulances and police arrived, they saw a car shoot out of the yard. But instead of driving uphill in the direction of University College Hospital, as might have been expected of any improvised transport for the wounded, the car headed downtown, straight toward the notorious Tivoli Gardens—the JLP headquarters, still a virtual no-go zone three decades on.

"Down in Trench Town we heard it as a news flash over the radio, and as soon as we hear it, we know what the source was, even if we didn't know the person till after. We knew what it was about," definitively states Bob's old Trench Town neighbor, Michael Smith, of the group Knowledge. "All of these things came from the politics, Bob deciding to do the concert for Manley when he had turned down doing a show for the JLP. At that time they had Bob Marley as an international star, and everyone wanted Bob on their side."

So Bob's best intentions for a nonpolitical concert had bitterly backfired.

Diane rushed out into the yard, where Rita was reeling, bleeding from the head. She begged, "Diane, take me to the hospital!" But seeing that Rita was still standing and coherent, Diane ran past her and into the kitchen. Just minutes before, it had been packed and buzzing. Now she was horrified to find an empty room and see a half-peeled grapefruit lying on the floor in puddles of blood. She breathed again only when she heard Bob call out to her weakly, "Is all right, Diane. Me here still."

Comforting the hysterical children, Nancy Burke watched as Bob walked out in his blood-drenched shirt between two policemen to the waiting car, holding his arm in its reddening bandage. The anguished self-questioning, as so often happens in the unfolding stages of trauma and grief, would soon come. He didn't look shaken or fearful. The Tuff Gong was angry.

Backstage in Europe, on their own exodus, the Wailers put past terrors behind them and enjoy getting on with the show. Manager Don Taylor, Bob Marley, Neville Garrick, Junior Marvin, and Carlton Barrett (l. to r.). © *Kate Simon. Germany, 1977.*

7

SO MUCH THINGS TO SAY

THIS TRAGIC VIOLATION was a defining moment of Bob's life, sending him on an unwanted, unplanned journey to an unknown destination. On the way, through the fourteen months between Bob's early-morning flight from his island home and his return to crowds at Kingston's Norman Washington Manley Airport in 1978, he was to encounter some of his greatest triumphs and bleakest pain. "You can't call Bob's stay in London an exodus," points out music journalist, astrologer, and screenwriter Neil Spencer, who had great difficulty tracking down Bob when he interviewed him for a *New Musical Express* cover story while he was recording *Exodus*. "He was in *exile*." True enough, but Bob himself saw the orbit into which he was sent as a mysterious trajectory that he could only believe would eventually lead him to his Father's home.

Although the shooting of Bob Marley in his own yard was one crime among many that occurred in Kingston in the lead-up to the election, it was a transgression of such proportions that it traumatized the island. More than just a favorite son, Bob had become the island's hope. Articulating Jamaica's aspirations, Bob had virtually single-handedly shattered the country's rigid class structure and united a population whose national motto was "Out of many, one people," but whose color-conscious inhabitants, still haunted by the British class system, rarely acted out that ideal.

No more could the light-skinned nabobs up the hills of fashionable, preppy St. Andrews automatically deride and ignore a ghetto population whose territory extended no higher than the old colonial clock tower at Half Way Tree, set among flower beds in a tropical echo of a British seaside town. Yet Bob was a curious anomaly in being a country/ghetto youth of the same complexion as many of the island's ruling caste. Had his white father not abandoned him, Bob might have been one of them, attending elite schools such as those to which he would later send his own children. Instead, he hacked his own way through the concrete jungle with music as his machete. The path he cleared led him to a crossroads where uptown and downtown met and sometimes clashed.

It could be said that the exact circumstances of his shooting remain a mystery, although there are two opposing views of the "invasion," as Family Man calls it, and those who hold to one or the other are equally convinced of the accuracy of their position.

"Through the years, all the questions I've been asked are pointing at who did it," summarizes Third World's Cat Coore. "But the truth of the matter is that there were other things involved, apparently, besides just the political thing." Some insist that Bob was the intended victim of a political hit by the JLP, incensed that Bob was endorsing Manley's PNP with the Smile Jamaica concert. Others feel that's a conspiracy theory and that the more mundane reality was that Bob became the fall guy for an alleged scam of Skill Cole's, in which he was reputed to have fixed a race by abducting a Caymanas Park racetrack jockey—in Bob's famous silver BMW.

A quarter century on, many people are still scared to talk, to name names; though everyone agrees all the perpetrators were either killed or O.D.'d not long after their perfidy, it's known that whoever they were, their equally reckless relatives are still very much around.

"I was never able to speak about that, because I really didn't know. I only heard these things," concludes Cat. "You don't want people to quote you in books if you don't know for yourself, absolutely, personally, what it is." He pauses. "But my impression was that most people round here were saying it was the work of the JLP."

"I heard one of dem was called Shabba," remembers musician, producer, and broadcaster Wayne Jobson, of the group Native. "I heard that sometime after, he went to see Bob to beg his forgiveness. Apparently him and Bob sat together for hours, and Bob gave him his blessing. I could believe that was true, knowing Bob. Then Shabba was shot and killed, going about his gunman business."

Others say that this penitent was known as Lips and that Bob alarmed the other Wailers by taking him on tour with the band.

When discussing his compassionate approach with friends, Bob always would declare, "Me no have to do nothing. His Majesty will take care of everything."

One thing's for sure—when Bob got shot, he never saw the faces of his attackers. Though he couldn't identify them, he sensed that he knew them, that they might well have shared ital food with him in the very yard they violated. "It was fucked up that it was our black brothers, some of the guys Bob had given handouts to," sighs Gilly. "It's a crazy world."

Again, it was a situation Bob had foreseen just two years earlier, on the justified paranoia of *Rastaman Vibration*'s "Who the Cap Fit": "Some will eat and drink with you / Den behind dem susu 'pon [gossip about] you."

Thinking of Bob's efforts at changing the ghetto dons' direction, Scratch Perry practically explodes. "You cannot bring peace to gunmen. From them men decide to kill for money, dem pick up a curse. Gunmen always kill for money, so gunmen cannot be healed. They are already dead, you understand?"

Call him cynical, but Scratch is adamant. "You can't support these people and they are never happy," he continued on a practical note. "They always have problems and when they want more, if the other man can give it to them, they will go over to the other side and fight against you."

That pithy summary of gangster relations, applicable anytime and anywhere, is usually linked to what the Mafia call *omertà*, the code of silence. Indeed, despite the shock that the attack on Bob's life gave the entire island, there has never been a successful police investigation of the invasion.

"That whole assassination attempt of Bob is still a mystery in Jamaica. Nobody has ever been tried. Nobody has ever gone to jail. If [there's been] any trial, it's been ghetto justice, but that is a case you can't go and find out about in books," muses Neville Garrick. "An attempted murder of Bob Marley, and there's no criminal arrest or nothing?" He shakes his head in disbelief.

Later, when Claudie Massop was visiting with Bob in London while he was recording *Exodus,* they spent an afternoon with reggae singer King Sounds. Talking to me years later in London, Sounds is vehement. "I was in the room when Claudie said to Bob, 'True, Skip, this coulda never happen if me was outta jail.'" In other words, Claudie the enforcer had been sidelined and forced into inaction as his fellow Labourites planned Bob's elimination.

Skilled at discretion and adept at compartmentalizing his life, Bob never publicly mentioned his knowledge of a startling fact that Syd Massop casually let drop while we were talking as snow lashed the windows of her orderly sewing workshop. "Bob definitely knew what was going on, before the shooting happened. Claudie told me that when he was locked up in Red Wall, he phoned Bob from the Gun Court and told him that people from his party were planning to come and get him."

In other words, Bob had been warned by someone he trusted and who definitely knew the "runnings" that the JLP were about to make an attack on his life. It's touching that true Rasta i-nity between bred'ren meant that Bob and Claudie's boyhood bond proved stronger than party politics.

Question marks will always hover over the mystery of exactly who tried to assassinate Bob Marley, this one in particular: Was it just by chance that Bob's close bred'ren, Claudius Massop, was captive in the Red Fort of Gun Court just when the invasion of Hope Road occurred? His charge was never proved; but Massop's absence created a convenient opportunity for the ambitions of the downtown don who would soon supersede him, one Lester Lloyd Coke, popularly known as Jim Brown, after the American football player.

The head of the Central Peace Council, Trevor Phillips, told writer Laurie Gunst of a conversation in which Bob, shaking with rage, said he'd recognized Jim Brown as one of his attackers. That would certainly coincide with the power struggle dividing the JLP at that time. "Jim Brown and Claudie didn't get on at all," amplifies Syd Massop. "Jim always felt he was in Claudie's shadow." The grassroots gunmen were suspicious of Massop's progressive qualities: his dignity and flair for leadership, his increasing commitment to Rasta and the unifying message of Bob Marley, and his active passion for the idealistic aspects of socialism and the power of the community. Though known as Labourites, the other gunmen had a simpler, more brutish ideology, supremacy at any cost. Massop had to be kept out of the way for Marley to become the sacrifice that signaled nothing would stop them, even the island's brightest light.

Regardless of the truth of the charge, Jim Brown paid the price for his years of psychotic violence. Having fled Jamaica when the PNP came into power in the vicious 1980 elections, Brown went on to terrify America with his sadistic "Yardie" gang, the cocaine kings known as the Shower Posse. He burned to death in a Jamaican jail cell while awaiting deportation to America in February 1992—on the same day that his son and heir, Jah T, was being buried in Jamaica. He had been shot on a Kingston street.

One thing's for sure, though: the traumatic events gave Bob an incessant hunger to know who his attackers were and which thugs were paying them, and sent him into a spiral of self-examination. Island's New York publicist, Charlie Comer, quickly positioned the shooting as an assassination attempt, thus switching Bob's public profile from musician to revolutionary. So this journey, both inward and external, gave birth to the *Exodus* album in 1977, and its sister release, *Kaya,* the following year.

A POLICE CAR took Bob to join Rita at University College Hospital, where Don Taylor lay paralyzed. Bob's wounded arm was easier to deal with. News spread swiftly round the island. Dermot Hussey heard when his broadcast was interrupted for the news report by broadcaster Charles Lewison. Halfway to Bull Bay, Neville Garrick also heard the news on the radio, and wanted to turn right round. But Judy begged him to get her home. Once he'd dropped her off, Garrick burned rubber speeding back, and blew a tire on Spanish Town Road. As he was trying to change it, a police car pulled up, recognizing Bob's famous silver BMW. "Is Bob Marley car dat!" They surrounded Garrick with guns ready, taking him to be one of the assassins. "Me is one of Bob Marley men!" Garrick shouted. To his amazement and relief, the cops helped him change the tire and gave him a blaring escort all the way uptown, back to Hope Road.

Neville was shocked by the same grim visual that had alarmed Diane Jobson—the yellow grapefruit lying on the floor in the pool of darkening blood. The yard was full of PNP men milling round, cursing and threatening the anonymous hit men. For whatever reason, no JLP followers turned up, appearing to corroborate the political motivation.

Immediately Neville was called on to act as Bob's representative. He tried to answer all the police's questions, but left Hope Road as soon as he could. "I just couldn't take it anymore. I had to see what was happening with Bob."

Dermot Hussey had jumped into his car as soon as his radio show finished, with the same intention. Speeding through the silent streets, he arrived to find the hospital corridor full of distressed well-wishers, including Lee "Scratch" Perry, Harry J, David Coore (deputy prime minister and father of Third World's Cat Coore), and Prime Minister Michael Manley and his wife Beverley, who were Bob's neighbors on Hope Road. Despite having effectively hijacked Bob's concert for his own political purposes, Manley was a huge fan of Bob's. Surprisingly often, the prime minister would slip next door to the Rasta commune and enjoy some reasoning with the Tuff Gong, and in the hospital Coore and the Manleys were among the few people Bob actually spoke to, thanking them for coming, and sketchily explaining his impressions of the assault. But his energy was low, and he spoke little and softly.

"I saw Bob with his bandaged self," Hussey recalls. "He looked very serious. He didn't say a word. Nobody did. Everybody was stunned."

Bob's reticence extended to his questioning by the police. When they asked if he'd experienced any threats lately, Bob just mumbled, "No, not really. Nothing in particular. Nothing you coulda really nail down."

But when he was alone with Lee Perry, Bob confided that though he didn't see the shooters' faces, he felt sure that "it was coming from Tivoli Gardens or something like that," Scratch says.

Once it was clear that Bob could be released that night, Prime Minister Manley asked the pertinent question, "Do you have anywhere safe to go?"

Neville had the answer. Chris Blackwell had purchased a gracious old property named Strawberry Hill, once a haunt of Lord Nelson's, and had encouraged Neville to use one of the cottages on the property as a painting studio. It was an ideal sanctuary, set three thousand feet up a peak of the Blue Mountains. Virtually the only more elevated public establishment at that altitude is the army barracks at Newcastle, where fir trees and brisk breezes, even occasional snow, recall a tropical Scotland.

For Chris Blackwell, Strawberry Hill had been as much a nostalgic purchase as a commercial one; some of his most cherished childhood memories were of taking English high teas with scones and the jam made from the property's own celebrated strawberries there on the plush green lawn with his glamorous, *sportif* mother, Blanche, the intimate of Noël Coward and paramour of James Bond's creator, Ian Fleming.

The property's long-established natural defense advantages were still valid—as Neville pointed out, you could control who was driving in from town, and the soldiers of the Newcastle Army Base would have your back. There was no safer place on the island.

Neville was assigned to drive Bob up the famous 365 precipitous bends of the road to Strawberry Hill in the silver BMW after they left the hospital. Bob was silent on the journey. The mood was fairly fraught, anyway, as their fellow passengers included not only two Twelve Tribes bred'ren there for extra support and security, but also a cop who'd been at the hospital. Seemingly the man people turned to in a crisis, it was Neville who'd been assigned to accompany that police officer downtown to the station, where he would pick up a gun to guard them en route to Strawberry Hill. With an irony appropriate for such an intense day, it turned out to be the same officer who'd arrested Neville a few hours earlier—and how long ago it did seem—for smoking a spliff in his car. On the way back to the hospital, the cop was thrilled with his new gun. Quite the action hero, he aimed it out of the window at hapless passersby, till Neville exploded. "Wha' you a deal with? You a idiot! You think you ride with dreadlocks so and wave gun! You mad, man!"

The cop was sulking, Bob was lost in his own thoughts, and the Twelve Tribes bred'ren knew not to break the silence. Eventually, most of the crew finally filtered up to the mountaintop, but as Gilly remembers, "None of us got any sleep that night. We didn't know who we could trust."

The general paranoia wasn't helped when Neville went to check on the police guard and found him nodded out over his prized gun. "Is so you a guard black man?" Neville shouted.

In the two days following the shooting, Bob remained at Strawberry Hill, where his companions were mainly top-ranking Dreads of the PNP and his close bred'ren, such as Lips, Tek Life, Frowser, Claudie Massop, Diane Jobson, Dr. Pee Wee Fraser, the tennis champion brothers Compton and Greg Russell, Minister Spalding, and singer Roberta Flack. The American crew who'd come to the island to shoot the Smile Jamaica concert with Island's West Coast representative, Jeff Walker, included a cameraman called Carl Colby II, whose presence there later fueled conspiracy theories about surveillance, as his father was the former head of the CIA. Colby junior appears to have been an innocent cameraman, but when accessing newly released CIA files for his *Catch a Fire*, author Tim White discovered that all those paranoid-sounding Rasta theories that skeptics thought were ganja side effects were indeed true. The CIA had labeled Marley a subversive who should be watched.

Though unaware of that fact, Bob certainly knew the rumors. At Strawberry Hill, Bob was quiet, brooding on the recent trauma. Trying to deal with the enormity of the attack and absorb the full implications, he couldn't decide whether to go on with the Smile Jamaica show. Was he setting himself up as a hero or as a target? Everyone in his think tank had his or her own opinion, and the wrong decision could be fatal.

Bob was tormented by the disturbing reality that people he'd thought his friends would conspire to kill him. He had always moved freely among all the top-ranking Dreads—powerful and volatile Rastas whom it was wise to have on one's side, if possible. Now it seemed he had been naive to believe he was beyond petty politics and loved by all the downtown factions—a nasty awareness that undermined his sense of self as an artist and a man. And having been unable to see his attackers' faces, he was taunted by the simple question of their identity, amid all the theorizing and half-remembered glimpses.

"'Im couldn't figure out who it was," recalls Neville Garrick somberly. "'Im was very upset, in the sense that [he wondered] which set of youth dem would pay a man fe come kill him. 'Cos now dem a say it is a political concert, and that was never our intention." A young band named Third World was scheduled to play support, but when they reached Strawberry Hill, Bob confided, "Bwaoy, dem say the concert is a setup fe mek dem come finish the job. Tomorrow we will know what fe do."

The following day, Heroes Park Circle was packed with thousands of Jamaicans who had waited for hours to show their support for Bob Marley. Backstage, about to go on, Third World's Cat Coore was called over to a police walkie-talkie. It was Bob. "Wha a gwan?"

"Come down, man," Cat shouted over the crackling line. "The whole place is ram [packed] and everybody want fe see you."

Finally, Bob strode into the show, flanked by Compton and Greg Russell. The crowds surged around him with hurricane force, almost knocking him over. Both big, broad Russell brothers were so intent on seeing Bob through to the stage that it wasn't till the music was playing that Compton registered he'd lost both his shoes.

It was a makeshift performance, but passionate. Family Man and Carlton were late, but their absence provided an opportunity for Bob's community of local musicians to pull together and show their devotion to the man, his music, and his message. Musicians from Third World and others all improvised. Within moments of Bob's arrival, they were in a huddle, working out which of the Wailers' greatest hits to play, swapping instruments. Holding the famous Rod of Correction given to him by Haile Selassie, and wearing a black leather jacket, Michael Manley came onstage to hail up Bob, then watched the performance standing defiantly on the roof of a van, surrounded by the sort of top-ranking ghetto Dreads—"rough house cats," as Cat Coore says—whose proximity might have threatened other politicians. "No Jamaican politician was better than Michael at dealing with everyone, from ghetto gunmen to visiting dignitaries," says Coore admiringly of the people's politician. "From they see him, the people just start shout, 'Joshua! Joshua! Joshua!' "

But Manley was not the hero that night. The survival of Bob Marley was the reason for celebration, and Bob did not let his people down. "The whole of Bob's humanity played out on the stage that night," says Cat Coore, who found himself passing on his bass and switching to keyboards and then guitar in that ad hoc performance. "You know how Bob is—every feeling showed on his face, from pain to anger to compassion. But for me, the moment I'll never forget was when we played 'War.' " Bob's most direct tribute to Haile Selassie, "War" appeared on *Rastaman Vibration*. Like our hunter ancestors coming back to the cave from the kill, those primal survivors, Bob whirled like a shaman onstage, acting out the events that had almost taken his life, delivering Selassie's excoriation of violence and ignorance with knife-edge clarity. Exorcising demons, he transformed the giant stadium into one community gathered round a campfire, gripped by the battle of good against evil, as humans have always been.

His locks flailed as Bob's head jerked from side to side so rapidly it seemed he was in a transport at a Pocomania session, seized by the powers. Tugging his shirt aside to show his bandages, Bob pointed to the wounds that, the eighty-thousand-strong crowd made him understand, had hurt his people almost as much as himself. His gaze at the audience was extraordinarily direct, mingled bewilderment and outrage. Turning away, he shrugged and flung his hands in the air in disgust, as if to put it all behind him. Then he was gone as suddenly as he had arrived, startling even the musicians.

Winding down, the musicians hung around a while, until warnings came that despite the night's elation, shooters were still running loose round town. Everybody scattered.

The Smile Jamaica concert had finally passed without incident, so the relief at Strawberry Hill that night was sweet, though still cut with caution. At two in the morning, Rita came to Neville. "Bob wants you to mek a move with him. Yuh ready?"

Tensely, Neville remembers, "From now on, it was not gonna be no star star business. This was serious and my life could be in danger. But there was no doubt in my mind. I had to go with Bob."

Neville raced down the hill to his parents' house in Mona Heights, where he kept his passport. That was all he carried, with a clean shirt and one change of underwear in a brown paper bag. Bob was always a light traveler, but for once he didn't even have his guitar as the two Dreads drove past Strawberry Hill's dozing security guards, zoomed down through Kingston town, and swung out along the sea to the airport, arriving just as the sun rose. It was blessedly quiet as they hurried onto the tarmac, where Chris Blackwell's luxurious private plane was waiting. As they lifted off at seven-thirty A.M., they prepared themselves for anything to happen.

Later that morning at Harry J's studios, Sylvan Morris checked that the tapes were properly filed. He expected that the Wailers would soon come back to finish off songs such as "Guiltiness." The rhythm tracks sounded very promising.

"It was amazing," muses Dermot Hussey. "Fifty-six Hope Road had this daily passing parade of people who came to Bob because he was this symbol—mothers with babies, all sorts of people with their sad stories, saying, 'Bob, help me.' He was always generous and gave money to this person, that person. From the shooting, I only saw Bob once again. A lot of people that used to be round him on a daily basis, we just dropped out, went underground. Fifty-six became like a ghost town. In a way, it just ended."

On the flight to safety, Bob and Neville were both quiet, thoughtful. The rest was necessary. As soon as the two Rastas tumbled out onto the tarmac, almost before Neville realized where they were—Nassau, Bahamas—a lineup of stern immigration officials was already waiting.

News of the attack had obviously reached Nassau. The immigration officers immediately inquired if Bob was seeking political asylum. "No, man," drawled the Dread. "Me is a tourist."

And so he would remain for more than fourteen months.

Never Go Down

THE BRIEF TIME that Bob and his inner circle spent in Nassau was a necessary decompression and an exhalation. A highly guarded society, quietly dedicated to the anonymity and security of the offshore accounts it sheltered, Nassau was relaxing to the point of somnolence.

Chris Blackwell had purchased a manageable compound: two villas scattered on a few acres by the sea, right under the flight path to the airport. The low-slung villa in which Bob was staying, which overlooked the pool, was named Seapussy. Blackwell stayed on a yacht moored at the property. Rimmed with palms and neon bougainvillea, the pool became the focus of the little household in exile.

Unlike turbulent Jamaica, Nassau was attempting to preserve the genteel image of the tropics that colonizers had impressed on folks back home in England—smiling black policemen in white solar topees, gingerbread houses in pistachio colors. Mercifully, in these controlled, manicured environs, the stress and easy assassinations that infested Kingston were absent. Nonetheless, Bob wasn't able to rest easy, even after his escape.

Following the early flight, they finally got to lay their heads down at Compass Point at nine-thirty in the morning. Sleep was brief. Some two hours later, they were woken up again by immigration officials, waiting with a car to take them back down to immigration at the airport. This time, Bob and Neville were forced to talk through the particulars of the shooting again. There was not much Bob could add to the facts in the papers. The men bursting in, the persistent nonstop gunfire—all that anarchy had literally shot by in a blur, and he had no clue as to the attackers' identities. Obviously, Bob was too wise to draw attention to the many speculations that were making the rounds of Kingston.

Yet, for whatever reason, the Nassau authorities remained unconvinced of Marley's suitability as even a temporary resident of the island; he and the others were only given a weeklong visa. "We actually had to go down to that visa office three times, and we were only there for three weeks," groans Neville Garrick. "They never gave us a visa for longer than a week."

Both Family Man and Neville point out that Bob always liked being on the road, enjoying the closeness of his team around him. So soon Bob and Neville were joined in Nassau by Family and Carly Barrett, Tyrone Downey, Seeco, Diane Jobson, Rita, Judy, Marcia, and Cindy Breakspeare; in a crisis, any potential hostilities between Rita and Cindy were sensibly suspended. They were all there to heal, and did so.

Keeping things lively, more police turned up at the door one day, carrying two bales of sodden weed just pulled from the sea. "Dem musta missed de drop," insisted one cop, determined to explore the viability of pinning ganja smuggling charges on the high-profile Dread visitors.

There was further harassment of a different form—paparazzi, hounding Bob and Cindy's newly public relationship. "Ughhhh, spying. Ridiculous," says Cindy Breakspeare with a shudder, re-membering the flashbulbs outside the window, and the notes slipped under the door of the supposedly secret suite the lovers shared in a nearby hotel. The thrill of being crowned Jamaica's first Miss World in London was quickly chased by the shock of her lover's shooting.

"I flew from England to meet him and spent Christmas in the Bahamas. It was nice, even though the reason [for being there] was horrible. We just hung around and had beers. Everybody cooked and wrote songs and got a little exercise. Go for a run on the beach, hop on a glider. The usual. Things didn't change that radically from one place to another. Just different geography."

Those weeks, including Christmas and New Year's, were a turn-ing point for Bob and his team. "The time we spent there was nice," chuckles Family Man, remembering. "Mostly we just meditate on what took place, the invasion, hoping that they would find all the guilty ones. Asking, 'Where do we go on from here?' "

Gathering around the swimming pool became the typical flow of the day. Usually the Dreads would read and reason about the Bible, passing the book around, each one reading a chapter aloud. "Vengeance is mine, saith the Lord," quotes Diane Jobson, remembering one biblical imperative that now had an extra resonance for them all.

"He was OK, you know. Not down, but very introspective," recalls Cindy Breakspeare. "Very thoughtful, trying to figure out what could have caused something like this to happen. His country he loved so much, his people he loved so much. I guess kind of thinking, you know, 'Did I deserve this? What have I done to deserve this?' " she continues evenly. "But then on the other hand, Bob had this very stoical approach to life, which said, 'You don't have to do anything to deserve this. It's the position you're in. It's the power and influence that people think you might have. Why they think you're dangerous. They don't want anybody out there waking people up and saying, 'Don't put up with this oppression. Stand up for your rights.' It was hurtful, but I think he understood. It was an occupational hazard."

Bob had never been more grateful for every minute, and relished every pleasure Nassau afforded a righteous Dread. "Me never gamble in life, me can't stand losing, because me born a winner," he'd cracked, but in Nassau he indulged in a light flutter on the slot machines at a nearby casino. Their stay's main entertainment was a concert by the Staple Singers, just the sort of soul injection he craved. When Mavis Staples hailed him up from the stage, Bob was pleased, but still didn't have the vibes to go backstage and socialize. He needed to preserve all his energy.

"It was from that time that Bob started to write," says Neville

Garrick earnestly. "It was his reaction to the shooting. He was not even putting pen to paper, because most of the time I wrote it down."

Music began to gush from Bob. A guitar was rustled up when they arrived, and he played constantly. The first song that tumbled out of Bob on the morning after he and Neville arrived is still clear in Garrick's memory. Nearly thirty years later his eyes close as Marley's amanuensis relives that day, vigorously singing in a minor modulation, with a strong Bob-style build, "Who gave them the order to shoot I down, Jah is I protector, I never go down." Three years later, "Never Go Down" was finally released as *Survival*'s "Ambush in the Night" with the lyric "All guns aiming at me."

Bob's composing methods could be spontaneous, or he could polish words and music for months. "Bob's approach to songwriting was like him have an argument, something to say, like an essay. I have experience of being around him writing, and he would change it, feel it around till he found the right thing," explains Neville Garrick. "'Im never sit down with a piece of paper and write down no song. 'Im do that after we get the song together. Every time 'im find a melody, 'im keep changing it."

While in Nassau, Bob was refining ideas he'd already sketched out and had even recorded basic tracks for in Kingston. He began amassing new material by letting his creativity pour and soar, ranging freely over a trove of musical and lyrical motifs.

"A lot of the germs for songs on *Exodus* and *Kaya,* like 'Waiting in Vain,' 'Heathen,' 'Jamming,' and 'Turn Your Lights Down Low' came in Nassau," affirms Neville Garrick. "Sometimes Bob don't write the whole tune one time. Sometimes 'im can write a tune and abandon it for a while. Then two years later, 'im can draw on it; the [old] words come back, and [help] write another new tune.

"There was no taping. Remember, this is just after the incident, so it's not like him brought up the band because him did wanna stay on a music vibe," continues Garrick. "Everybody knew what was going on; everyone just wanted to be near him, you understand? So in Nassau, we just spent the time strumming around, feeling around. I remember Bob working on 'Waiting in Vain,' 'Turn Your Lights Down Low,' and 'Three Little Birds.' We decided, well, we'll just go to England to work on the next album."

However, Fams remembers one day when the musical energy got so strong that they had to record. "I wanted to take up more time than just hanging out. I was getting the vibes, putting the words together with Bob."

But the Wailers found themselves without any means of recording—Blackwell's Nassau studio, Compass Point, was still a couple of years away. So Family Man borrowed Blackwell's tape recorder and set up a few mikes around Seapussy's open-plan living room. Carlton played the kete drum, while Bob played acoustic. "After a while, even Tyrone and Seeco got involved in grooving on that song," Family Man remembers affectionately. Built around the somber propulsion of the kete drum, the song they worked on finally surfaced eighteen months later on *Kaya* as "Time Will Tell."

The weeks of meditation and recreation worked well. Bob and the band flew directly to London refreshed and eager to tackle the next recording. Though the plan had been to lay down at least the basics of the next album in Jamaica, it was now decided that what came to be known as "the Jamaican Reels" would be flown to London to form the basis of the new album. In fact, they turned into two new records, released thirteen months apart.

"ME REGARD LONDON AS A SECOND BASE," Bob said to me, "and when I am in Jamaica, anything happen in London, me know it right away." Adds Neville Garrick, "Bob felt safe in London. He liked the fact that the police didn't carry guns."

Bob and Neville's generation were the youth who lived through the tail end of British colonialism, and even though he was a graduate of the pan-African school of Marcus Garvey, the Black Power movement, and Rastafari, the London nightspots such as Piccadilly Circus that Bob name-checks in "Kinky Reggae" on *Catch a Fire* were still familiar, part of his cultural formation and childhood mythology.

To make things cozier yet, mid-1970s London also had both a thriving sound system and a Rasta scene, and even an outpost of Gad Man's Twelve Tribes, the Jamaican organization/church to which Bob belonged. Jamaican Dreads who'd visited England had come home with photos of the Twelve Tribes house in St. Agnes Place, Kennington, and the Dreads who were keeping the organization going, such as Pepe Judah and Norman Adams, aka Jah Blue. There was an immediate cultural as well as musical context for Bob to slide right into.

But even while there were new situations to engage him and plenty of work to do, Bob was still constantly processing the invasion. Locked in an internal debate, he looped the same questions, watched the same freeze-frames, over and over again. The haunting and self-questioning often emerged as songs that sounded as if the man was debating himself, pondering out loud, such as "Running Away," which eventually found its home on *Kaya*. Bob's voice descends to a low growl, as if his subconscious is shouting out. Ever tending toward the lateral, balanced with an appealing directness, Bob's current experiences and reflections showed in his vocal technique. Despite the nightmares, Bob was energized, directed, and writing constantly. To all outward appearances, Bob had bounced back in London.

Before and during the recording of *Exodus*, Bob enjoyed the novelty of chilling in front of the TV. "Bob was never one to brood about things. I saw him in London and we just had the best time," remembers Nancy Burke. "I remember we watched ballet together on TV, *Swan Lake*. You know Bob, he was a great admirer of physical fitness, and I was surprised how much he enjoyed the ballet, every aspect of it. He looked at them leaping and everything and he kept saying, 'Bwaoy, dem fit!' "

On another afternoon, some kids were in the room with Bob and Cat Coore, watching cartoons. Bob started sneaking glances, then got lost in giggling at the cat-and-mouse antics. "It was such a surprise to me, frankly," Cat recollects. "Bob was a funny guy, but I'd never seen him laugh out loud like that, at this kid's stuff. I loved it. Even for me, who was round him quite a bit, it was another side of the man."

London had a liberating effect on everyone, Family Man included. The bass player enjoyed going round the record shops in Soho and flipping through secondhand bins looking for surprises. One afternoon he wandered back to Chelsea with the day's purchases and found Bob waking from a nap and ready to reason. "Here, Skip, check dis," announced Family Man, and carefully positioned the stylus on a particular track of one of his new bargains—a collection of movie soundtracks. With a great cymbal crash and a swoon of surging strings, the familiar theme from *Exodus,* composed by Ernest Gold, filled the room with its haunting minor modes. The muscular ripples of piano, and the plaintive theme, with its echoes of a universal folk soul, entranced both the Jamaican musicians anew. Drawn in once more to the instrumental's narrative of pain, rage, and hope, Bob listened more and more intently.

When the song was over, the two Dreads talked excitedly about its grandeur, the epic way it evoked a tribe's struggle for survival, the way it suggested the possibility of hope in the dreadest times, and how its resonance embraced everyone, all the fleeing sufferers.

The *Exodus* theme sparked a memorable conversation. But still,

Fams was surprised when Bob walked into his room two days later with a guitar and sat down.

"Fams, you ready fe dis?"

He strummed a chord and began to sing percussively. "Exodus! Movement of Jah people."

At once Family Man heard the bass in his head, a riff on the piano of the *Exodus* theme.

The beaming bassie nodded. "That irie, Bob."

Meditation and reasoning in the yard at Hope Road at "Kaya" time. For Bob and his bred'ren like Gilly (l.) smoking ganja in this chalice means more than getting high; it is a sacred communion with Jah and the crucial inspiration for a spiritual grounation.
© *Adrian Boot/Bob Marley Music. Kingston, 1978.*

8

EXODUS VIBRATION

"He Made Old Pharaoh Understand."
— "Go Down, Moses"

An Exodus Grounation

Supremely transcultural, though rooted in Jamaica, Bob well understood the underlying links between belief systems. "When you say Rastafari, it's Jesus Christ, just [with] a new name, just like reggae used to be ska. So it really is the official thing for earth," he explained to me, "and reggae is the music the Bible speak of."

Now, far from home and unsure of the future, the idea of exodus inspired one of Marley's most enduring songs. By writing his Rasta anthem, Bob was consciously taking his place in a chain of creation drawn from the Bible's Book of Exodus.

"Everybody got a little Moses from school coming up, in church, in Sunday school," chuckles Fams, who built the song together with Bob. "We just put in the knowledge, what we have learned along the way."

Indeed, between church, school, and home, where all the Wailers were raised in some form of Christianity, the whole idea of exodus was intimately familiar. Individual characters and roles, like the love-hate between the siblings Moses and Aaron, and the adversarial role of Pharaoh, were closely identified for Jamaicans with the narratives of contemporary world leaders, from Ghana's much-respected first independent leader, the pan-Africanist Kwame Nkrumah, to Queen Elizabeth or, indeed, their own area leaders.

Certainly when Bob mentions Brother Moses in "Exodus," he's not referring to himself, or even positioning himself for that big assignment. Still, the man was known for directly or indirectly supporting several thousand poverty-stricken sufferers in the most literal sense: they depended on his work for their daily survival. As an additional responsibility, Bob was charged with a mission. The commitment he felt to the sufferers was total, and he urgently wanted to communicate Rastafari and a message of progressive unity to his rapidly expanding tribe of fans round the world. It went beyond the external packaging and what Rastas, with their wicked wordplay, call "isms and schisms." Thus, Bob was stuck with being a Moses figure, as Gandhi was for Indians and Mandela was for South Africans, galvanizing huge social transitions and shifts of consciousness while still being quite private people.

Indeed, with characteristic humility, shortly after the release of *Exodus,* Bob insisted to the writer John Bradshaw, "Me no leader, me just a sheep in the pasture"; nonetheless, the shepherd's crook was thrust into his hand. Bob had to lead his motley people from one mentality to another, even while he was still scanning the horizon for another Brother Moses. Beyond its central theme of liberation, Exodus and its key human player, Moses, have as many symbolic levels as an archaeological dig in the Old City of Jerusalem, and Bob was not the only seeker who yearned to dig deep.

To really understand the pull that Exodus exerted on Bob, it was essential for me to reason with Bob's Rasta guru, Mortimo Planno. Known as a prophet in the Kingston ghetto, Planno graciously permitted me to visit him at his bungalow by the University of the West Indies, where he had been appointed Folk Fellow in the late 1990s.

Now frequently confined to his room, the eighty-three-year-old

Dread sage lolled on his bed like an emperor on a palanquin, crowned by dreadlocks gnarled like great thick tree roots. Three bulbous growths on his lip, the result of an accident, gave him a distinctive demeanor; one friend said that Mortimo appreciated the effect of these marks, making him more fearsome, like a true lion of Judah.

The day Planno finally agreed to speak to me about exodus, he seemed particularly thoughtful, and at first seemed keener to listen to the news on the radio than to talk. But I was leaving the island the next day, and had only managed to visit him by borrowing a car for a couple of hours. Eager to reason, I managed to get Planno to turn off the radio. The moment our talk stopped, on it went again, and I realized with a shock that he was listening to news reports of that day's death toll in tribal street fighting and police shoot-outs, as he must have done innumerable times before. Mortimo was all too aware that the struggle is ceaseless.

Planno's speech is slow and slurred, and his disciple Nabbie Natural is his interpreter. They tell me that the movement of Jah people Bob invokes in his "Exodus" is the journey to fulfillment as told in the Bible. Nabbie speaks of the burning bush that made Moses marvel when he was a shepherd in Midian as being a portent of the plagues to come. As they say in Jamaica, "Everyt'ing is everyt'ing," and the two Rastas note cosmic connections wheeling between the Bible, Bob Marley, and the lush foliage framing the windows.

"What is Exodus?" Nabbie asks rhetorically. "We can never, ever, remove the fact that planetary cycles govern everything we read about and discuss in the Bible. All the pass-overs Exodus refers to mean the planetary movements and what they bring, and the reaction of the people on the land to what they bring. Say we see there's bad weather coming. How do we deal with it?" For Planno and Addis, then, Exodus is almost synonymous with change and how we respond to it, whether it's the supple flow of a life in tune, a seamless shift between seasons, or a painful death and rebirth.

The Rastas' take on exodus does indicate that, despite the strength of destiny or whichever higher power we may relate to, we still play a part in forming our own transitions and development. The essence of Exodus is knowing how to righteously ride life's rhythms, as Nabbie concludes: "The Exodus refers to a general [skill at] moving away from incoming disasters, governed by passovers; and preparing for each change in due season."

But Planno is eager to hear a cherished verse again. "Now," he commands me, his voice between a whisper and a growl, "[reach] where I'm trying to get. The time is running out, for me soon have to go away, and you too. So, we want to reach the stage where God tells Moses his God name. Look, and you'll find the part." I scramble through the pages of the Bible, till Addis shows me the way to Exodus 6. "Go on, read it, read the book," instructs Planno.

So I start to read from Planno's well-thumbed black King James Bible that his grandmother gave him "back in the old village," noting that it's been adorned with pictures of Rasta lions and H.I.M., just like Bob's. " 'And God spake unto Moses, and said unto him, I *am* the Lord: and I appeared unto Abraham, unto Isaac, and unto Jacob, by *the name of* God Almighty; but by my name Jehovah was I not known to them.' "

Planno leans back and listens, eyes closed. He evidently relishes the flash of recognition between Moses and the Divine Presence, in which the One God finally reveals himself fully to Moses; like a flirt who first gives out a false number, but then realizes there's something in the chemistry worth pursuing, and braves revealing his or her true identity. When he hears God actually introduce himself to the human race by name, Planno summons his strength, rears powerfully, and, flashing his dreadlocks like a lion flinging back his mane, gives a mighty roar: "*Jah!* Rastafari!"

With that shout to the heavens, the identification between Jah and Hashem is clear and complete and the universality of Exodus is confirmed.

"In a sense, it's the Jews' story, and they probably have more right to it than anyone else," comments writer and activist Richard Holloway, the former Anglican bishop of Edinburgh. "The film *Exodus* captures that, and the sound track to the movie was wonderful. But of course, Afro-Americans, Jews, and Martin Luther King all used it. Exodus is in some of the old Negro spirituals, like 'Go Down, Moses.' It's got all those resonances."

Indeed, the Exodus trail leads through virtually every liberation struggle in the Western world. African Americans have a special link to Exodus. In her preface to her popular abolitionist novel from 1852, *Uncle Tom's Cabin*, Harriet Beecher Stowe almost automatically referenced Exodus, bundled in with her hopes for a wholly Christian Africa with "Western" values. "May then the scenes of the house of bondage be to them"—the "enlightened" Africans of a theoretical future—"like the remembrance of Egypt to the Israelite—a motive of thankfulness to Him who hath redeemed them!" For Stowe, Exodus's central message was more the power of the Divine than the passage to freedom.

As Holloway notes, Martin Luther King Jr. frequently invoked Exodus. At a service celebrating the second anniversary of the Supreme Court's ruling to overturn segregation in schools, held in May 1956, when he was twenty-seven, King referenced the parting of the waters of the Red Sea in a sermon entitled "Death of Evil on the Seashore." He quoted Exodus 14:30: "Thus the Lord saved Israel that day out of the hand of the Egyptians; and Israel saw the Egyptians dead upon the sea shore."

This popular passage, known in Hebrew as Shir Hayam, or the Song of the Sea, was sung by the rejoicing Hebrew men, with a women's chorus led by Moses' sister, Miriam. King knew he was in a tradition; he was fond of a celebrated sermon, "Egyptians Dead upon the Seashore," by a Boston preacher called Phillips Brooks, quoting the same text. The preacher father of the singer Aretha Franklin, C. L. Franklin, also turned to Exodus for a mid-1950s sermon, "Moses at the Red Sea." As always, Exodus's cast of characters and story line can be inflected to reflect quite different perspectives. For example, where Martin Luther King Jr. used Exodus to explain the end of European imperialism and the cyclical recurrence of liberation movements throughout time, Franklin more specifically identifies black Americans with the oppressed Hebrews.

But every sufferer who hears Exodus knows it as his or her own. Richard Holloway observes, "Whenever a people has been imprisoned, kept down, captured, and longed for release—longed for exodus—that book has given them all the metaphors, all the symbols that they need, whether or not there's any historical accuracy behind the story."

Historical accuracy or not, Exodus certainly offers insights into eternal aspects of human nature, contradictions that enrich the thrust of its story line. While Jesus Christ and Allah are regarded as perfect beings, role models to aspire to, the lessons we learn from many Old Testament characters include their struggle with their flaws, writes the lawyer and teacher Alan Dershowitz in his book *The Genesis of Justice*. Indeed, after slaving in Egypt for their onions and leeks, one would have thought the Hebrews would be happy to harvest the new food source, manna, that dropped so conveniently from the skies. But even that intriguing food group, whose flavor rabbis said changed according to taste, turned out to be another reason to kvetch.

"It is a telling moment when they all regret having left slavery and rebel against Moses. Because at least there was a security in slavery," elaborates Holloway. "There's that bit where they go, 'At least, back in Egypt, we had our needs met. We had shelter. Now you've taken us out into this wilderness and we don't know where the hell we're going.' So the wilderness is another one of those great metaphors. It's a motif that all leaders have to learn from, because invariably, before they go from captivity to the Promised Land, they have to go through the wilderness." History confirms his point: leaders must expect to go through both the political and ideological wilderness, dissent and social upheaval.

And the escapees weren't the only ones moaning. "Moses was constantly complaining to God, 'I can't do anything with these people,'" observes James Russell, the Mashtots Professor of Armenian Studies at Harvard University. "Really, the people wanted slavery. It was Moses and God who were trying to free them. If you look at the Bible in Hebrew, the main adjective they say about Moses is *anav*, which means 'humble.' Moses' real virtue in leadership is not conventionally political or military, but in his sense of morality and humility."

That was exactly the sort of leadership role, if any, that Bob aspired to. He was all too familiar with the tension inherent in leadership: how to steer without becoming authoritarian. On the night they were mixing "Exodus," Bob and some bred'ren were reasoning angrily about South Africa, and Bob asked me why I didn't write more about apartheid in *Sounds*. I pointed out that I did what I could, but my rag was mainly music. Bob nodded and added wryly, "And if you *did* write about it, the editors would probably take it out."

Bob was tired of interviews, muttering, "There come a stage when I check that these writers purely defend Babylon, just a pure different blood claat *Babylon,* although dem smile and laugh at me every day." He spoke of his urge to keep experimenting musically, as with the love songs on *Exodus*. Regarding the media's expectations of him as purely a musical warrior, he said forcefully, "Me no gonna sing [strictly] about dat. Me is ahead—" and then he broke off, just to make sure he wasn't being misunderstood, although it was just a casual chat by the foosball table. Correcting himself, he said, "Not a *head* of a people, but mindful of certain things." He might have had a real gift of prophecy, one that did not always feel easy, but Bob didn't need any more projections pinned onto him.

The prophets' club is very elite, and you have to be invited to join. Most members lead very turbulent lives. But the narratives of some prophets are so meaningful that their examples transcend any differences between beliefs. As Professor Ibrahim Malik of the City University of New York explains, "Our holy book, the Koran, compiles revelations that came to the Prophet Mohammed over some twenty-three years. All of the prophets of Judaism and Christianity, like Moses, who we call Moussa, are prophets in Islam. The Koran tells us repeatedly that we are enjoined to honor all of Allah's prophets, both named and unnamed. That means we are not to put any one of them above the other."

But one of the most pervasive metaphors arising from Exodus is the transformational journey itself. For Muslims, the original Old Testament Exodus that Bob refers to as the movement of Jah people is refracted in the Prophet Mohammed's travels. However, the closest parallel is not with the well-known Hajj, or pilgrimage, to Mecca that righteous Muslims are obligated to experience at least once in their lifetime.

"The first thing that comes to mind is the Prophet Mohammed's own exodus, which in Islam we call the *Hijra*," explains Professor Malik. "Soon after he began receiving his revelations, the Prophet and the early Muslims experienced persecution. In order to escape, he actually sent some of the early Muslims to relocate in Ethiopia, under a Christian king. Eventually, the persecution prompted him to leave his home in Mecca, and go to a city called Medina, which was some two hundred miles away. There he was able to flourish with his followers. The *hijra* is seen as so significant that it marks the first day of the Islamic calendar.

"But Exodus also raises another question that, to me, is broader and deeper," continues Professor Malik. "What the brother Bishop Holloway says about Exodus being emblematic of liberation and opportunity is true. But bringing it down to an almost personal level, I think that we all see Exodus not only in terms of physical movement from one place to another, but also as an intellectual or spiritual journey, a change in attitude. You can have an exodus from a certain attitude which keeps you imprisoned and in the dark, and you come into the light, or a greater sense of awareness."

An inward journey and process of self-examination is also part of the Kabbalistic view of Exodus expounded to me by Rabbi Larry Tabick, an American whose own journey has led him from New York to a quiet, leafy crescent in north London.

To secular Jews who thought of themselves as rational and enlightened, Kabbalah was a primitive hangover of their religion's occult roots, and new immigrants generally forgot it quickly in their rush to fit in and secularize. Fresh off the boat, your old Granny's habit of swinging a hapless chicken over her head by its scaly legs because of some obscure superstition was regarded as a rather embarrassing heritage. Nonetheless, rediscovered—and, some feel, deracinated—and reborn as a New Age healing and therapy system, Kabbalah's power, the foundation of so many ancient magical systems, still throbs uncontrollably.

In terms of an artist such as Bob Marley, whose work deftly straddles the often disconnected topics of revolution and romance, one of Kabbalah's central explorations has a particular relevance. In Kabbalah's celebrated cosmic map known as the Tree of Life, in the quest for the *tikkun,* or healing of the universe, certain stages are specifically male or female. The ideal of a blessed union and balance between the two genders, which Eastern thought calls yin and yang, is one of Kabbalah's main aims. Tabick speaks of the Shechinah, "the presence of Hashem," the female energy that blesses the Sabbath, beginning as an abstract idea but around the thirteenth century taking on an increasingly female aspect, transmuting into a king's daughter who falls into a mutual enchantment with the king's son, who is himself in some way a prisoner. . . . The ideas and images tumble out, convoluted and refined as a DNA sample.

"A *sefirah* is one of God's ten aspects, links in a chain of being that connect God's most unknowable aspect with the 'real,' created universe." The king's son is the *sefirah* of *Tiferet* (Beauty), which is masculine, and the Shechinah is the *sefirah* of *Malchut* (Sovereignty). When these two are in union, positive divine energies flow into our universe. As the next paragraph says, " 'The Shechinah is held captive by the *Kelipot,*' " the rabbi explains. "And it's our job to liberate her. A number of the Kabbalistic meditations are designed to do that, particularly on Friday nights and festivals, which are said to be the points at which the Shechinah can be at least temporarily liberated and reunited with her masculine counterparts."

In his study lined with bookcases filled with spiritual texts, we sit at a dining room table with a lace cloth. Rabbi Tabick listens to Marley's *Exodus* for the first time, carefully, his head cocked to the side as he sips his lemon tea. He is intrigued and quickly gets the connection between the Jamaican musician's quest and the questions posed by other thinkers and channelers of belief throughout the centuries. Having heard the music, he explains how within both the mainstream and the more exotic, arcane Jewish interpretations of Exodus, ideas of freedom play out on several levels at once, couched in mystical abstractions that read like *Star Wars*. The sacred symbols of the Exodus myth are no more required to function on a literal level than, say, a dream analyzed by Freud or Jung. As the rabbi speaks, levels and layers of liberty unfold like the opening petals of a Buddhist chrysanthemum. Vividly, Tabick evokes the specifically Kabbalistic imagery of shells, seemingly fragile but tensile constructs that shelter and conceal.

"There is a recurring notion that historically, liberation from slavery also points to a cosmic liberation. Humans are in partnership with Hashem, and our souls are divine sparks that need liberation. Because we are also captives of the shells."

Fondly, Tabick talks of the late-sixteenth- and early-seventeenth-century Kabbalist Chaim Vital, from Safed and Damascus, who interpreted the opening chapters of Exodus as "a personal journey about being born and growing to adulthood. The basic message is that the world is a seriously unredeemed place and that we all have the potential to further the process of redemption."

Exodus is an extraordinary unifier. Sitting with Rabbi Tabick in north London, I watch him search for references in his extensive library, and my mind wanders to Mortimo Planno and Addis in Kingston, with just a small shelf of books at hand, but so much knowledge. They would love this library. Then Rabbi Tabick spots the right page and looks triumphant. He has found what we have been looking for.

"Yah is one of the ten names of Hashem in Hebrew that must not be erased or destroyed, which means you mustn't throw whatever it's written on into the garbage," he explains with a smile. "*Jah* is basically a form of *Yah*, as in *hallelujah*, which means 'to praise Yah.' When *Yah* was translated into English it came by way of Latin, and at certain periods Latin used our letter *J* for a *Y*. So you get *Judah* for *Yehuda* and *Jah* for *Yah*. Instead of the four-letter name that we're not allowed to say that's become known as Jehovah, we can also say Jah."

Exodus Ancestors

"SOMETIMES YOU HAVE TO DO THINGS. You *have* to leave," Bob Marley said decisively. I'd just asked him what had finally made him choose to leave Studio One, his new bride, Rita, and the other two Wailers to join his mother in America in 1966. But on that placid Kingston afternoon ten years later, Bob answered me with a particular firmness, as if the feelings of urgency and desperation to be gone were still very immediate to him. To emphasize the point, he repeated crisply, "If you have something to do, you do it." As it turned out, Bob's antennae were dead on; we were talking just days before the invasion, and he was about to have to leave once more.

You have to leave. With those words, Bob summed up the refugee imperative. And when you have left, you have to do something. It sounds so simple, but it's a big, scary wilderness to people struggling to reach safety. Can it be just chance that so many of these exodus creators experienced so much international movement in response to political forces?

Perhaps the definition of the courtly composer may be Georg Frideric Handel (1685–1759), who wrote *Israel in Egypt* in 1739. He's famous for big set pieces, such as *Music for Fireworks,* designed to be enjoyed by nobility in powdered wigs and satin breeches at lavish royal masques. Like all artists of his time, Handel was vulnerable to the vagaries of patronage, his only source of income.

Bob Marley suffered for being perceived—wrongly, I believe—as supporting a political party. Patronage, real or imagined, has its costs. To stay one step ahead of any downturn in his fortunes,

Handel instinctively followed Exodus's teachings about the necessity of flexible response and speedy adaptation to any change you see coming.

To become a musician, Handel rebelled against his father, surgeon to the Duke of Saxony. Lured by an invitation from the grand duke of Tuscany, he moved to Italy to soak up its oratorio and frothy opera buffa scene. But a mere three years later, aided by Ludwig, the elector of Hanover, the ambitious Handel fled again, this time to England.

It may seem strange that a sponsor would encourage a favorite artist to leave town, but there was a regal subplot involved. Ludwig was in line for succession to the British throne. Even while England was fêting Handel as the foremost composer of opera buffa, he was spying on his aristocratic social circle for his early benefactor.

George Ludwig became King George I of England in 1713, and he commissioned Handel's beloved *Water Music*. Further aristocratic patronage led to his controversial *Israel in Egypt* in 1738. Blending the rich vocal harmonies of Italian oratorios with the drama of opera, Handel answered the public's new thirst for music in English by lifting blocks of text directly from the Bible. He abandoned all characterization and concentrated instead on wringing feeling from individual verses, isolated like haikus. Exuberantly plundering the plagues for their sonic potential, Handel's music rattles ominously to portray locusts and his plucked violins jump like frogs.

When it was first performed, *Israel in Egypt* got a lukewarm reception. The work did find some fans, however. As historian Sir Newman Flower wrote, "A Jew on the stage as a hero rather than a reviled figure was a thing practically unknown in London, and [after *Israel in Egypt*] Handel found himself possessed of a new public." Subsequent centuries proved the appeal of Handel's male and female voices swooping through his stately harmonies.

Recognition did not always come easy. Like so many of these musical masters, including Bob Marley, personal flight would inform and inspire their turn to the Exodus story.

IN HIS PARTICULAR STRUGGLE, the opera buffa maestro Gioacchino Antonio Rossini is a typical link in the Exodus chain of creation. European politics was even more torturous than it had been in Handel's time. Monarchies in every small nation shuddered at the beheading of their fellow aristocrats. In Italy, Rossini's homeland, opposition to the democratic ideas of Napoleon and the French ignited political turmoil, with Italy being tossed back and forth between the warring superpowers of the day, France and Austria. His musician father was fired from his municipal orchestra and often jailed for his support of Napoleon, leaving mother and son to struggle for survival as itinerant singers. A speedy composer, Rossini wrote seven operas in sixteen months, including the opera buffa *Barber of Seville,* by age twenty-one. Shortly thereafter, he was forced to flee Venice for Naples because of his republican ideas.

By 1818, when Rossini's *Mosè in Egitto* opened, he was on fire, burning like Moses' bush to tell some of the truths he'd lived through. Still, Rossini, having seen his father suffer for his political beliefs, tried hard to appear apolitical, like Bob Marley in Kingston years later. Nonetheless, as in Marley's case, the public immediately found political relevance in his variation on the exodus theme, identifying the repressive Bourbon princes as a pharonic regime. As Stendhal, Rossini's biographer, observed of the opera's premiere, "People stood up in their boxes and leaned over the balconies, shouting. . . . I had never known such a triumph."

FOR CAPTURED AND TRANSPLANTED Africans and their descendants in America and the Caribbean, the slave masters followed by postcolonial governors would be recognized as the pharaohs of their day. That parallel was spread by one spiritual in particular, "Go Down, Moses," which became the anthem of the anti-slavery movement.

Born in slavery, so-called "Negro" spirituals became the cornerstone of African American music and spread through every outpost of captivity, naturally reaching the Jamaican hamlet of Nine Miles, where Bob Marley would sing them in the church in the 1950s. "Spirituals are like the first music," Bob said. "But when I find the Rastaman now, I find I am one of them. The original teaching of Christ is Rasta."

Escaped slave Harriet Tubman, known as "Black Moses," often used the spiritual "Go Down, Moses" to convey directions in code as she returned repeatedly to the South to set more captives free. Perhaps because of the localized area of its field research, the landmark anthology "Slave Songs of the United States" failed to include "Go Down, Moses." Its incalculable influence might never have been felt but for the transcriptions of another exodus channel, pioneering African American artist Harry Thacker Burleigh.

The spiritual first came to wider attention when it was sung by escaped slaves who had made it through to Union lines at Fortress Monroe in April 1861. Among those who heard and were touched was a visitor, the Reverend Lewis C. Lockwood, on a YMCA mission to assist the people called "contraband"—slaves who'd gotten away and were being harbored by Northerners and sympathizers. Moved, Lockwood sent the lyrics to his bosses. At a whopping twenty stanzas long, the text appeared in the *Tribune* newspaper, and "Go Down, Moses" became the first spiritual to be printed in sheet music form. Its sales raised funds for the anti-slavery movement.

Born into slavery and thus forbidden to read, Burleigh's grandfather was found with a child's primer under his shirt and whipped till he lost his sight. Nonetheless, he succeeded in buying his freedom and raising and educating a family. He took his son Richard and grandson Henry on his rounds as a firelighter, and the three generations would sing spirituals together.

While still a student, Burleigh became a protégé of Antonín Dvořák, the Bohemian composer, and introduced him to the spirituals. Thus Dvořák included "Swing Low, Sweet Chariot" in his *New World Symphony*. Evidently born to build links, Burleigh was also the first black cantor in New York, at Temple El-Emanuel, Fifth Avenue's Jewish cathedral, so Burleigh sang Exodus in the original Hebrew.

In his last years, Burleigh attained sage status and continued to lecture. He was still compelled by "Go Down, Moses," which he sang in one of his final concerts, and told a group of students that while many spirituals lent themselves to being transcribed in a "black" southern dialect, the importance of "Go Down, Moses" demanded expression in classical English—a natural comment, perhaps, from one whose dream was the creation of a classically oriented black music academy.

Committed to supporting younger talent, Burleigh mentored an honors graduate from Rutgers University named Paul Robeson. The older musician was present at the landmark performance on April 19, 1925, in which Robeson sang "Go Down, Moses," which was to virtually become his theme tune, in the first concert of spirituals and secular music ever performed by a black soloist.

But Burleigh later broke with Robeson, appalled at what he saw as a slovenly descent from civilization into black nationalist explorations of patois and African roots by Robeson and his sympathizers. Nonetheless, by transcribing the spirituals, Burleigh had furthered a development process of cultural expression that was now questioning his values.

Indeed, as the Harlem Renaissance gained confidence, a new,

more specifically African-identified consciousness was forming. The artistic giant of the Harlem Renaissance, Paul Robeson was the son of escaped slaves. As brilliant as he was handsome, Robeson was a gifted athlete, and one of those rare talents whose physical and intellectual aspects seemed evenly matched. As he was raised in the classical tradition, it took a leap of perception for Robeson to rediscover the spirituals of his ancestors and make them his own. In many ways, his gravitation to the spiritual mode matches Bob Marley's affection for the old folk sayings of Jamaica, which he often adapted for his songs—a visit to the ancient well of folk/race memory.

That decision was to cost him dearly. Even after he'd scaled the heights of social and financial accomplishments, Robeson's insistence on identifying with the disinherited and their struggle would put him on a collision course with the political and artistic establishment of the time. Throughout his transformation, Robeson never forgot "Go Down, Moses," and his delivery of the venerable spiritual as a metaphor for the struggle of black people in white racist America literally inflamed a riot at a civil rights concert in Peekskill, New York, in 1949.

Malcolm X, the black American Muslim firebrand, made a spiritual journey from his Nation of Islam exclusionism to a more inclusive form of Islam after traveling the world. Similarly, Robeson's political perspective broadened to embrace Communism, while his musical aesthetic grew to include singing folk songs in Russian, Yiddish, Spanish, and Hebrew.

At the London School of Economics, Robeson studied African languages, and said, "Now I find it easier to express subtleties in languages like Swahili, rather than my own." Yet the more of a world citizen he became, the less popular Robeson was among America's all-white, all-right ruling class.

Like so many others, including Handel, Selassie, Garvey, and

Marley, Robeson experienced exile in London, where his extraordinary talents received appropriate acclaim. To silence Robeson, and remove him from the international scene as a spokesman for the African American cause, the American government rescinded his passport in 1950. He would never see the Africa of his dreams, just as Moses never trod the Promised Land. When later Black Power generations ignored his significance in the struggle, it was a further blow. Paul Robeson died in 1976, at the age of seventy-seven.

After Robeson had really popularized "Go Down, Moses," the spiritual continued its journey and received the masterful treatment of New Orleans trumpeter Louis Armstrong, already anointed as America's musical ambassador when he played it on his 1958 album, *Louis and the Good Book*. Fond of saying that he was raised a Baptist, always wore a Star of David, and was friends with the Pope, Armstrong in his hungry youth was the protégé of an immigrant Russian Jewish couple who loaned him money for his first cornet. Though as Michael Cogswell, curator of the Louis Armstrong Foundation, explains, the selection of "Go Down, Moses" was very likely made by his manager, Sid Glaser, Satchmo's blithe urbanity dons a becoming gravitas on the track. The whole arrangement expresses a new musical age, blending both Burleigh's black classicism and Robeson's affinity for Africa.

One of the more left-field interpretations of "Go Down, Moses" came from an artist whose music, attitude, and beliefs were profoundly impacted by Bob and who had recorded with Lee "Scratch" Perry. London punk rocker Joe Strummer reinterpreted it as "Get Down, Moses" on an album he made with the Mescaleros, the eclectic outfit he formed after leaving the Clash. The idea came to Strummer when he was touring with his band and picked up a budget reissue Satchmo CD en route, explains his biographer, Chris Salewicz. Strummer's lyrical take puts a new, reg-gae/hiphop spin on the showdown between Moses and old Pharaoh: "Carve the message on the tablets of LSD . . . get down Moses, with the Dreads."

Like Bob, Strummer was looking for another brother Moses. The punk's rapport with the prophet was likely informed by Isaac Hayes's hugely popular two-record set, *Black Moses*, which was essential listening while Strummer was first forming his punk ideology in 1973.

A believer in reincarnation who's sure he was once a king—and is one now again, in Ghana—artist and activist Isaac Hayes has fulfilled many roles with excellence. Among his most resonant was that of Black Moses, striding the stage in black leather, shades, and chains at 1973's Wattstax music festival.

At high school in Memphis and as a gospel singer in the 1950s, Hayes used to sing "Go Down, Moses." "I think people love that spiritual because it shows Moses had faith in God when he was coming out of the land of Egypt. He led the people to the Promised Land, he saw it, but he didn't make it himself. There was a message in that, to be proud of our achievements. We were overcoming at that time," Hayes recalls with feeling. "I used to hear those Negro spirituals in church when I was a kid. We'd sit on the porch in the country and sing them. It was inspirational for me. I think it kept a lot of blacks [together] in the South, especially guys in slavery."

As he was coming offstage at a show, after getting four encores, Hayes recalled that a security guard told him, "Man, you need to give them another song. You're the Black Moses!" Still mindful of his church roots, Hayes replied, "Dude, don't say that. That's sacrilegious."

But despite his misgivings, the name took on its own life. Standing onstage hearing eighteen thousand people in the audience exultantly shouting, "Black Moses!" Hayes knew he had to explore the persona.

"When I realized the relevance it had to black people at that time, I said that as long as it means something and people can be proud of it, I'd wear 'Black Moses' with pride. Black people were needing some unity. We had just come through the civil rights struggle with Dr. King, and here's a guy with a bald head and chains, and I'm standing here [in such a strong way that] what once represented bondage and slavery now represented power. They knew I was leading them in song. But when the press started trying to make it a novelty, then I took it off and put it on the mantel."

Interestingly, the romantic, heavily orchestrated tracks on *Black Moses* don't seem to match the militant and spiritual aspects of the title. But there's more than one way to be a soldier.

"My marriage was breaking up and I was really brokenhearted," confides Hayes. "Most of the titles on *Black Moses* were related to breakups and affairs of the heart. It was sad. I used to stand in front of the mike and I would cry. One time, I had to have my secretary hold my hand while I was singing songs like 'I'll Never Fall in Love Again.' They named it *Black Moses* because of the influence I'd gained. But the subject matter, the music, was reflecting a man mourning his relationship that had hit the rocks."

In short, despite the chains and warrior stance, Hayes's *Black Moses* was manly but not macho. He was fighting on the emotional front line, unafraid to stand emotionally naked and reveal his vulnerability.

So Moses can embody different messages, all urgent to the musicians who portray him and his story. Arnold Schoenberg, who wrote *Moses und Aron* in the early 1930s, was drawn to the relationship between the siblings: Moses the leader, the boss really, who was nonetheless still dependent on the somewhat capricious Aaron as his mouthpiece. One interesting side effect of Moses' verbal limitation is that he sings in *sprechstimme*—a half-spoken, half-sung drawl that foreshadows Jamaica's sing-jay style: DJs who shift swiftly between singing and rapping.

Schoenberg's music had a challenging complexity. The avant-garde composer and creator of the Conduction musical system, Butch Morris, says that Schoenberg's twelve-tone system is "constructed according to the principle that twelve notes of the equal-tempered scale are arranged in an order forming a series or rows that serves as the basis of a composition. Each note-row has the possibility to form forty-eight forms." This lateral approach results in sudden, spiky changes of tone and note.

The composer's provocative approach alienated people. At the premiere performance of his *Pierrot Lunaire* in 1907, one audience member shouted, "Shoot him! Shoot him!" Such reactions encouraged Schoenberg to set up his version of an independent label, creating his Society for Private Musical Performances so that he and his avant-garde peers had somewhere safe to play.

Some might assume that Schoenberg, a refugee from Hitler given to Old Testament themes, was obviously Jewish. Not so. Born a Jew, Schoenberg converted to Lutheranism—an ironic choice, as Martin Luther had restricted Jewish liberty. After the war, Schoenberg switched back to being Jewish.

He confided to friends that he identified with Moses, and for Schoenberg, *Moses und Aron* had a special meaning, particularly as he felt that it represented a refining of his twelve-tone system. Yet just like Moses, he viewed the promised land of actually finishing the opera from afar. One among many German artists fleeing Hitler, Schoenberg wound up living in Los Angeles, where he applied for a Guggenheim Fellowship in 1945 to enable him to complete *Moses und Aron,* but got turned down. Still, Schoenberg did not expect to be justified by the laws of man, as Bob sang on "So Much Things to Say."

"The mind of the musician and audience have to mature so they can comprehend my music," Schoenberg said in 1947. "I know I have personally renounced an early success and I know that success or not it is my historic duty to write what my destiny orders me to write."

Perhaps the twentieth century's greatest popularizer of Exodus was Cecil B. DeMille, whose grandiose movie *The Ten Commandments* (1956), with Charlton Heston as Moses, was widely accepted as a literal representation of the Bible. Its sound track was by Elmer Bernstein, who'd revolutionized film scores with his jazzy sound track for Frank Sinatra's *The Man with the Golden Arm.* Like many of the artists blacklisted by Senator Joseph McCarthy, he was Jewish. A committed leftist, Bernstein actually met his wife at Paul Robeson's Peekskill concert, the one stopped by riots. In those Red-baiting, Commie-hating days, only the immense power of DeMille, well known for his hatred of Communism, enabled Bernstein to take the commission.

Bernstein liked to tell people how the flood of Jews departing Egypt was actually Egyptians marching to a tune that DeMille wanted to sound as much as possible like the hymn "Onward, Christian Soldiers."

One of Bernstein's composer friends in Hollywood was a Viennese refugee named Ernest Gold, who channeled the Exodus story for the score of producer Otto Preminger's film of that name.

"I remember Elmer Bernstein and Dad talking about musical authenticity. They did a lot of research figuring out what Egyptian music was like and basically had to make it up," says Gold's musician son, Andrew.

Though Ernest Gold was only a teenager when he made the

risky sea voyage from Germany to Los Angeles with his parents, the pianist was already an acknowledged prodigy. Like Schoenberg, he was ostensibly a Lutheran. "Dad's father was an agnostic Jew and his mother was a Czechoslovakian Lutheran Protestant. They raised him in the Protestant church, but they didn't take it seriously. My father used to joke that if I ever told Otto Preminger that his mother wasn't actually Jewish, he'd kill me!" laughs Gold's psychiatrist daughter, Martha.

Ironically, like Schoenberg, Gold's family had converted to Lutheranism. But nonetheless, they still associated with Jews, and that was enough to put them on the Nazis' hit list. When the teenage Gold arrived in Los Angeles, he was eager to put all the totalitarian traumas of Nazi Germany behind him. Soon he established a reputation and a career in Hollywood as a sound track composer.

When he got the call from producer Otto Preminger, a fellow refugee, to score the new film Preminger was making based on the best-selling Leon Uris novel *Exodus,* its topic was of interest to Gold. But he was unprepared for the assignment to become a life-changing experience.

"When he was doing the music for *Exodus,* I think he really felt a surge of pride and anguish that had been hidden when he came to Hollywood. He connected with the joy and pain of being Jewish, the horror of the Holocaust, and the pride in setting up Israel as a state," remembers Andrew. Specifically, Ernest Gold flashed on childhood experiences he'd suppressed: his neighbors in Vienna who disappeared one night; seeing open truckloads of Jews rattling through the city streets.

Ernest Gold delighted in telling the story of the recording of the movie's theme, which was to become such an enormous global hit. As the music unfolded, Preminger, who was known for being explosive and even abusive, became more and more agitated and screamed, "Ernest! What have you done to my music? What are you doing to my picture? You're wrecking it, it's awful!"

"Otto was up in the control booth, pacing. He was a wreck," laughs Andrew. "My father was totally humiliated, of course, but he had a cool head about him and he started thinking about what Otto was saying and that he couldn't really explain himself very literately, musically anyway. So what Preminger really meant was, 'It's not the same! It doesn't have the emotion!' "

Gold stopped the orchestra and walked round, softly asking every musician to make notes on their score, and then play everything again, but at half the volume. "Otto began beaming and saying, 'That's it! That's my music. That's my picture!' Preminger thought that my father was a genius for being able to rewrite the music on the spot. So my dad had pulled a fast one on him."

Says Gold's first wife, the glamorous chanteuse Marni Nixon, known for dubbing Audrey Hepburn's singing in *My Fair Lady* and Natalie Wood's in *West Side Story;* "Although it was the main theme of the picture, I know Ernest thought other songs in the movie were better. He was totally shocked when Pat Boone wrote words to it, and suddenly the *Exodus* theme was on the charts. Ernest was going to sue. He was furious. He called Otto Preminger, complaining that he hadn't given permission, but neither had Preminger. My husband just hated the words—until it became a huge overnight hit, and then, of course, he cried all the way to the bank. But he still grumbled and grumbled every time he heard it."

There followed innumerable cover versions. But ubiquity failed to diminish the song's grandeur, and the tune made a huge impact in Jamaica, where various versions were recorded in the early 1960s.

The popularity of both the movie and the music indicated a public hunger for the Exodus saga. Island Records' U.S. radio promo man in the mid-1970s, a Jamaican named Lister Hewan-Lowe, was a child when he saw *Exodus* at Kingston's Carib Theatre. "In all Third World countries, people would have responded to the film just like Jamaicans," he says emphatically. "They are actually making the movie. They are the extras, the actors. In the movie, a boat full of Jewish refugees from the Nazis is held offshore by the British, and if they can't land, they'll be sent back to die in Germany. Paul Newman stars as the Jewish freedom fighter, and he slips and slides around things and outmaneuvers people, and manages to get all those people out. They go on hunger strike, and at the end, he's willing to let them all die right there, except for the children. Then a mother comes with her baby in her arms, and when he says, 'All women and children off the boat,' the mother answers, 'No, we'll stay here. We'd rather die than live in slavery.'

"If you think of Bob Marley's life, he's identical to that Paul Newman character," Hewan-Lowe continues. "He's trying to survive and the music is the mantra of the tribe. It's a summary of the whole struggle."

As he did on so many ska recordings, guitar virtuoso Ernest Ranglin played on the Skatalites' version of the *Exodus* theme. "I saw the film of *Exodus* in Kingston," recalls the soft-spoken maestro from his Kingston home. "A lot of people went to see it. I know it was a moving movie, with its moral about oppressed people fighting for their existence. I guess that's why I did the tune, too."

Right after Ranglin played on Millie Small's prototypical ska hit, "My Boy Lollipop," in London, he cut the *Exodus* theme again, this time for himself. The session happened at the BBC studios in St. John's Wood, with a band including jazzman and club impresario Ronnie Scott, whose house band Ranglin played in. There was just one other Jamaican player. "The English musicians had never played ska before and it's an offbeat, not on the downbeat as they're used to," Ranglin recalled. "But they're great musicians, and after a few go-rounds they were right there." Returning

9

PUNKY REGGAE PARTY

THE QUALITY OF QUIET DYNAMISM that Ranglin, the veteran, had spotted in Bob as a teenager was to be tested now in this period of London exile. As a conscious people's artist, Bob's job was to articulate the sufferers' issues to the world and make it listen, while still remaining a simple, humble bred'ren. In addition, Bob had to sustain that communal Rasta environment on the band's travels, a process not unlike leading a wandering tribe in the wilderness. It was a challenge Bob rose to as he found himself in a London bubbling with culture, conflict, and change, which he would sing about in a slightly clumsy but affectionate tune, "Punky Reggae Party."

His self-styled "second base," London, was a valuable decompression chamber. Though unplanned, the shift in locale allowed Bob to relax and enjoy things he'd be unlikely to get a chance to appreciate in Kingston, with all the pressures. Nonetheless, everywhere he stayed immediately became a big social center— almost a re-creation of 56 Hope Road, minus the soccer and the warring gangs. Some things never changed; Bob still spent a good part of his day dealing with a line of—perhaps slightly less desperate—people, all hoping for a financial or spiritual handout from the Tuff Gong.

As the Wailers record *Exodus* in exile, Bob's presence blesses London's buzzing young Rasta and punk scenes. This rare shot shows the Peace Committee members who flew in from Jamaica to work with Bob for harmony among Kingston's warring political gangs and formulate the Peace Concert: Claudius Massop, Tony Welch, Bob Marley, Earl Wadley (aka Tek Life). London, February 3, 1978.
© *Caudley George; Courtesy archive of Norman "Jah Blue" Adams.*

Of course, Bob already had a standing army of Dread bred'ren to plug into in London. Mikey "Dread" Campbell and his partner, King Sounds, were two bred'ren he saw often. "When Bob spoke of the shooting, he was always bitter," remembers Sounds. "He didn't speak of it frequently, or in public, but he knew who did it and why they did it."

But one of the secrets of survival is resilience, and Bob was determined not to let the trauma dominate him. After all, he was alive. "I saw Bob soon after he reached England, and we never talked about what had gone on. Everybody knew what had happened, and Bob was ready to move on," states Campbell.

Before the invasion, Bob had told me he rarely left Hope Road in Kingston; equally, apart from attending the odd Twelve Tribes celebration, Bob didn't hang out much in London either. Anyway, as always, the world loved to come to him. Awareness of Bob's very presence in their area energized the growing young black British communities, although he was not actually seen "up and down" too much. This period of Bob's life was proving to be *livicated* to meditation, consolidation, and creation. Apart from his regular soccer matches in Battersea Park or Wormwood Scrubs, Bob spent most of his time indoors, at one of his homes or regular hangouts. But behind closed doors, away from friends, musicians, reporters, or the public eye, Bob Marley was making some of his greatest conceptual leaps.

After all the turmoil and change he had undergone in Jamaica, it was a welcome respite to live through each day with a blessed simplicity and familiarity, without too much excitement outside of the recording process. Of course, there were the logistics: Bob had to divide his time between various households and establishments.

"Wherever we stayed there had to be one place that he could see all those people, the Ethiopian community and the Jamaican bred'ren who were always there, and then somewhere else that we could go to have some peace and quiet and privacy," recollects Cindy Breakspeare, then pauses. "Otherwise it was really stressful."

But that was part of Bob's gig, bridging worlds. His headquarters was the ranch, the band hangout, at 33 Oakley Street, a renovated Georgian four-story terrace house with an open-plan kitchen in the basement. The round pine table became a daily hang, while the Wailers' cooks continued their endless round of preparing juices and ital food.

In the Oakley Street ranch, Bob's bright room, almost a small conservatory, could only be reached by a white wrought-iron spiral staircase. Tyrone's attic bedroom, next to Neville's, was full of keyboards and gizmos. The highlight of Family Man's décor was one of the big boom boxes of the day, with travel speakers, and cassettes strewn everywhere. The large, gracious ground-level room, a typical modernized space with high ceilings, original moldings, and a fireplace, was the mass hangout that came to function as a sort of Dread party central. The presence of the Rasta superstars was a spiritual and social magnet. I remember being there on an ordinary weekday and having to politely squeeze up and down the crowded staircase, as if you were at some packed party. There always seemed to be masses of Dreads sitting smoking and reasoning, waiting for Bob to grant an audience. Twelve Tribes members such as Bob's bred'ren Pepe Judah, Malachi, and Jah Blue were usually in the mix, eager to involve Bob in a new development in Ethiopia or to ask him to fund some Dread celebration.

"I don't really remember any particular girl other than Cindy being around, because there were just so many of them," remembers Suzette Newman, who ran the Fallout Shelter studio at Island and worked closely with Bob. "All over the floor, the stairs, everywhere you went, you'd step over girls, just hanging around, not talking much. There were Rasta girls or just girls. You know, all kinds. Thin, tall, big, pretty, not pretty . . ."

"They weren't all there to see Bob," adds DJ Leroy Anderson, Rita's half brother. "All the band members had friends, and there were others who just wanted to be round the Wailers, begging for an autograph."

For many of these young acolytes, spending time round Bob was a life-changing experience, if only because he had a flair for unlocking their musicality.

As always, he made music for and with the people. While living at Oakley Street, he was developing the track "Work," which ultimately came out on the *Uprising* album. Sitting strumming in the living room, he got everyone so involved with singing the chorus, "We Jah people can make it work," that even when he wandered out of the room, everyone carried on.

"Someone would tap a glass, someone else would shake a box of matches, grabbing anything that could make a percussion sound," recalls Breakspeare. "I don't think Bob was gonna sit there and be bored, or anything other than what he really wanted to be, because he ran things. But he really felt like he had an obligation for people to come and be there, and listen to reasoning, be a part of the songwriting process. Because they needed hope. And this is where they thought they were gonna get it. So he would *never* send them away."

But Marley needed the contact, too, observes the Trinidadian writer Isaac Fergusson, a friend of both Marley and Tosh. "Walk into Kingston and talk to any sufferer and you're likely to get a lively mixture of religious philosophy, international happenings, and poetry; analysis, in other words, the runnings. It's one of the greatest Jamaican attributes. Jamaica has more philosophers per square mile than any other place in the world, and the groundings with the bred'ren fed Bob and his fellow reggae musicians. All they had to do was put it to music," he explains.

During the time I spent with the band and Bob in the studio, it was never appropriate to tape an actual interview, although from the journalist's point of view that was obviously desirable, or rather, necessary. As the nights rolled on, and I became part of the regular crew supporting the musicians' work, a proper professional reasoning seemed ever less likely. So when I was going to Oakley Street one Saturday afternoon, I popped my Walkman into my bag, just in case. Here's what happened when I arrived and, for once finding the place quiet, tentatively began to look round to see if Bob was home.

Sounds: **London, April 30, 1977**
Another bright Saturday, this time in Chelsea.

I'm climbing the white wrought-iron spiral staircase to Bob Marley's eyrie. When my head reaches floor-level, I see Bob asleep after a hectic soccer game in the park, on the beige couch, legs dangling over the end in their faded khaki trousers, militant-style, one foot bandaged from a soccer mishap.

On the colour TV the Saturday afternoon sitcom is playing away to itself. The floor's covered in cassettes, a bag of cashew nuts. The room basks in late Saturday stillness, light rippling through the trees outside in waves that wash over Bob asleep.

Hmmm. Asleep. What to do . . .

Just then, Bob looks round. Sees me. Closes his eyes again, as if to sort out whether he's awake or asleep. Decides to be awake.

Sorry to disturb you, Bob, but you said I could call by . . .

"Na. cool. One minute . . ."

. . . and vanishes downstairs to collect his thoughts.

Moments later he re-appears, and establishes himself cozily back on the couch, ready to talk . . .

"You see me here? The first thing you must know about me is that *I always stand for what I stand for.* Good? The second thing you must know about yourself listening to me is that words are very tricky. So when you know what me a stand for, when me explain a thing to you, you must never try to look 'pon it in a different way from what me a stand for."

He's an unusually participant interviewee, always asking *me* questions—

"What you think about now? How you feel in life? You feel like you gonna *live,* or you feel like you must die? . . ."

I feel . . . movement.

"You feel like you're gonna live . . . that's a good thing. You have people feel seh, yes bwaoy, they gonna die so nothing makes any difference . . ."

Basically, this interviewee's as interested in checking out the interviewer as vice versa (and that's unusual). Reason being:

"Speaking truly, when people write about me, me no specially like it, y'know. Me no really deal with—*make and break,* that type of word. Whatever I have to say, I wouldn't like it to be a personal thing, like what me think about meself.

"If you want to do some good, you should say some good things about Rasta, so that people can get some enlightenment."

Though he always shied away from talking about anything personal—Bob was always happiest talking about Rasta—that day he spoke fondly about his childhood and how he enjoyed feeding the chickens in Nine Miles. He grinned as he reminisced about the talent shows he used to play with Peter and Bunny at the Carib Theatre, and for a moment he seemed unusually nostalgic. He broke off and muttered, "Nice. It was nice." He glanced over at me, eyes twinkling in conspiratorial fun, when he described the young Wailers cutting "What's New Pussycat," the theme of the raucous Peter Sellers and Peter O'Toole comedy.

The unusual emptiness seemed to echo through the house that afternoon. It struck me that even when we spoke alone, there were usually people hovering next door, waiting for a moment of Bob's time. Thinking of how busy and public his life always was adds a poignancy to something he said, almost as an aside: "They call me a dreamer. That means I always meditate. Quietness is a strong part of my life."

TO PRESERVE HIS PRIVACY, Bob had at least one other bolthole at all times. Throughout the *Exodus* period, Cindy Breakspeare was based in London while fulfilling her Miss World duties, and when he could, Bob spent time with her in her rented flat. Other times they actually sneaked off to the luxury of Claridge's Hotel, when privacy was at a premium. When the I-Three spent some time in town to lay down their backing vocals, Bob tried to be there every day to see the children. It was no problem for Bob to be a nomad; he was already a soldier.

While Rita was still Bob's wife, there was no doubt that during the *Exodus* period, the King of Reggae's consort was Cindy Breakspeare. "Bob almost never used to go out to the clubs at night," remembers Neville Garrick. "Why should he? 'Im have 'im woman at home already." Virtually pitching the pair as a West Indian Beauty and the Beast (oddly, that was the title of a film project they discussed at the time), the press happily mated Miss World with the wild-maned Lion Man. The relationship was so media-ready that some observers tended to dismiss it as a fling, an attraction of opposites. But in reality, the connection between the uptown girl and the downtown soldier was profoundly grounded. Not only had they been housemates at 56 Hope Road and known each other amicably for some time before their intimacy developed, they both had a passionate interest in exercise, health, and diet.

Sighs Breakspeare, "He had this gruff exterior and he had to keep it out there to get things done, keep the bred'ren in line and the soldiers on time, make sure everybody was at rehearsal, or on the bus when they're supposed to be. He did have a very sweet, soft, playful, vulnerable side. It was wonderful, but he couldn't indulge it too often, because he had too much to do."

For Bob, Cindy's flat was a place where he could relax and recharge without having to keep up his troop's energy. She would cook for him at three in the morning, mostly ital-style steamed fish and vegetables, but Bob also appreciated calves' liver, for the iron, lightly sautéed with onions, tomatoes, and hot pepper. "He would put the cassette of that day's recording on in the bedroom, and dance the whole place down," remembers Breakspeare with a smile. "You could see he was just elated by it. His pleasures were few and his demands were many."

Breakspeare herself had an extremely busy schedule as Miss World, entailing a lot of traveling and public appearances. Their meetings weren't always straightforward; when Breakspeare was booked into one West End hotel, the front desk wouldn't let the wild-looking dreadlocked musician join her in the room. Disgusted, the couple split for Oakley Street.

In their intimacy, both parties relished smashing the island's rigid class boundaries. An obsession with complexion has blighted Jamaica since the massacre of the indigenous Taino Indians, but though Marley and Breakspeare were both light, she was a privileged princess, of the island's elite, while the island's postcolonial social system was structured to keep Marley down in the ghetto, where he was reckoned to belong. Already quite independent from her family, Breakspeare was a rebel in her own way, just like Bob. "The best times we spent together were alone together, one on one," she recalls nostalgically. "So there wasn't the pressure from his side, who disapproved of me, or my side, who disapproved of him and thought he had bugs in his hair and all the rest of the rubbish that they thought about Rastafarians at that time."

Pressure from the hard-core orthodox Dreads meant that returning from being Miss World at some event, like Superman using phone boxes to turn back into Clark Kent, Breakspeare would find herself having to transform in freezing, drafty British Rail lavatories, destination London. "There's a little sink and you have to hold the tap on because it's a spring faucet; you let it go and the water goes off. And it's ice cold water, and I'm trying to get the makeup off before I get back to Oakley Street. Because you didn't want all the bred'ren to see you looking like this painted doll and give you shit for it," she remembers. "So I used to wear the long skirts, tie up my head, look as dowdy and as frumpy as I possibly could whenever I was in their camp. Then when I had to go and do my thing, I'd break out the props. For Bob I would do it. Now I don't think I could do it again.

"One night I didn't get to do that. A car brought me straight back there, and I walked in, shut the door, and I'm just going down the hallway at the entrance when the door opened and Bob walked in right then—he was the first one in the door. He looked at me, broke out in a big smile, and said, 'Caught you!' " and Cindy jabs her finger at me with a saucy expression that obviously mimics Bob's pleasure at "winding up" his beloved.

On one of the rare nights out, Bob, Popsy, and all the crew went out to Tramps, a popular West End disco, all silver and mirrors whose very walls seemed designed for sniffing coke. Everyone staggered off at the end of the evening, and Bob and Popsy found themselves alone as the waiter handed them an astronomical bill. Bob raised a quizzical eyebrow as he checked the total—enough to feed his old Trench Town yard for months. "Well, Pops," drawled the Gong, "looks like is we going to be washin' dishes tonight."

The more people flocked around the Wailers, the more Bob would find himself in these positions, before the word *entourage* was popular. Some might have wanted to withdraw, keep their wealth to themselves. But as a Rasta, Bob felt a commitment to a communal life and the building and maintenance of the community, on macro and micro levels.

"Bob was always the last man to eat dinner, last man to go to bed. Many times when he got there for dinner someone else had eaten it, and he would just say, 'Well, maybe they needed it more than me.' He gave a lot that way," Cindy remembers.

Sometimes Cindy would arrive at Oakley Street while Bob was still dealing with his many bred'ren, family, and supplicants, and she would sit chatting with Leroy Anderson, Rita's half brother, till the Skip was through. Emerging very late one night, Bob joked, "So, Leroy, you trying to chat up my woman now?" Leroy denied it stoutly, but they all knew Bob was just teasing; regardless of Bob's various kinds of relationships with different women, his and Cindy's love was palpable. "You could see it. He was different when Cindy was around. A lighter Bob," Al Anderson says.

Not that Bob's life was ever simple. Rita was in town to record for a time, and he had other familial responsibilities, too. "Lucie Pounder came around, too, the mother of Bob's son Julian," Anderson continues. "Of course, every woman Bob had a child with, he loved in their own way."

We sit in Leroy's old car outside Honest Jon's record shop in Portobello Road, while his posse sells old-school reggae tapes from a stall. Bob became close bred'ren with Leroy when the younger man was a teenager. Leroy and his sister Pauline, aka BBC reggae

DJ Miss P, and Rita Marley had the same father, the jazz musician Leroy Anderson. First, their father moved from Jamaica to England, where he played in Liverpool's Cavern club, of Beatles fame; then he became part of the jazz exodus to Sweden. The first time Leroy met his father was as an adult, in New York, around the time of *Rastaman Vibration,* when he first heard of Rita, his half sister, who was married to a Jamaican fellow named Bob Marley. As he'd promised his father, Leroy made sure to connect when the Wailers came to London. Now he was part of the tribe.

At that time Leroy was still seeking direction, and Bob took a somewhat big-brotherly interest in his development. Bob told Rita about her brother's progressive ideas and encouraged her to help him, a move that was to help transform the British musical landscape and help spread reggae. With a little help from big sister Rita, and his other sister, Miss P, Leroy launched Britain and the world's first pirate radio roots reggae station, Dread Broadcasting Corporation, known as the DBC, in a riff on Britain's venerable BBC.

"Yeah, so we're hanging out in Chelsea, in his little place, first on Kings Road, not for very long, then on Oakley Street," recalls Anderson. "I'd watch guard until Bob fell asleep, then I'd come back to the flat about eleven in the morning. After cleaning up, he'd eat something, pick up his guitar. Constantly with his guitar. Most of what I saw, he was practicing, he used to seriously concentrate. He'd have a spliff there and be feeling something out, always smoking and strumming away and scribbling on pieces of paper, working on tunes and chords. I heard him working on 'Jamming,' and other songs that weren't released.

"Then the crowd would start coming and he'd put the guitar down and deal with the day's runnings. So that was most of his routine. I was in the front room or the passage and sometimes there'd be a passage full waiting from seven in the evening till one in the morning. They were all wanting something, and he would deal with everybody in turn. The Bible was always prominent, laid out in his room with two candles, open to whatever page he was reading. Every night, no matter what time people came and went, he'd find time to read his chapter. Literally. Yeah. I think he wanted that space when he was alone. He'd say, 'You can't run away from yourself.' But maybe he was going into himself with all that time and space.

"He gave away a lot of money, too. It just went up in smoke. And I'd say to him, 'Why are you giving away your money?' And he would say, 'For a peaceful life.' He'd say, 'It's not my money anyway. It's just passing through me.' He so didn't care."

BUT BOB WAS RECEIVING as much as he was giving. One offering he was particularly glad to make was the money he gave to the Ethiopian royal family. Following the footsteps of their grandfather Haile Selassie after Mussolini's invasion, they were in exile in London. Many of them had escaped with nothing after Selassie's regime was overthrown by the Marxist forces of Colonel Mengistu Haile Mariam in September 1974. Bob was surprised to discover on a visit to one family member's hotel room that they were about to have to decamp yet again, and realized that they were forced to keep on moving, trying to evade possible assassins.

This relationship with the Ethiopian royal family was one of London's positive experiences for Bob, and as well as his affinity with Haile Selassie's granddaughter Yeshikassa, he maintained a strong relationship with Selassie's grandson Prince Asfa-Wossen, whose advice he always took to heart.

"For Bob, 1977 was the best and worst of years," Garrick muses. "But there was something of a change for the better, because now he was endorsed by the Ethiopian royal family. It gave him a stronger leg to stand on than just [being] a Rastaman who said, 'Haile Selassie! Jah!' We got to meet these girls who were

H.I.M.'s granddaughters, and one in particular, Yeshikassa, she was young and she really loved Bob."

The regal visits made an impact on the Oakley Street Dreads. "His Majesty's grandson Prince Asfa-Wossen and the two princesses came and visited. They were really beautiful black empresses, and they were very humble," recalls Jah Blue. "When they came amongst us, they would take off their shoes and cook Ethiopian food, just free up themselves. They weren't Rastas, but dem know we say their grandfather is God, and sometime they ask us questions about it."

Prince Asfa-Wossen gave Bob an oblong imperial ring that had belonged to H.I.M. It became the unpretentious star's sole jewel.

Much though he loved being part of his community, Bob was happy when the Wailers were at work in their hermetically sealed cocoon. Neville remembers how Bob loved being on the road and in the studio. "That's when everyone was closest," guitarist Junior Marvin agrees. "Bob was happiest when we were moving together like a family."

The delicate ecology of the Wailers, a band of brothers who'd come up from the ghetto to stay in luxury hotels, dance at Regine's, and not worry about the next meal for their youth was altered by an introduction made by Chris Blackwell—guitarist Junior Marvin. Wearing slick Jheri curls, as opposed to knotty dreads, his screaming rock guitar was a sweet-and-sour contrast to Family Man's bass notes, smooth and round as black pearls. But such superficial cultural differences didn't disguise Marvin's talent. In what must have been one of the most ego-boosting days ever had by any guitarist, Marvin had to decide whether to go work with Bob Marley or Stevie Wonder. When Marvin had to make his excuses to the Motown genius, Wonder was gracious. After all, he so admired Bob that one of Wonder's catchiest songs, "Master Blaster," was a tribute to his Jamaican inspiration.

Known as the "British Hendrix," Marvin came from a gifted family; his elder sister was a dancer on the seminal TV pop show *Ready, Steady, Go.* While still a young boy, Marvin was in *King Kong,* the South African musical first made famous by Hugh Masekela and Miriam Makeba, and also had a long run in *Hair.* Drama beckoned, but the dearth of roles for black actors encouraged Junior to explore other skills, and music soon became paramount. Though he had left Jamaica for England as a kid, Junior was exposed to Jamaican music by his uncle's sound system. Marvin was a natural rocker, though, and adopted the surname of singer Cliff Richards's guitarist, Hank Marvin of the Shadows.

In some respects Marvin could be said to have picked up where the previous non-Jamaican Wailers guitarist, Al Anderson, had left off. But while Al's aesthetic was rooted in R&B, Junior was a straight-up psychedelic rocker. Before Junior, any rock-inflected lead guitar in the Wailers' music had been played by guests who had little connection to reggae.

Soon Marvin's star was rising within the band. It provoked some murmurings, but nonetheless, within weeks Bob had come to rely on the cosmopolitan guitarist, and he became the unofficial band spokesman. Bob understood that the link he provided was crucial. "Junior was a good transmitter for Bob," observes Chris Blackwell. "Bob never really felt at ease meeting with people he didn't know well, or know their understanding, so he liked to have an intermediary, don't you remember? And Junior could do most of the talking."

New Wave, New Craze

A CULTURAL TRANSLATOR was particularly useful at this time. While Bob told me he regarded England as his second home, his flight from Jamaican turmoil had landed him in the middle of a very different kind of social clash, as he experienced at first hand the devolution of the country that used to be Jamaica's "motherland," and the epitome of all that was once considered proper by the ruling minority. Only four years had passed since the Wailers had been to England as a three-man harmony trio, and now a revolution was happening, on the streets and in music.

A jolt was desperately needed in complacent old England, still wallowing in the afterglow of having run colonies across the globe. There was a terrifying sameness about a Britain where everything closed at five-thirty and stayed shut all day Sundays. Gripped by garbage strikes, power cuts, and the three-day workweek, the country was sliding deeper into unemployment. Since coming into power in 1974, the Labour government appeared to have succeeded only in deepening the social inequities it had planned to prevent. Destabilizing things further, regular IRA bombs ripped the capital. The specter of the queen's Silver Jubilee in 1977, an orgy of establishment reverence, seemed to symbolize everything that was stultifying about the British system. It was definitely time for a new groove.

Before the dawn of the punk era there really was a darkest, dreariest hour where pop was concerned. Tedium ruled in the editorial meetings of the feisty little underdog rock weekly *Sounds,* where before becoming features editor, I was an ace cub reporter in the mid-1970s. The big names we were supposed to salivate about and scrap over with our rivals, *Melody Maker* and *New Musical Express,* were the same old roll call that had been around since the seemingly ancient 1960s. Teen culture had been reduced to a few rock icons, locked away in limo luxury land, all seemingly on an inexorable collision course with middle age and increasing irrelevance: the Rolling Stones, Genesis, Pete Townshend, Led Zep, Pink Floyd, Stevie Winwood.

So it was like dynamite when the call to the punk barricades came, via blurry photocopied flyers, for midnight gigs in bizarre and exotic locales—a disused warehouse, a transvestite club, an X-rated flea-pit cinema. In such arcane venues, the weirder the better, the new punk groups such as the Sex Pistols, the Clash, the Buzzcocks, and the Slits would play all night, and it might cost a shilling to get in.

A fascination with reggae also marked the punk era. At the first punk club, the Roxy, a budding dreadlocked filmmaker named Don Letts spun reggae, on the pragmatic grounds that there was no other good music around; none of the punk bands had recorded yet. Many of the artists starting out in those dingy dives went on to incorporate Jamaican music, notably dub, in their audio palette; the deconstructed remixes of vocal tracks that re-invented a song's whole sound, transforming melodies with unexpected jolts of ghostly horns or heavily reverberating voices that refracted and echoed like a ghost train's sound effects. A truly modern, even futuristic music, dub versions became practically de rigueur for punk bands: Generation X, with guitarist Tony James and lead singer Billy Idol, was the first to do a dub, swiftly followed by a stampede of punk dubbers. The Clash covered "Police and Thieves," Lee "Scratch" Perry's edgy production of falsetto singer Junior Murvin, and also collaborated with Jamaican DJ Mikey Dread. Fronted by a fourteen-year-old dreadlocked banshee named Arri-Up, the Slits delivered deep dub-influenced tunes, and internalized reggae in the bones of their grooves such as "Shoplifting," "New Town," and "Typical Girls." Their deliberately dissonant look—ballet tutus with "bovver" boots, white-girl dreadlocks tied in ribbon, torn fishnets over colored tights—was a visual manifestation of the way they aimed to rip and slash the status quo. For their accomplice, they chose Dennis Bovell to produce their LP, *Cut*.

Three months before Bob was shot, the streets of Ladbroke Grove in West London had erupted in a very British riot, when the police enforced an early evening close to the annual West Indian Carnival. The Lenten festival was started in 1959 by Trinis, people from Trinidad and Tobago, home of the original Caribbean Carnival. In those days, before it became Europe's biggest street party, Carnival was a rather more ramshackle, spontaneous, and homey affair, an opportunity for all the local West Indian chefs in the family to jerk chicken or concoct creamy curds of ackee and salt fish flecked with red pepper. Cottage industry and private enterprise flourished amidst the music and licensed licentious behavior. Almost invariably inspired by the Wailers, the reggae groups springing up in Ladbroke Grove would perform. Equipped with the obligatory spliff and a Red Stripe, a sunshine amble past sound systems, from strictly rockers to ska specialists, was heaven for a reggae lover. The frisson of possibility in the air was delicious and fraught with intriguing adventure. For one day a year, we owned the streets. From my window, I could watch wave after wave of rainbow-colored glittering costumes, and floats of steel pan bands whose silvery cascades of sound made their Tchaikovsky and Beethoven melodies seem to shimmer in the warm air.

The Rough Trade record shop down on the dodgy end of Kensington Park Road was often the scene of a cool wind-down at the close of Carnival, when insta-mates would drift into each other's arms like the leaves that always started to fall on the exact day after Carnival, with staggering regularity. The lettering on the store window was very Haight-Ashbury, but the head space of this shop was different. Distributing the newly minted independent punk and reggae singles and distributing younger indies, in some senses Rough Trade was taking over from where Island had been ten years before.

In later years, we Carnival regulars came to recognize when the action might turn to aggression. The change of mood would blow through a mellow crowd. That year, 1976, overaggressive policing curtailing our one-day-a-year party flared into a battle between black and white youths against the police that became a turning point.

A precious cultural collision occurred in England during that era, when reggae was our religion and dub our sacred sacrament. Two decades after large-scale Caribbean immigration began from the newly independent islands, yesterday's colonies, the first generation of black British youth claimed their right to an all-night life. Their parents had come to the so-called motherland to do the hard slog work of keeping the country running that the homecoming World War II heroes hoped to avoid. But a good portion of their restless children, not content to fit in and slide unnoticed through the status quo, started to make their own music and invent a self-determined world within a sometimes hostile community. Money was scarce, but this generation had plenty of energy, and if regular clubs wouldn't have them, their own basements and empty houses surely would. Starting with Duke Vin in the 1950s, West Indian house parties became blues dances and then shebeens, where British youth molded their own version of Jamaican musical innovations: sound systems, DJs, and their sidekicks chatting on the mike in the shebeens, where Boy George and the Clash would skank alongside Aswad and Steel Pulse, the laboratory for a new groove.

The atmosphere was volcanic, particularly round the area of Basing Street Studios, which had been a crucible for British race relations since the first generation arrived from the Caribbean on the ship called *Windrush* in 1948. Its quaint church building was just one block below the front line, All Saints Road, home to the Mangrove Café, which became a center for progressive black activity. Within minutes of Basing Street was a network of shebeens, the most popular being Weasel's, on the ground floor of a house, which became a crucible for the scene that Bob and Scratch Perry were to call the "Punky Reggae Party." Although a shebeen could become the location for the acting out of grudges and disputes, and knives were known to flash, it was still a remarkably peaceful scene—luckily, as every shebeen was almost inevitably a fire department's nightmare, with a shaky staircase leading to a basement crammed to near immobility, and a luxuriant, mysterious darkness that hid sins of all sorts as couples slow-danced round the room, fused into one slowly writhing, four-legged, two-headed being. The shebeen drinks of choice, other than the inevitable Red Stripe and Guinness, constitute a quaint roll call, each stiff with sugar, but given a veneer of healthiness by their energetic attributes: the adrenaline fizz of Lucozade; or the pastel sludge of Nutrament in its various flavors, a meal in itself; and queen of them all, Babycham, fake champagne with ladylike overtones lingering from their old advertisements featuring doe-eyed ingénues. This nectar was bubbly and golden enough to make a hip-grinding, waist-winding rub-a-dub dance become an occasion for vertical orgasm, concealed by darkness from the public gaze.

The *Exodus* album fed off that energy. Family Man, Neville, and keyboardist Tyrone Downey went out quite often to the dives where reggae ruled, such as the narrow subterranean darkness of the Four Aces Club in Dalston, Columbo's in Carnaby Street, or Paddington's Q Club. But they all realized the usefulness as well as the fun of dances, and sometimes even the Tuff Gong would stop working for a while.

"Yeah! This is exclusive from Bob Marley!" growled DJ Dennis Bovell with a flourish as he twirled the faders on his amp, making the bass thud and the dance floor tremble as if a Dread giant were out there, skanking among the youths. It was a celebration of Haile Selassie's birthday, July 23, 1977, at the Metro

Youth Club, a forgettable gray one-story box of a building behind the Westbourne Park tube station, with an interior that
looked like a basic school gym. Dennis Bovell's Sufferers Sound
System had the privilege of playing the Wailers' "Exodus" in public for the first time ever.

The tune Dennis dropped that night, a twelve-inch white label—
a dub plate with no information—was the raw result of the previous night's session at Basing Street Studios, with just a touch of
vocals and no horns, but tons of drums and bass. The latest Wailers scorchers, soon to be polished to pop perfection, also had to
work in a packed dance hall if they were to succeed. Certainly,
Bovell had no problem with getting the heavy, heavy sound that
roots fans sometimes missed in the Wailers' polished Island releases. "I didn't have to fiddle with nothing," the burly bassie
cracks. "I was playing it at, like, twenty-five thousand watts, know
what I mean? Just raise up the volume and your trousers will fall
off."

Throughout the hall the profound growl of the bass dominated
every exchange. Dennis Bovell with his DJ Sufferers Sound System
was one of the most popular communicators of culture through
music. Along with the Cimarons, the band Matumbi, with Bovell
on bass, spearheaded the first generation of British reggae bands to
have dread up, inspired by Bob Marley and his Jamaican bred'ren.
Bovell's productions were launching the popular sweet harmony
style, lovers rock, and his DJ setup was a heavy Rasta ambassador.

This audience was not the long-haired student sector Bob's new
music was being groomed to seduce, but the core, the converted,
the first generation of home-grown British Dreads and their cohorts, whose parents had tried unsuccessfully to banish locks from
the family living room: schoolgirls in fat headwraps, scant makeup,
and the demure dress of the day—high round necks and shirts with
collars, just-below-the-knee skirts, knee-length socks, and clumpy

Clarks shoes; the youths in slick slacks, suede desert boots, peaked caps, and knitted tams stuffed with dreadlocks.

Impressing one another with bold "steppers" moves—jumping alternate knees to waist height, as if juggling a soccer ball—or sensuously wind 'n' grinding in an intimate connection, the young dancers were unaware that the Tuff Gong himself was in the house, leaning quietly against a wall at the back of the main room, observing the impact of his new rhythms, blocked from prying eyes by his more gregarious bred'ren, Family Man, Seeco, and Neville. The man liked to move in a humble, low-key way, and even the admirers who got to spot him sensed they should give him space.

"He liked to see how people were dancing to the music," specifies Bovell, sitting at the big country-style table in a north London kitchen full of family photos. "We'd drop it a couple of times, try to rip up a storm about it in front of him, and then he'd go back in the studio and adjust it, or keep what he had."

Bob never conversed with Bovell at those sessions, but with a serious expression, he would direct the DJ a nod, meaning, Respect. Dennis had a small history with Bob. When the original Wailers trio were trying to make it in London in 1973, on the cold tour that turned Bunny off permanently, Bovell's band, Matumbi, found themselves on the same bill in some poxy club in Harlesden. The London lads got a sound check, but the Wailers had to make do with a totally untuned PA, and it could be heard. The ensuing screech prompted one music journalist to big up Matumbi versus the Wailers. "Our drummer wanted to find that journalist and beat him up," elaborates Bovell. "We were all gutted. Bob was our hero."

Indeed, having Bob's blessing helped crystallize the new community, and awareness of his presence helped promote what Delroy Washington called "Wailerism," a nonaligned movement whereby the Wailers were revered as figureheads of Rasta, a belief that some youths found to be not just an inspiration but also a transformative identity tool.

But despite the pleasures of the night, among many young West Indian Brits, especially the males, there was an expectation of regular harassment from the police, notably by the implementation of an antiquated law designed to control vagrants in Napoleonic times, the charge being suspicion of loitering with intent, commonly known as "suss."

The old law was being applied for purposes never dreamed of when written. Lanky and doe-eyed beneath his big peaked cap, I remember Aswad's Drummie Zeb mournfully sloping into the studio, lamenting that he'd just been picked up for suss in London's busy shopping district, the West End. "I should have known better than to go to Oxford Street on a Saturday afternoon," he concluded.

Bob's star status conferred no immunity from police scrutiny. So placid was the Wailers' time in London that the one dramatic incident everyone remembers is the famous pot bust, and its surviving protagonists still bicker amicably about it nearly three decades on, as old friends and family will. Given the time and place, perhaps it had to happen, but since the outcome was comparatively relaxed, it's become one of those old war stories to which rosy hindsight has given aspects of a Keystone Kops farce. The band was leaving the Basing Street studio, and Neville was slightly tetchy, having been away most of the night and returned to find the source of weed dried up. He's still annoyed that though they'd denied him a spliff, his bred'ren were twice damned when the cops produced joints from Family Man's socks and Bob's pockets.

Although he chuckles at the memory now, Family Man clearly still remembers how extremely unhappy he was at the time. "Me is a mechanic, you know," he insists, "and me did tell Neville Garrick to get in the car early to mek sure it warm up. But instead 'im have to stay in the studio and keep warm. So when the police drive past, they see all a we sorta hanging around in the street while the little car stuck on the road. Naturally dem 'ave to stop and search us."

When the police wanted to know who owned the weed they found under the driver's seat, Bob grandly declared, "Me claim all herb." Still grateful, Neville Garrick comments, "That got me off the hook." But sadly, Bob's philosophical gesture failed to impress the cops.

Bob had the presence of mind to give his address as the Chelsea rental apartment where Marcia and Rita—the I-Two, as Fams jocularly called them—were staying with Marcia's little boy. When Bob arrived in the police car, he tried to announce himself in an unusual way, by announcing, "Is Robert," instead of the usual "Bob," to warn the girls—but sure enough, someone opened the front door, admitting Bob, Fams, Neville, and the cops, who were greeted by Rita and Marcia in their dressing gowns. His story was lent credence by the fact that Bob actually had clothes there, because Rita was doing his ironing. Happily, Marcia's little boy leaped into Bob's arms. The adorable tyke cooing, "Bob! Bob!" melted the cops, whose perfunctory search of the Wailers' real ranch in Oakley Street missed the stash.

Island Records chairman Tom Hayes was charged with defusing the situation. Humorously, Hayes reenacts his introduction of Bob to his defense lawyer. "Mr. Bowler had a very Oxbridge accent and he was very respectful, but Bob for some bizarre reason decided to answer him in semi-patois. Bowler kept asking, 'I'm sorry, Mr. Hayes. Do you understand what he said?' So this whole interview was conducted through me. Bob was obviously having a bit of fun, because he could speak perfectly 'clean' English when he was in the mood to. Then near the end, it was classic." Bowler, the lawyer, asked what Bob's defense would be in court. Bob reached in his bag, produced a Bible, and pointed to a psalm about everything being put on earth for use—one of the favorite Rasta lines explaining why weed is a sacrament.

"Bowler kind of looked at him and said, 'Hmmm . . . very good, Mr. Marley, but I don't think the judge will accept that somehow. Perhaps that might not be our best line of defense.' But when everyone boogied off to court, Bowler kept the emphasis on the religious aspect, with the backup from the Bible."

Bob got off with a £30 fine.

The whole landscape of seething London and awakening England meant Bob's lyrics fell on ready ears, and the musicians he was inspiring, such as Aswad, Steel Pulse, and Black Slate, were keen to spread his Rasta message. The Southall collective Misty in Roots was perhaps the reggae band most associated with the front line; their manager, Clarence Baker, almost died after being beaten by the police in an anti–National Front demonstration in Southall in 1982.

The scene fascinated Bob. His bred'ren, Pepe Judah, took him to Ladbroke Grove to meet Joly, the white dreadlocked founder and proprietor of Better Badges, whose lapel buttons were an effective guerrilla punk PR medium. The Rastas' plan was to flood Marxist Ethiopia with badges of the overthrown monarch, Haile Selassie. One particular button on the shelves caught Bob's eye. In the Rasta colors, it read, "I Shot the Ferret," a hilarious twist on "I Shot The Sheriff" for whimsical Brits. That surreal humor came from the cosmos of TV series, *Monty Python's Flying Circus,* where a ferret was automatically funny. Joly watched Bob study the curious legend for a long time, pleased but slightly puzzled by this strange homage.

Most enthralling to Bob was the emergence of the first generation of children of immigrants from the Caribbean. Before he'd ever been to England, Mortimo Planno had shown him the photos he'd taken showing, literally, England's first Dreads—including Jah Blue. Now the Twelve Tribes were becoming organized. There was much need for Bob's involvement: among other things, they were actively engaged in organizing repatriation to the land Haile Selassie had set aside in Shashamane, in a literal fulfillment of Marcus Garvey's edicts. Says Bob's close bred'ren footballer Skill Cole, "That's where the idea for 'movement of Jah people' came from at that time, because we were talking about moving out, like in Exodus. Like we called it: movement. We had started sending people to Ethiopia already."

The Twelve Tribes organization had acquired property in St. Agnes Place, Kennington, and their calendar offered a round of spiritually based social activities, which were welding together a British link in an international community. They were expanding, engaged in opening new chapters, and festivals on the Twelve Tribes calendar were observed with due ceremony and celebration. Bob's presence at any of these functions, of course, was an extra blessing.

Twelve Tribes functions were virtually the only outings Bob went on. As the organization began to spread outside London, Bob and Popsy would drive up the motorway to Birmingham or Manchester in Popsy's Volvo. Suddenly dragged from the womb of the studio, Bob would be so tired he'd stretch out and doze in the backseat, and wake with a start when the car hit a bump in the road.

One warm Saturday afternoon near the end of the *Exodus* mix, I found myself alone with Bob and Scratch Perry upstairs at Basing Street in Chris Blackwell's futuristic apartment, where Scratch was staying. There was a slight edge of hilarity to the exchange between the two longtime friends, whose bond had survived all manner of human conflicts. They were slapping each other on the back, and whenever Scratch got excited, which was often, he would jump up and wave his hands for emphasis. Their enthusiastic talk was a real

Rasta reasoning, about the superior contribution of the black race. With some amusement, Bob described a young man he'd seen on Portobello Road, whose bizarre trousers were buckled and belted so extensively that he looked like a trussed rabbit, and whose rainbow hair jutted at mad angles. Scratch and Bob chuckled at these crazy baldheads. Of course, I felt impelled to explain to the visitors that the youth was not actually a filthy loser but in fact a punk. As such, he belonged to Bob's own constituency: the disadvantaged, disaffected, and unjustly stigmatized. Indeed, they constituted the very sufferers and rebel souls of whom Bob was the eloquent bard. Punks were playing on the same team as Rastas.

Both Bob and Scratch really got it when we listened to the Clash's version of Scratch's Junior Murvin production, "Police and Thieves." The scathing lyrics numbering corruption were twice as fast as the original, with Strummer's brash, hoarse shout replacing Junior Murvin's silken harmonies. "That's a group that stand up and speak the truth, me really appreciate that. 'Cos 'Police and Thieves' not a joke, y'know. I like they try, mon, I appreciate the move. If we could have some more white band play reggae, that woulda suit me even more. Me no criticize the way dem do it as long as dem don't alter words. Because they do it inna feel of how dem feelin', and as long as dem a tell the story right—that's movement. I feel them a try earth movement. I like the move. Me make a tune, y'know, towards the whole movement, named 'Punk Rock Reggae,' " Scratch said excitedly, in the first glimmer of the upcoming "Punky Reggae Party." Not long after, Scratch produced the Clash on their song "Complete Control," and joined a white punk band in London called the Assassins.

Excited by the synergy of the times, I wrote a two-part article called "Jah Punk," which turned out to be a controversial name that stuck for a while. The articles recall those moments heightened with creative intensity as different communities in London experimented with music and one another to try to express how they wanted the world, and themselves, to be.

Sounds, London, September 3, 1977

The Clash go into the CBS Studios with Lee Perry, the magical mystery Jamaican producer, whose crystalline star wars productions are impossible to reproduce, and cut "Complete Control."

That same week Bob Marley's in town, recovering from yet another football injury to his big toe. I walk into the room carrying a copy of the Clash album with their Westway rocka "Police and Thieves" on it—remember, Lee Perry not only worked with Marley but also cut the original version of "Police and Thieves" with falsetto-swooping Junior Murvin.

Marley grunts, clocking the long player and my newly bleached hair. "Wha'appen, Viveen? You turn into *punk-rocka*?" he teases, inference being it couldn't be more uncouth. "You shoulda change your hair to *red, green and gold!*"

That's next week, Jah B. Now, just check these sounds awhile . . . Marley and Scratch are both surprised. Impressed.

"It *good,* t'raas claat!"

And the week after that, I'm in a listening room at Basing Street Studios, and Bob's voice is rolling in magical command out of the huge speakers: "We're gonna have a party, and we hope it will be hearty, it's a punky reggae party . . . the Wailers will be there, the Slits, the Feelgoods and the Clash . . . rejected by society, treated with impunity, protected by their dignity, it's a punky reggae party . . ."

I'm not sure how many punks, in it to have fun, would recognize themselves in Marley's typically emotion/politics-charged description, but it sums up the crucial reason why punk and reggae are linked—when you get right down to it, punks and dreadlocks are on the same side of the fence.

Bluntly, who gets picked up in the street by the police? Answer: those natty Dreads and crazy baldheads.

Bob Marley and Lee Perry both said it, sitting in the thick white-carpeted luxury of Basing Street. "The punks are the outcasts from society. So are the Rastas. So they are bound to defend what we defend." Marley paused, flexing his arms. He's wearing a bright blue tracksuit, and he'd just finished telling us why he wears just tracksuits and faded denims onstage. It's because he doesn't want to wear flash clothes that the youth will admire, envy and feel frustrated 'cos they can't have.

Remember all those declarations in the early days of punk that echo his sentiments? Anti-chic, poor people's fashions, dustbin-liner chic. If you can't afford a packet of safety pins you can pick them up in the street . . .

"In a way, me like see them safety pins and t'ing," Marley continued. "Me no like do it myself, y'understand, but me like see a man can suffer pain without crying."

It seemed that in this new transcultural lovefest, it was left to punk's most prominent reggae fan, the Sex Pistols' ever-bolshie singer, Johnny Rotten, to voice reservations. "I don't like the idea of emphasis on punk and reggae. That way both the musics could get diluted," he said, shouting to be heard over the heavy bass of a reggae prerelease twelve-inch spinning in his Fulham ranch.

The bass player of the Clash, Paul Simonon, was the only white kid in his school and thus raised on ska and reggae, and their music demonstrated it. "Reggae, punk, it's not like most of the stuff you hear on the radio, it's something you can relate to, kids your own age," said Simonon at the time. "Black people are being suppressed, we're being suppressed, so we have something in common. But personally, all that about Rastafari bores me. I don't think there would ever be a God-music punk band, because punks want to tear down everything that's establishment, like church and police."

To cut the spunky twelve-incher "Punky Reggae Party," a local all-star crew was recruited that combined the best of London and Jamaica. Aswad was well represented; Drummie Zeb was deeply flattered to be asked to play with Bob and Scratch. Musicians from Third World, also recording at Basing Street, were playing, too. For that much-discussed session, held at Island's Fallout Shelter, the studio was packed.

"Bob was standing in the middle, conducting, holding everything together," recalls Aswad's singer, Brinsley Forde. "Rumor had it that it was really Scratch's song, that Bob was singing it because he dug his old bred'ren and wanted to work with him." Maybe the exact allocation of labor will never be known, but it seems possible, if only because Bob's lyrics tended to be smooth and sparing, understated and insightful, while Scratch went for a stream-of-consciousness babble. Bob manfully tries to inject some swing into the first line of the bridge—"No boring old farts / Will be there"—and he manages, but barely. More typically, he would have split the line smoothly. Ultimately, the record seemed to work better as a conceptual art piece, a zeitgeist homage.

"The session for 'Punky Reggae Party' was absolute chaos, mad, like a sort of insanity," remembers Newman. "Bob was kind of not that keen at first to do it. But though it wasn't very well recorded, it was great."

Discussing it three years later, enjoying being in his own studio at 56 Hope Road, Bob looked back on the episode and concluded,

"Me no care what people dem a seh. Me want to do 'Punky Reggae Party,' so me do it."

But in the end, Scratch wound up taking the "Punky Reggae Party" concept down to Jamaica, to his regular Upsetters crew. "We tried that with Third World, but they were the smooth type of musician. The players for 'Punky Reggae Party' need a rebel feel, like a warrior. You see when the dog bite something and shake its head because he want to kill the thing that he bite, tear it apart? That has to be the energy. You need a wolf, lion, or a bad dog to do it," he explained laconically.

"We were trying to put the punk, the English vibration, and the Jamaican vibration together, for an international sound and power," Scratch continued. "That was the master plan, the positive plan. And it couldn't have happened in England. It did have to happen in Jamaica, because that's where the energy came first."

Ultimately, this old comrades' side project wound up taking up more studio time than any track on either *Exodus* or *Kaya*. When Scratch was happy with the Upsetters' result, the two bred'ren met in Miami. "We take it to Criterion Studios, and Bob Marley did the vocal just one time, in one take. Then he told me he was sick with cancer. I believe in healing. And I said to him, 'God can make the impossible possible.' So they cancel the operation to cut off his foot, with the healing power of 'Punky Reggae Party.' "

In Bob's absence, the island was shaken by another bloody trauma that musician and DJ Wayne Jobson described as their generation's Kent State. The Green Bay Massacre occurred on the night of January 4, 1978, on a beach in an army firing range. In a deadly game of bluff and counterbluff, twelve JLP members were advised they could get guns and jobs by traveling to Green Bay in an army van for some guard work on a construction site. But when they arrived, the men were ordered out of the trucks and onto the

beach. Blood soon stained the sand. They were met by an army firing squad who immediately opened fire, killing five men out of, it
was said, ten. Amazingly, the survivors were able to crawl through
the underbrush to freedom.

"Dudley Thompson, the government minister of national security and justice, sent his thug soldiers to kill the Green Bay guys. It
was pitched as a gang thing," Wayne Jobson bluntly states. Despite
suspicions, the government might have got away with it. But in-
criminating photos were lifted from the desk of one Major Ian
Robinson, who'd led the attack, and deposited on that of a journalist at the *Gleaner,* David D'Costa, as writer Laurie Gunst reports in
her book *Born Fi' Dead.* Examining the shots, D'Costa swiftly realized that the soldiers' long shadows indicated the position of the
sun and proved that the army had been lying in its version of
events, and the massacre became public knowledge.

Lamented in a flood of singles by artists including Tappa Zukie
and Big Youth, the extreme gravity of the massacre seemed to
prompt extra-eloquent, angry music. It marked a grim coming of
age, even for youths seemingly hardened to daily gunfire and the
apparently inexorable eradication of their generation. Conspiracy
theories were everywhere. Was it Manley's team, putting the fright-
eners on the opposition? Or was it Seaga himself, callously discard-
ing a few of his followers' lives to ensure a further term?

Dudley Thompson, the PNP minister for national security and
justice, appeared to support the mutterings of those who said his
office was implicated, by making a most unpolitic statement to the
press: "No angels died at Green Bay." The sheer derision of that
quote about slain youths who might have been his constituents had
they been born mere blocks away remains staggering.

Even by the comparatively violent island's standards, a line had
been crossed. It could be argued that the extreme cynical savagery
of Green Bay helped lay the foundation for the cocaine wars of the

next decade, organized by JLP gangs such as the infamous Shower Posse, in which expat Jamaican bad-boy gangs became known for their psychotic brutality in England and America.

But before the individual enforcers threw off their political controllers and struck out on the cocaine business, a catharsis had to come. Used to being each other's nemesis, enforcers and area leaders from rival factions finally confronted each other in a place where they couldn't just pull out knives or guns to settle the argument. Two downtown dons made the momentous commitment to peace, Labourite area leader Claudius Massop, who had tried to alert Bob to the invasion, and the PNP's Aston "Bucky" Marshall. The reasoning happened in perhaps the only place it could—a jail cell.

There was one transcendent night in which all of downtown shared a mutual rediscovery and barriers went up in the smoke of giant ganja "cutchie" pipes, whose smoke sealed the new deal. When morning came, longtime opponents were on the same side— the people's.

Bob sent Claudie a ticket to London. Out of all the area leaders, feared and revered, Massop was perhaps the best primed to lunge for peace. Respected in their Tivoli Gardens community, Massop's father was an odd-job man, his mother a homemaker, and by virtue of both imposing physique and intellect, Massop naturally gravitated to a leadership position in the community that Seaga had brought out of the slums. His particular responsibility as area leader was children and the elderly. Despite a fearsome reputation and eleven charges of murder, Massop was never once convicted of anything except illegal possession of a firearm, for which he paid a J$200 fine.

One of the greatest flaws in a party system that reflexively rejects all of the previous government's initiatives and leaders is the human waste. It was typical that when Manley replaced the JLP government in 1972, Massop's family considered that Kingston was now too hot for Claudie. Having recently been acquitted on a murder rap, Claudie came to London.

Says Jah Blue, "When Claudie Massop came to England as a young man, long before the Peace Concert time, we didn't know who he really was or what he represented, to be honest. At the time, him was just another black youth that come up from Jamaica. He was young, played football and cricket with us. We know him come from Tivoli, but we never identified him as an area leader or activist then. Not until after, when some of us started to go to Jamaica." By that time, Massop had gone home and become a Tivoli Gardens area leader, backing Seaga.

In London, Massop fell in love with a teenager called Sydoney Williamson who worked as an intern for designer Mary Quant. They married and he whisked her off to a very different world in Jamaica. At first they stayed with music producers Tommy and Valerie Cowan, and soon Claudie drove her round the ghetto areas. Coming from leafy West London, Syd was shocked by the alleyways of fetid hovels lashed together out of garbage, the grime romanticized by names like Rose Lane and Love Lane. Tivoli Gardens is still a flashpoint three decades on; but back then, Claudie explained how much better the brutalist neo–Eastern European concrete projects were than the shanties Seaga had bulldozed. Thoughtfully, Syd says, "He spoke about Seaga studying poor people because he was an anthropologist, and how important this was in knowing where black people came from. Now I think maybe he was a little bit ignorant about the [wider implications of the] whole political thing."

At Bob's invitation Syd came to stay with Claudie in London in early 1978, when they all stayed with Bob in a suite at Blake's Hotel. Bob and his bred'ren were preparing the next phase of the exodus strategy. The long-term plan was repatriation to Africa, ending apartheid, and building up the Jamaican Rasta community in Shashamane; but right now something needed fixing in Jamaica. While Bob was trying to heal his island, he was ailing. In their service flat, Sydoney would see him wince as he moved around and was concerned. Although he kept cheerful, he seemed to be in pain, moving slowly. He was between hospital stays. "I was worried about his foot," she says with a grimace. "It didn't look like it was cared for. He was limping around with that bandage and his toenail was too long and the whole thing didn't look healthy at all." However, nothing would stop Bob pursuing the Rasta plan.

A number of meetings were held, including one at the Keskidee Centre, where a very young Linton Kwesi Johnson, one of Britain's leading poets, was working the front desk. At one session, with no area leaders present, Marley met with his Hope Road neighbor, Prime Minister Michael Manley. The gangsters and the island's leader had the same aim—to assure Bob Marley that it was safe to come home to Jamaica. To Manley, Bob made one proviso: he'd come home if Skill Cole was allowed to return safely. The footballer had split for Ethiopia right after the invasion and was unsure whether it was wise for him to go home.

Michael Campbell's partner, the entertainer King Sounds, was present at one of the meetings. "Claudie was very insistent that if he had not been in jail when they came to shoot Bob, it would never have happened," recalls the man who used to tailor the Wailers' stage suits in the 1960s. "Bob admired the way Claudie operated. He was one of Bob's mentors—in fact, I think Claudie's influence stood out more than anyone else's. He felt more safe to come home to Jamaica when Claudie told him it was OK."

When Bob realized that Jah Blue, the London Dread he'd met through Mortimo Planno, was also an old friend of his longtime bred'ren Claudie, they became even closer. As Blue walked into the hotel room where the Peace Committee meeting was being held, one of the few Dreads permitted to enter, Claudie hailed him with an exuberant, "Soldier!" Pleased at the link between his worlds, Bob urged Jah Blue, "You must come to Jamaica, mon. Help with the program after the Peace Concert. The Rasta government."

"The idea was to involve the Rasta community in the social, political, activist vision," clarifies Jah Blue with dignified emphasis. "I tell Bob seh, 'Yes.' "

"The plan was Claudie's, but Bob was the strength behind it," interjects Bob's childhood Trench Town bred'ren Michael Knowledge, who sits with us in Blue's living room in a typical Victorian west London terrace house. "The Peace Concert came about because of that idea.

"The plan was to set up an opposition that would be truly popular, and eliminate the old, corrupt parties, in the name of Rasta," continues Jah Blue, who now lives in London and Ghana. "At that time in England, the mainstay of the Rasta community didn't really see Africa as the central focal point. I read a lot about Africa, but my general preaching was that Rasta must come back to Jamaica. There can be no repatriation to Africa until we have representation in the parliament in Jamaica. So as a young Rasta community in England, we were educating ourselves spiritually, politically, and economically, fi come back to Jamaica and involve ourselves."

Aswad's manager, Michael Campbell, was one of the few aware of the extent of these radical secret meetings. "Downtown Kingston was already divided up politically. After the Peace Concert, now, the people who were controlling the areas were gonna stop fighting one another. Then they, the area leaders, might become the MP of that area, and they'd get out whatever political parties were in power. So that means Tony Spalding, the minister of housing, and Dudley Thompson would be out. Seaga would be out. A lot of people didn't want to let that happen."

10

EXODUS: THE INTRO

BOB HAD ANTICIPATED IT, dreamed it, and even written prophetic songs about it, but still, the assassination attempt killed off his old life. The making of *Exodus* was an exorcism, a tuneful howl that burst from underground in the Fallout Shelter, a cramped basement studio under the offices of Island Records in leafy Chiswick, and took its final shape in the converted church in Ladbroke Grove's Basing Street, on the Caribbean Carnival route.

"*Exodus* was really a big turning point for Bob. Basically, *Exodus* is a concept album. The songs were definitely Bob's reaction to the shooting, his fear, his anger. And at the same time, 'im was in love with this girl named Cindy," recalls Bob's close bred'ren Neville Garrick.

All these extremes of human emotion find their balance in *Exodus*. Digital listeners might not even be aware that in its original incarnation, Side A, flowing on from the haunting "Natural Mystic" through "So Much Things to Say," the thunderous "Guiltiness" and "The Heathen," and soaring to a finale with "Exodus," was officially perceived as "heavy." In contrast, Side B was "up," kicking off with "Jamming," then moving into the love zone with "Waiting in Vain" and "Turn Your Lights Down Low" before feeling a more universal love with "Three Little Birds" and the sunny

Holding back the Heathen: How Bob Marley and the Wailers recorded
Exodus.
© *Adrian Boot/Bob Marley Music. 1977.*

"One Love" combined with Curtis Mayfield's "People Get Ready." The duality was much commented on.

Heard in the digital age, however, *Exodus* unfurls seamlessly on a compact disc. The album's mythos stands out more starkly as the primal movie itself, the infinite cosmic wheel of death and rebirth. Listening to the *Exodus* album in an uninterrupted flow, going through the hurt to the fun, from the darkness to the sun, can actually function as a therapeutic exercise. Its ten-song round can be experienced as a manual to recovery and emotional rescue. It can help prepare the perturbed and perplexed to deal with painful or poignant eventualities. As an exodus, the flow of the tracks can also represent a transition from one state of being to another. On this journey, Bob dons his Moses persona completely to act as a guide, leading listeners through their worst fears, confronting betrayal and disillusion, to finally attain a place of joy. Like an old quilt from the South whose pictograms of houses and rivers hide another meaning—the route from slavery to freedom—listening to *Exodus* can suggest a way to make it through to the other side with sanity, humor, and reverence intact.

Matching all cultures' emergence from winter dark to the promise of a new year, the recording of *Exodus* and *Kaya* spanned January to August 1977. The track sheets given to me by a colleague, compilations maven Bill Levenson of Universal Records, were a valuable guide to the anatomy of an album, particularly as every interviewee seemed to have a different recollection of the album's construction. Some said it was partly recorded in Jamaica before the invasion, but then all those tracks were discarded and redone in London. Everything on *Exodus* was inspired by the shooting, others opined, and the album was built between Miami and London. Then there was the further theory that *Exodus*'s earliest tracks had been cut in Nassau, but as we know, Nassau had no recording facilities at the time.

Having no luck asking so many people involved about the origins of the tracks described on the tape boxes as being "Taken from Jamaican Reels," I'd always assumed that these were tracks Bob had mentioned he and the band were recording in a nonspecific way and storing up for future use.

Perhaps the realization of the meaning of that cryptic inscription had to come from a session musician. Guitarist Earl "Chinna" Smith, who played on these and many other Wailers tracks thereafter, was amazed to find that he was the only person who specifically remembered that, in the true thrifty Wailers tradition, three tracks on *Exodus,* "Guiltiness," "Three Little Birds," and "One Love," were all outtakes from the *Rastaman Vibration* sessions.

Having built up the tracks in three countries, the Wailers were eager to lay them down in twenty-four-track splendor. There were other benefits to recording in London as well, including a sense of ease. "Everyone felt safe at Basing Street," says Dick Cuthell. "They knew the sound. Blackwell used to like those late sessions because he would drop in very late to have an earhole and show some celebrity around, and you'd have some film star like Catherine Deneuve, or Phil May from Queen, who would be in awe of a tape op."

Managing the Fallout Shelter at the time was Suzette Newman, the young Island employee who'd first greeted Bob and Brent Clarke when they came to meet Chris Blackwell with a tape labeled "CBS." "I was in all those sessions. I used to stay until five in the morning, mainly because I was terrified there would be a breakdown in the studio, and everything would go wrong and I'd get the blame," says Newman. "Anyway, Bob used to say to me, 'You no go home tonight, Suzette, you stayin' till we done.' And it was something special. Incredible times."

"Basing Street was more posh, but the Fallout Shelter had more of a rootsy sound," proclaims Dick Cuthell, who, as a session musician cum engineer cum tape op who doubled as a delivery boy, shuttled nonstop between the two studios. "Bob used to like to go out and record in the tiny corridor between the control room and the main studio. He said it had an excellent echo."

Though the Basing Street studio was on a lower floor, its atrium lobby made it feel spacious. In the case of the Fallout Shelter, where the first tracks for *Exodus* were laid, it was literally a case of descending into the basement like Orpheus into the underworld. The muffled thud of the fire door banging shut at the top of the stairs, sealing off the outside world, marked the passage from one state of consciousness to another, and going down the stairs meant entering a physical expression of the subconscious, home of creativity.

The studio was unusually full every night. It really felt like the best party ever, with all the music being built around you, so loud you could drown in it. Bob liked it that way. If he brought the ghetto uptown at Hope Road, he gathered another community round him at Basing Street. "One evening I had to leave early on some Twelve Tribes business," recalls Michael Campbell, the Twelve Tribes Dread who managed the group Aswad. "Bob really didn't want me to go. He was disappointed, like I was letting the team down. He liked to have that energy around him, being part of a community." Although Bob appreciated solitude for meditation and strumming the initial sketch of a song, on another level he really was the expression of a people's artist; he enjoyed having the people around him and creatively fed off them, and he relished hearing casual expressions that would later pop up in a new song.

Having written and performed the song, the hands-on mixing aspect of the process was a moment for Bob to sit back slightly and monitor the work of the sound men he trusted. "Family Man was the man mainly at the desk. Chris would suggest something and they'd try it out. Bob would say, 'I don't like that' or 'I do like that,'" recalls Leroy Anderson. "The big bag of weed was there, and it was open for everybody to just get a spliff. Sometimes it took days on one track, specially 'Exodus' and 'Waiting in Vain.' And somewhere they found time to do 'Punky Reggae Party.' " Anderson shakes his head and wonders, "I don't know how they did it."

The combined energy of the local Dread artists and Twelve Tribes members were a kind of soul food for Bob, and he liked to encourage young new Dread bands, such as Steel Pulse, whose members he ran into at Island, and Aswad, Ladbroke Grove's reggae spearhead. At that time, the young Rastas were feeling somewhat beleaguered. Recalls Brinsley Forde, Aswad's original singer and guitarist, "Every time we went into the Island offices there was this atmosphere like people were watching us, expecting us to nick something," he says, anger still in his voice. "One night we went down to Basing Street and found there were no balls on the foosball table. We got really upset and thought the balls had been taken away to stop us playing. We were getting a bit excited when Bob suddenly came out of the control room and laid the balls on the table, and went back inside. It was just him making sure he got a game."

Such were the dramas of the little late-night world that *Exodus* created in an old West London church; a safe space where survivors of shootings and the regularly harassed were permitted to work together and enjoy one another.

In the Rasta way, there was much apocalyptic, millennial reasoning about politics. At the time, NATO was discussing the Strategic Arms Limitation Treaty (SALT) in terms that Bob viewed with some cynicism. During a heated reasoning about it at Basing Street, I remember Bob interjecting with a snarl, "Ha! Let them perish in their own fucking SALT." That was a particularly neat critique, as it punned on Rastas' rejection of salt in their diet, and all the Dreads there got it. But the main message was Bob's distrust of the traditional system. It wasn't just in Jamaica that he was unconvinced by the political establishment.

Recent events had made Bob even more determined to be on guard and in control. His early ghetto training never deserted him. Instinctively he knew how to position himself for security, even in the studio, where he should have felt at ease. "When he worked at Hammersmith, Bob would take up position," recalls tape op Dick Cuthell. "He liked going to sit down on the settee in the front of the control room, where the monitors were really close to you, in front of the big window looking through to the main studio. When you sat there, you were hidden by the mixing desk, so people couldn't see you when they walked into the control room. But you could see their reflections."

"I remember the sessions were very hush-hush," recalls Stella McLaughlan, a transplanted American who ran the canteen at night. "We weren't supposed to go and talk a lot about the sessions outside the immediate crew. But looking back, I'm surprised at the lack of security. Now he'd never be allowed to not have a body-guard, after they tried to kill him."

Indeed, Bob enjoyed the odd stroll in Portobello Road Market, right by the studio, and Aswad sometimes came across him in Lancaster Road, "wearing his football shirt and trainers with one leg of his pants rolled up, rude-boy style," remembers Brinsley with a smile.

So for those London months, the Wailers' rhythm was set. "I remember it so clearly. I remember the carpet there and rearranging certain things in the studio to give them more space. I remember everything about those sessions," reflects Suzette Newman. "A lot of people used to come and hang around where the TV and the pool table were. Everyone [in the extended family] knew where Bob was when he was recording. His sessions started in the afternoon, and they'd go on until four or five in the morning."

There was little time for socializing on their schedule. Priding themselves on their professionalism, the Wailers had a fierce work

202 | The Book of Exodus

ethic, particularly Bob, known for being first on the bus and last in the studio. As each Jamaican team member was an established winner in Kingston's competitive studio circuit, efficiency was part of the kick of a job well done. A star herself since her 1970 hit duet with Bob Andy, "Young, Gifted and Black," singer Marcia Griffiths recalls how quickly she and Rita were laying down backing voices. "It depends on how the song goes, how the vibe is in the studio. Because it's Bob, we want it to be perfect. If the song is not too hard, then, you know, we would knock that one off and go on to other songs."

"It's probably obvious to people, but the rhythm track goes down with bass, drums, piano, skank, and Bob playing the guitar. Maybe Seeco doing some percussion. Maybe Junior playing, maybe not. But the basic unit is four people," Terry Barham sums up. "Without even a hesitation, once one track's picked—'Yeah, that's a good one to go with'—straightaway, without even stopping for breath, it's straight out into the studio, and down goes Tyrone's organ part on top. They work out how to concentrate the rhythm of that organ, 'cause it gives a lot of the bounce to the track. It's not just an instrument, it's another piece of percussion, and it's gotta be right into the rhythm. That makes it a complete reggae rhythm, 'cause you've got the chop, the bubble, and the rhythm section. As quickly as it's finished, you're done, and that happened every time. So when you're listening back to it later, you've got Bob's guide voice, and a full rhythm track. And then you can set a course on what you might just add to it, you know?"

Although Bob was the big boss, the band all enjoyed the creative energy, feeding off one another's ideas. "A song would start and everyone would throw in their own contribution, because the singer gave them the glow of confidence," explains producer Karl Pitterson. "Everybody would listen to the track, then do horns, percussion, and voices. They used to make adjustments, OK, but by then I already knew the operative formula of what they expected and could go on from there."

Sitting in his sparse, immaculate living room in Miami's suburban area of Kendall, where so many Marleys have found a home, Pitterson has no visible mementoes of the years he spent working with the Wailers, Rico, Steel Pulse, and Third World. He grew up not far from the Wailers, in Kingston's winding downtown alleys, and now he enjoys sitting out by his pool. He likes to look at it, but doesn't swim.

"Remember *Exodus* was also in the mix with *Kaya*. It was a ton of songs done [at] one time and they arrived at the studio with their songs ready. Some got modified in the studio, but plenty songs Bob had in his head and they were done just like that," recalls Pitterson. "Some songs he sang straight through, others he would know the chorus and then they'd start figuring out the best way to run the track, whether Carly's drums would be one drop or straight four, or a different style. Plenty of songs were done like that, it would be normal in Jamaica. From that point on, the song was the song and they'd practice it. When they finish a song, it was straight on to the overdubs, horn section, vocals, and stuff. If it took the whole night, when the session was done, the song was done. They never really do one song and come back to work on it again tomorrow."

"I had no control over what Bob recorded," remembers Chris Blackwell. "It was just delivered to me and we would mix it together."

Bob's plan was to draw in people who'd never appreciated reggae, without alienating the faithful. "Being the clever artist he was is why Bob did 'Exodus,' 'Waiting in Vain,' 'Could You Be Loved,' all those kinda songs, because he realized that there was a fight," explains Neville Garrick. "We wanted that drive time, and we wanted black America; so by having the 'foreign musicians,' the Al Andersons, the Donald Kinseys, the Junior Marvins to add that blues and R&B texture, Bob was being a clever fisherman."

Indeed, *Exodus* was a creative leap, a journey from one familiar style and technique in search of an unknown other, retaining the music's reggae patois while making it intelligible to a broader community.

Studio engineer Terry Barham agrees. "Everyone was trying to make new sounds. Then, you only had a small palette of sounds, so if you could make something sound interesting, but it came from a kind of organic source, like a piano, then it was quite good really. You'd made up your own sound."

"One of the things they were trying to do was have something that was not just totally roots, because they knew that totally roots was at its peak," says Karl Pitterson. "It wasn't just the band. Chris had a lot to do with it at that point. He had this thing where they could get into the wider market—and it worked. It happened as it happened. I knew what direction they wanted to go into, to have room. I'd been working with them for years in Jamaica."

The music was morphing, perhaps even more swiftly than they'd imagined. "Bob would give keyboard player Tyrone Downey and myself money and we'd go out and buy everything. Tyrone had everything available, a Fender-Rhodes piano, a Clavinet, and a Hammond C-3 organ, Moogs and mini-Moogs," details guitarist Junior Marvin. "There was no budget problem, no limitations to what we could buy, we had freedom and we'd only buy the best."

Bob was protective of his band and their musical developments and definitely didn't like Wailers playing or sharing their sound around. "He was quite articulate that we don't spread this thing too thin so that everybody has it. It had to be unique as well," Marvin affirms.

"What Bob had more than all these other guys was melodies.

Each song have a different tune, they don't sound alike," Neville Garrick explains. "Bob was the first one to decide he wanted a band, and he pay them a retainer so they don't do sessions— although Family Man woulda sneak out every now and then and do a session for somebody. It used to be, when Jamaican groups went out on tour, they had to see which backing musicians were available. But Bob had him band, so by having your band you can build a flavor and a sound."

The upgrade of the Wailers' sound was progressed by a friend of Junior Marvin's, guitar technician Roger Mayer. The wah-wah pedal guitar effect that Jimi Hendrix deployed on "Purple Haze" was made by Mayer, and he had worked with Stevie Wonder, too. When he saw the Wailers, Mayer loved the music but was underwhelmed by their "raggedy island sound," and told Bob he could help.

"Bob explained that he wanted the Wailers to stand up, quality-wise, to anybody's record," the jovial Mayer explained. "For himself, Bob wanted the perfect *chuck* guitar sound. Once you get that *chuck* and its echo perfect, it drives the songs. That's what Bob did better than anybody else."

Marley was making sure that the Wailers could rank alongside the world's best. For him, the success of not only himself and the Wailers, but reggae itself, was a constant struggle. "Watch me, baby," he once said to me sharply, "nobody tried to make reggae come. All they do is try and stop reggae from creation. Reggae reached on its own strength. But dem can't stop this. Reggae is the music the Bible speaks of, in so many places."

The fresh, ambitious musical approach reenergized a team so familiar with one another that they might as well be family. "You know what was so interesting? Every night I went into the studio, the experience was just so wonderful. I looked forward to the variety of these tracks, I had no doubt they were good," asserts singer Marcia Griffiths, who sang backing vocals with Rita Marley. "It's like you're walking through life; every night there's another song saying something different, taking you on a journey. So when you go to the studio you want to know, what part of the road will you be on and where are you gonna be tonight?"

MY EDITOR at *Sounds,* Alan Lewis, used to grunt when I came into work somewhat on the late side after spending nights with the Wailers as they recorded *Exodus* up the road from my place in Ladbroke Grove. There wasn't much he could say, though, as we rock scribes were supposed to be around the musical action. Soon enough, Lewis was sure that the paper would benefit from my off-duty hours spent around a creative process he knew was extraordinary.

As for me, why would I have chosen to be anywhere else? Just hearing the layers of music find their place and form a thrilling whole was a sensual pleasure. And the buzz, the high, in the studio went beyond the sizeable ganja consumption. People with a sense of doing something positive with their lives are generally happier, I've found; and the heady ambience of those *Exodus* sessions was as loaded with purpose as sea air is with ozone.

Sounds, London, May 28, 1977

In the studio, Family takes control. You think he's asleep, leaning back in the padded swivel chair, with hands folded on his tum. Then oh-so-slowly, he leans forward, eyes half-closed, rests a well-shaped finger on an echo button and pushes briefly. The music shifts, deepens, as Family closes his eyes with a satisfied half sigh, and folds his hand on his tum again, settling back into meditating on the music like a shiny black Buddha.

And outside, Bob's playing table football.

The table football machine's a welcome variant in the Wailers' on-the-road staples of life: food and colour TV. The patterns repeat, like Wagnerian leitmotifs—after a while it seems like one long round of watching a Clint Eastwood movie on TV (when a hapless soldier falls from the top of a building in flames, Neville cries exuberantly, "See it deh: Catch a Fire!" and everybody yells "EXODUS!" when the prisoners escape from the dungeons . . .) while tucking into ackee and saltfish and dumplings 'n' drinking that Life Protoplasm . . . so the table football machine becomes a cathartic mirror for the emotions of the day. When everything's going well, when a track's near completion, Bob plays a keen attacking game.

"Come, Aswad," he shouts, "I-man gonna' mash up all o' dem!" Angus Gaye jumps to the table, and balls fly towards the coffee dispenser as they rock the machine. At 5:30 in the morning, when "Jamming" is into what seems its 18th mix, Bob muffs shot after shot. He's tense; he can't understand why every track takes so *long* to mix . . . "Energy low," he mutters, as he turns away.

Other nights the energy's so high it seems as if the whole studio's about to fly on wings to the sky.

This reproduction of Neville Garrick's sleeve design is black and white, but the real sleeve is solid gold, like the music it represents. 1976. *Album cover design by Neville Garrick.*

11

EXODUS: A SONG CYCLE

1: "Natural Mystic"

THE ESTABLISHING SHOT, the track that takes you there. An album's confidence and majesty is assured in its first seconds, as *Exodus* begins and the steady lope of Family Man's bass creeps into the listener's consciousness by stealth. The distinct figure, moving at a low five-one interval, is aerated by Family Man's trademark stutter, a way of leaving a gap between the notes that inspired Robbie Shakespeare, Dennis Bovell, and every aspiring reggae bass player. So distant it seems like a half-remembered dream infiltrating the psyche, the bass line takes four deliberate bars to build up to its full potent stroll. Instantly, the song occupies a very different territory from the original version of the tune, recorded by Bob with Lee Perry in 1975.

"Sometimes me just like record old songs," Bob told me. "Yes, mon, we used to have some *nice times* singing."

Interestingly, *Exodus* is topped and tailed by its only versions of old songs, "Natural Mystic" and "One Love," indicating that aspects of Bob's core values, his fascinations and beliefs, had remained constant throughout his career. The character shift in the handling of both songs is revealing.

Prior to the invasion, Gilly used to drive Bob on Sunday nights to Scratch's studio, where he listened to a variety of jamming with Scratch's Upsetters. Gilly would play the drums, and he clearly remembers working on "Natural Mystic." "We made the first track for 'Natural Mystic' on a drum machine," remembers Scratch, still struck by the innovation. "I added the machine pop drum, which give it that popping sound. Then he did it over again with Carly and it sounded good. On my version we had a horn section which sounded better to me."

In common with the early recordings of Burning Spear, Scratch's "Natural Mystic" showcases doo-wop based all-male harmonies and a sonorous horn section that sounds so ancestral it might have been blowing down the walls of Jericho. Designed to suggest the red dust of Africa, "Natural Mystic," à la Scratch, was strictly roots.

"The first 'Natural Mystic' we recorded was from early times fe sure," recalls Family Man. "Soon after the Wailers, Scratch Perry, and the Upsetters decided to work together. That was the early vibes within that time and that energy in which we come out with a music they call *riff*," he chuckles, remembering the discovery, "and the timing, and get that sound, not like any other . . . a *we* sound. That's why it still stands up till today, because it's outstanding.

"We knew it was a great song and also knew it could be expressed much wider and deeper, that we could take it to a higher level of heights. Even at the time we were [first] doing it we knew we could move it from that standard to another standard." Fams laughs again. "In those days there was just four-track recording. Then we did move to eight, sixteen, twenty-four . . . we did just utilize it, take the music, spread it out, then drop it."

Just so, on the Island album version of *Exodus*, Bob sounds both elegant and stately, singing alone; and the horns are more muted and subtle, with a touch more swing, though still as melodic. The new feel demonstrates a thoughtful refinement that may be the factor some critics labeled as being too polished and smooth, for *Exodus* was an extremely controversial album. Roots reggae fans, Bob's original constituency, felt that the Wailers' new sheen was a sellout. While *Exodus* became a multimillion-seller around the world, in the Ladbroke Grove punky reggae record shop, Rough Trade, it was outsold by Culture's strictly rootsical *Two Sevens Clash*.

When some criticized Bob for redoing his own material in this way, Bob scoffed, "These people! My inspiration come from the Most High. Me a free being 'pon this earth and me do what me want to do. The world don't control me. Them songs great and me love them, that's why I do them over. And me might do them over *again* 'pon the next album if me feel them nice still!"

The emotional force and precision of "Natural Mystic" is the sound of the Wailers' maturity. "Maybe because they're brothers, but when Bob got the Barretts, with their individual style, they created their own form of music," comments Ira Heaps, bandleader and bass player of the Jammyland All Stars, New York's popular reggae band. "Family Man pioneered this type of playing, coming in on the third beat with a bit of delay, holding the bass behind the beat, and that's what gives it that reggae mellow laid-back feeling.

"This track has the rhythm pattern that defines Jamaican music. It is a classic Carlton Barrett one drop; he's the king of that beat, it's his trademark. Instead of the regular rock 'n' roll four/four beat, there's no beat till the third count. Carly hits the snare at the same time, and it's all carried on the hi-hat. Normally the organ does the bubble [that bouncy keyboard sound] that follows the bass line, making a double pattern, whereas here it's doing the skank [the rhythm chop], which is quite unusual."

Adds tape op Terry Barham, "In Carly's drumming, when he does the fills, it's a bit like a kettle drum, even though it's the snare drum, you know? It's that nice kind of answer sound."

The night of the mix, there was much discussion in the control room about how to start the track, though no one knew it would eventually be the album opener. All concerned, including Family Man, Karl Pitterson, Junior Marvin, and tape op Dick Cuthell, clearly recall that the intro's subtle seduction was a specific brainchild of Chris Blackwell's.

"Personally, when I first heard 'Natural Mystic,' I just loved the groove of it, the riff of it," Blackwell recalls, clearly still in love with the memory of the moment. "It's a trick beginning, the way it creeps up on you. What I did was, I tripled the length of the intro, so we could just fade it up, because I loved the idea of it coming out of the air, building up, building up; then the drum comes in, *rakakaka,* it's right in your face. 'If you listen carefully now you will hear,' " he quotes. "The drumroll comes out of the air, building up, building up—and then the voice comes in. It's so quiet that you're not quite sure. You tend to turn up the volume on your record player, so when it really comes in, it whacks you."

For Blackwell, that slowly growing intro has great emotional resonance, a sense of romance. "It was the perfect beginning of a record, introducing Bob as a natural mystic poet, then going through a journey. That was the idea."

The idea of the album as journey was not discussed as such; the ultimate order of the songs that Bob unfurled before his peers in intense all-night sessions was still unknown. Yet that sense of what mythologist Joseph Campbell called "the hero's journey" was always implicit, precisely because each song, in whatever stage of its development, offered a progress through such distinct worlds of experience and emotion, going through the darkness to the light.

If "Natural Mystic" serves as any sort of guide or portent to what lies ahead, its note of caution reminds us that, just as the track's lyrical beauty camouflages the knowledge of pain, there are no guarantees in the seemingly smoothest of lives. Ultimately there is no protection from the perennial menace that surrounds us, as Bob has learned so dearly: "Many more will have to die, don't ask me why." The tone is elegiac but not mournful. Rather, it is a call to action, invoking ancient symbols to incite future revolutions.

In recording the track, the band worked like the crack corps they were. The newest Wailer, Junior Marvin, remembers, "Laying 'Natural Mystic' down wasn't like laying it down, then fixing it. It was very tight, just get in there, and do it. I could do no wrong, playing on top of these guys."

The music also contained subtle elements, ghostly imprints of sounds made but not heard. The Wailers' percussionist, Seeco, as the elder Dread master drummer, was something of a guru to Bob. As the man who first taught Bob elements of music and had actually carried him to meet Coxsone Dodd at Studio One, he was still a special bred'ren for Bob and played the Rasta drums to keep the rootsical grounation spirit alive in the Wailers.

"When you're recording, you like to do the percussion after the drums, because you can keep control of the sound," explains Terry Barham. "You want it separated, because the hand drum's very loud, so it leaks over onto the drum kit. For 'Natural Mystic,' we overdubbed Seeco playing that Rasta drum. While the others were recording, Seeco would play along in the control room, not miked up, just checking that the music all worked."

In the true Rasta spirit, Bob invokes the Bible on "Natural Mystic," as he does repeatedly throughout the album. Frequently in Jamaican music, use of the Bible and old Jamaican proverbs are virtually interchangeable as familiar hooks, signifiers of authenticity and of keeping it real; and Bob was adept at deploying both.

Heavenly thoughts obviously preoccupied Bob when he first

wrote the song. With its metaphysical reference to the Book of Revelation, the lyrics seemed specially relevant to the singer. Junior Marvin deconstructs: "When Bob sings, 'This could be the first trumpet, might as well be the last,' it's like he's saying, 'This could be the last call for all of us.' But he's actually telling us we all have a chance." Marvin continues to quote the lyrics: "If you listen carefully, now, you will hear." Marvin repeats for emphasis: "Now. Listen carefully *now,* and you *will* hear."

Hope, then, is woven into the tune. With that heady sense of optimism that paralleled the first days of Jamaican independence, when anything seemed possible, Bob was shaping up another new contemporary Jamaican blend of music, designed to be more accessible on a mass level than roots, but still soaked in a very Jamaican feeling and flavor.

It seemed as if everything was gonna be all right, as Bob sang in "Three Little Birds." Indeed, some beneficent spirit did seem to hover over the recording of "Natural Mystic," judging by the strange synchronicity and spiritual flash experienced by Junior Marvin. "It was only years later that I realized some of these songs were recorded three or four times already, like 'Natural Mystic,' for example. It's so weird because I ended up playing a horn line from the old version on guitar, though I'd never heard it. Bob must have thought, 'This guy's heard this song before.' I had to think, 'Wow, that must've come to me through God.' "

Despite his familiarity with the song, its deceptive simplicity seemed to overwhelm Bob the night it came time to lay down his final vocal. Exulting in the possibilities of his voice, kicking tone and timbre about like a football, was a part of the recording process Bob particularly enjoyed. But when Dick Cuthell dropped by Basing Street Studios late one night, he found the place deserted except for Karl Pitterson and Bob, looking glum, sitting on a speaker in the studio, smoking a spliff. In the control room, Karl kept busy mixing a dub. "It was really simple, no extra instruments, just bass and drums, and he might put in a little guitar now and again," remembers Dick Cuthell. "He's a tasteful dubber, Karl." Though Bob was about to do a vocal, Karl explained, "He doesn't feel right. But we'll leave him and he'll get into the vibe."

Dick wandered into the main studio and started chatting with Bob. He was touched that the singer agreed to let him share his spliff—a big deal for a Rasta. Cuthell elaborates, "No man shares his spliff really, but he's very gentlemanly about it." Bob's headphones were lying on the floor, and Dick could hear "a cacophony" coming through. He offered to check the sound and urged, "Bob, you ought to listen to what Karl's got in there. It sounds fantastic. He's got a dub, he's got it stripped down." Bob acquiesced. Setting up the sound feed of the monitor mix into the main room was no simple matter, and it took all their combined ingenuity to do it, but finally Bob could hear a radical, sparse new take on the familiar rhythm.

"He put his headphones on and he started listening and rocking," Cuthell reminisces. "Then he got up to the mike, a few feet away from where I was sitting on some equipment, and he did it. That was it, man. One take. It sounded fantastic." Cuthell pauses and laughs. "So that sticks clear," he continues. "That is one of the privileged moments in my life."

"I love all Bob's songs, but to me 'Natural Mystic' is who he was," says Cindy Breakspeare. "Every time I hear it, I think, 'Little did you know you were singing about yourself.' "

2: "So Much Things to Say"

FOLLOWING THE SIREN SONG OF "Natural Mystic," which uses its haunting melody and atmosphere to sweeten a confrontation with life's uglier aspects, the jaunty one-drop tone of "So Much Things to Say" seems like a diversion. It's deceptively simple, the old one-two chord progression, going major to minor, suggesting a child's musical primer. But like "Natural Mystic," the song's message nicely contradicts its format. As its verses skip blithely along, Bob toys with the meter, almost scatting his way through the crowded syllables of complex tongue twisters such as "I and I no come to fight flesh and blood," and then stretches languidly, stretching the next words like black-brown Jamaican molasses.

These intriguing dualities are so subtle that "So Much Things to Say" is perhaps *Exodus*'s most underrated track, often perceived to function just as a segue between the potency of "Natural Mystic" and the heavy, heavy throb of the following track, "Guiltiness." But Bob uses "So Much Things to Say" to clearly articulate his position as he now understood it, after months of deep meditation and agonized self-questioning.

Discussing the *Exodus* songs with many of those involved, it is "So Much Things to Say" that people such as Junior Marvin and Family Man Barrett tend to quote at length, savoring the compression of ideas and information into a pop song format.

As Fams says, "'Cos they got so much things to say, so very very much. Dey think it so easy for them to find me guilty, but is only Jah Jah can prove that I and I innocent," he concludes, with a laugh. He launches back into the past, talking about his bedroom in Oakley Street, where Bob would sit on the edge of the bed, strumming his guitar, and Family Man would saunter around, adjusting the levels on the little home recording setup that he traveled with on the road. Then, with the knowledge that late at night, interruptions would be kept to a minimum, they would discuss the events that had propelled them to London. "So we speak of these terms, then we scratch them round and set the music to it. That's what makes our music so special.

"On 'So Much Things to Say' and 'Exodus,' notice how those tunes move, notice the concept of the bass line; it's a melodic line, singing, almost like a baritone harmonizing with the lead, and the first, second, and third harmonies. They carry the lyrics and message to the four corners of the earth," Family Man concludes.

Here Bob name-checks the Jamaican national heroes Paul Bogle and Marcus Garvey. It was unusual for Bob to reference individuals quite so specifically, but the names he conjured were absolutely key in the rebel Jamaican tradition. A farmer who built his own Native Baptist Church and trained a volunteer army, Bogle and his comrade George William Gordon led the pivotal Morant Bay Uprising in 1865. Among their demands was the abolition of the instrument of torture, the treadmill, which was meant to have been abandoned when slavery ended. Later that same month, Bogle was court-martialed and hung. "Bogle was a Jamaican legend," affirms Marvin, then returns to his recitation of the well-remembered words, " 'So don't you forget now, youths, who you are and where you stand in the struggle.' " Junior pauses to let it sink in, then continues, "It's the struggle of life, self-realization, and discovering the truth about yourself and your history."

Matching Bob's self-exploration was the urge to explore new sound that is a hallmark of *Exodus*. While *Rastaman Vibration* and *Natty Dread* had both been breakthrough albums internationally, it was now a quest for Bob to forge a new Wailers identity, one that was quite separate from the old partnership with Pete and Bunny, and he was confident enough in its roots to be able to reach out and explore selected elements of what was happening in the wider pop scene, including disco, the genre that was seemingly swallowing all other styles and putting musicians out of work.

Up till the appearance of Junior Marvin, Tyrone Downey was the band's most enthusiastic seeker of new musical technology, and his room in Oakley Street was full of every interesting keyboard he could lay his hands on: Moogs, mini-Moogs, and various primitive synthesizers. In one of Blackwell's late-night drop-ins at the sessions, he found Tyrone quietly experimenting on a small electronic keyboard. "He wasn't saying 'Do this, do that,' but he was listening to Tyrone playing it in his lap and spotting some sounds. 'That's a nice one, that one there,' " recalls Barham. "It was just a gentle little pointer to a few sounds that might be interesting. And they wound up being used at the start of 'So Much Things to Say.' "

In addition to all the new gear, Barham remembers one of the improvisatory techniques used before the advent of sophisticated samplers: "Putting a piano through the phaser, turning it inside out so it ceases to sound like a piano and instead becomes like a bigger chop sound. The treated piano makes the basic skank sound fatter, and then you put on another straight piano, but they blend into one sound. The first piano is so screwed up, you can't recognize it. It sounds absolutely brilliant."

Very late one night, in the days before "So Much Things to Say" was laid down, Terry Barham wandered into the recording area and found Bob Marley alone. "He was mucking about on his own on the piano, and he was playing 'So Much Things to Say'; he already knew how it went. So he's just singing, and in a sense, he's waiting for more lyrics to come down. I've heard this from singers before, but I think it's particularly relevant here. Bob's actually a conductor of the words, like an aerial, so the words are already in existence and he's pulling them down. He's playing the song and he's halfway through the line 'When the rain fall . . .' And he kind of just hits it. 'It don't fall on one man's housetop.' And it's obvious that he's hearing it at the same moment I'm hearing it. I was just standing there watching him, and then he just bursts into laughter"—Barham laughs out loud himself at the memory—"because of the actual joy of the line, you know?"

By squeezing an unusual number of words into a beat, the track is unusually wordy for a Bob song. Usually he's almost haikulike in his verbal economy. But with its rich cascade of the I-Three's voices framing Bob's dashing brio, this tune leaves an impression of lightness and cheer. The transition between the song and its successor, the imposing "Guiltiness," is a vertiginous shift of pace and mood.

The innocent skank of "So Much Things to Say" almost screeches to a halt, as Bob's voice is snatched away almost before he quite finishes chanting "They don't know what they're doin', yeah." A beat of silence follows like a gasp, like breath catching in your throat—and then "Guiltiness" drops.

3: "Guiltiness"

BOB WAS WELL AWARE of the gravity and import of "Guiltiness." "I don't have to sing no more song, just that one line, 'Guiltiness rest on their conscience,'" he told me.

Indeed, the dense, magisterial rhythm of "Guiltiness," with its sonorous horns swinging like a New Orleans back line, asserts *Exodus*'s challenging direction. No regular album, pop or reggae, dared be so far removed from the usual idea of entertainment. In numbering the wrongdoers, Bob sounds beyond wrath; vengeance is his, sayeth the singer. Although there can be little doubt that his attackers at Hope Road and their backers were in his mind as he lambasts their brutal betrayal, the lyrics take personal responsibility to another level. Like the Bible, which opposing factions have always used to support their conflicting ideas quite well, "Guiltiness" can be used to apply to all too many scenes of exploitation, too many wars. It is an all-purpose song of Job-like defiance and faith in the face of disaster, and a belief shout-out in a karmic comeback, protecting the righteous.

According to the track listing, "Guiltiness" is one of the few to be "taken from Jamaican reels," and Jamaican engineer Sylvan Morris's memory bears this out. Certainly, as previously stated, I myself was present when Bob was working on the song in Jamaica, days before the invasion.

" 'Guiltiness' wasn't one of my favorites at first but I grew to really like it. I think we caught a really good mix of the feel of the track; it just has a great loping rhythm; it just swings," comments Blackwell. "Also the lyrics are very serious, not like pop lyrics. There's a lot of thought in the song, and it provokes a lot of thought when you hear it. 'Guiltiness' followed 'So Much Things to Say,' suggesting that we're going to cover a lot of different issues; and then Bob talks about [serious things like] guiltiness, and later, about exodus.

"I remember a couple of people saying that they didn't know if 'Guiltiness' was strong enough, or popular enough—if it was too thoughtful, if you like—to be the third track on the album. But I'm a big believer in the album concept as a body of work with a beginning, a middle, and an end. I just felt that part of the [power] of any good piece of art is, it's a little bit challenging at times. It gets you to think, and it doesn't give you everything you want right away. Perhaps that's part of what pulls you in and exercises you a little bit. I thought 'Guiltiness' really performed that function and helped set up the whole tone of the record."

Musically, the sound was a rich brew. "On 'Exodus' the horns are quite thin compared to the horn sound on 'Guiltiness,' " comments Terry Barham. "I think it gives it a nice setting. It sounds like everything is playing at once." Ira Heaps breaks it down differently. "It's interesting how the keyboard skank is put through a flanger here. Lee Perry was the first to use the flanger in reggae. The Wailers use this one-drop rhythm that they pioneered a lot; it's like an independent producer recycling a rhythm with different artists. Here the bass and snare drum are both behind the beat, with the hi-hat on the beat."

Junior Marvin says, "We started 'Guiltiness,' like most of our tracks, at, say, about one, two in the afternoon. We'd go to bed about four or five in the morning, and we'd sleep for six, maybe seven hours, then come back and start all over again.

"I found myself using this wah-wah pedal on 'Guiltiness,' which gave it that kind of shivery feeling. It made you feel guilty, like, 'What did I do that I need to confess about? I know I did something wrong, because none of us are perfect.' A lot of people actually copied my wah-wah style from what they heard. It wasn't notes all over the place. It was tastefully put in."

Rita Marley and Marcia Griffiths found that certain more complex tracks made them work hard to sound easy. " 'Specially 'Guiltiness,' it was a difficult song," recalls Marcia. "The harmonies are not just one thing throughout, they're different sounds and styles in one song."

However, the rhythm guitar posed a problem on "Guiltiness," finally solved when Family Man played Junior's guitar and retuned it lower. "The only effect I use was a little reverb, tremolo, and speed. Not like today when we have all these big pedals. It was a natural sound, a true sound, with just a little reverb to wet it up." Always responsible for tuning Bob's guitar, Fams also helped out here on keyboards, piano, and percussion.

4: "The Heathen"

LEADING ON FROM THE thunderous denunciation of "Guiltiness," "The Heathen" is a psychological preparation for not just battle but victory. A defiant war chant with the rhythm of a Zulu prebattle stomp echoes in the percussive elongation of the lyrics.

The repetition of the refrain, with the I-Three's gliding mellifluously behind Bob, works like a mantra or a positive affirmation, giving courage the more it's steadily repeated. All the while, Carly's supple wrist action on the cymbals keeps the top end of the track skittering edgily, countering the sturdy foundation of the bass.

This martial air, a warrior whoop, is suitably stirring, and on one level works as a direct pep talk for Bob and his extended family, intended to heal any feelings of being weakened and destabilized by the invasion. On a broader level, "The Heathen" is like a psychic suit of armor, readying the listener to deflect life's several sorts of body blows. The method of attack that Bob references as he urges the fallen fighters to rise and ready for battle suggests the stylized moves of the kung fu flicks that were as popular in Jamaica as they would prove to be two decades later on Staten Island, uniting the many members of hiphop's Wu Tang Clan. The unexpected minor note in Family's bass line startles and gives an ominous frisson, as if gathering energy for the attack. Subtly treated with the technology of the time, Junior's fuzzy guitar slides and weaves around Tyrone's sci-fi keyboards, edged with a buzzing drone reminiscent of Sputniks coming in to land.

"This is by far the most brilliant rhythm on the record. A lot of dancehall tunes are being written on this rhythm right now, twenty-five years later," observes Ira Heaps.

"At that time, there was no keyboards that you could play like a string section. You could only play a line," recalled Terry Barham. "But there was a thing called a poly-Moog, which was a really new toy, and Tyrone had got hold of that. So it gave birth to some of those synthy parts on 'The Heathen.' "

Clearly, Bob articulates his survival strategy, observing that running away can actually be a wise war tactic, not a cowardly cop-out. A war is more than just one skirmish.

Again he dips into the ancestral well, running his version of the familiar biblical quote from Galatians 6:7, "Whatsoever a man soweth, that shall he also reap," together with the old maxim "Talk is cheap," to create a couplet that sounds as if it's always been there. Scratch Perry insists Bob lifted some early biblical stories of "Heathen" from him, and the producer still performs it onstage. Yet even while he was putting familiar island and biblical expressions together and making poetry, Bob was adjusting to the possibility of life as an exile, some would say a refugee, and was collaborating in a process designed to open his music up to a wider market without losing his authenticity—a contradiction in terms, it might seem, but it was time for Marley to bust out of his usual milieu, both geographically and creatively.

"I really liked 'Heathen' because it was so different and had so many rockish elements. Remember, my concept was always that Bob was a black rock act, not R&B; forget about R&B, later for that," Chris Blackwell says. "The audience I felt he could really reach, apart from Jamaica, was the rock audience: college kids, liberal kids interested in culture, people's lives, and what was going on."

Smart and sophisticated though he was, there was a lot that Bob hadn't been exposed to and new ways to absorb. "Early on after I signed Bob, I took him to a couple of shows on a tour with John Martyn, Traffic, and Free, and he could see how all those shows were sold out, and Traffic had never had a single," Blackwell continues. "In his experience of what music was all about, you needed to have a single and then go on and do shows."

The recasting and marketing of Bob Marley was always controversial for his initial core following. Subtle though the changes set out to be, and effective though they were, perhaps inevitably they had the effect of alienating some of the roots fans who'd been mad about Bob since their earliest ska days.

Though still relevant to Jamaica, and expressed in very Jamaican terms, Bob's lyrical palette had become more general and universal, less concerned with immediate community occurrences than they were in the days of cutting "Mr. Brown" with Scratch Perry, packed as it is with colorful local references, incomprehensible to anyone "from foreign." However, despite its close commentary on recent events, *Exodus* has no tracks specifically or overtly relating to Jamaican *livity*. Instead, each song directly relates to our human condition and universal emotions, thus commenting on both Jamaica and the world.

Exodus's planned accessability to rock ears was the latest stage in a process that began with Wayne Perkins's plangent pedal steel and Rabbit Bundrick's keyboard overdubs on *Catch a Fire*. The addition of first Al Anderson and then Junior Marvin to the band was all intended to help the Wailers in their challenging task of crossing over without losing their Jamaican integrity and identity. That direction manifests in different ways in the span of *Exodus* but is first noticeable on this track, with Marvin's simply delineated strutting rock guitar solo. Marvin himself sums up the power of that brief but intense solo thus: "I actually put melody on top of that aggression as well. They used to call me the young Jimi Hendrix, some kind of angry Jimi Hendrix. So when I heard Bob say, 'De heathen back deh,' it was like a statement, a wake-up call. I felt the guitar needed to be like a rock guitar. The actual solo, every guitar player I've met since *Exodus* comes to me and goes, 'How did you get that sound?' "

The imagination was progressive, but in certain respects the instrumentation was traditional. Barham says, " 'Heathen' hasn't got any modernisms about it. Like in some of the other tracks you get a bit of synth playing, bubbling around the track, and you get wah-wah guitar, you even get vocoder. Nowadays people have got polyphonic keyboards, so you can play chords and do huge amounts of sounds and samples and generate a lot of sounds quickly from a lot of different little things. At that point in time, though, it was still technically quite hard."

5: "Exodus"

"THERE WAS ALWAYS SOMETHING SPECIAL about 'Exodus,' a magic, right from the beginning. Everybody was excited, talking about how they were all going to sing on it. I remember that it was recorded very late at night," says Suzette Newman, whom Bob always liked to be in the studio. She followed as the entire Jamaican contingent thundered enthusiastically down the narrow stairs to the Fallout Shelter and squeezed into the studio to lay down a unique mass male vocal for the chorus.

"During the recording of 'Exodus' I said to Bob, 'This is gonna be such an important song for you. It's really magical.' And he always used to wink at me and say funny things, so he just teased me and said, 'Yes, a big t'ing dis, Suzette,' " Newman continues, still chuckling at Bob's mock gravity.

Indeed, "Exodus" was special, from the moment Bob first strummed its initial sketch to Family Man in his bright bedroom at Harrington Gardens. Fams instantly picked up on the resonance of the Ernest Gold sound track, the theme from *Exodus,* that he'd just played to Bob. "I knew it from the movie and Bob from the Bible," says Fams. "We wanted to project the Bible story in music, with those big, grand epic sounds [like Gold's]. It was to inspire young singers and players of instruments to move on up."

Movement was a key word for Bob at that time. He used it approvingly, as if motion inevitably meant progress. "It's movement time!" he would cry, sounding as if he was keen to be off and away, doing his job.

" 'Exodus' was one of the last songs written in Oakley Street,"

Neville remembers. "It began with the line 'Movement of Jah people.' The whole irony of the situation was, when everybody jumped on the bandwagon, the word was, 'Rastaman gone soft, Dread gone funky,' and all dem kinda t'ing," remembers Neville Garrick, yesterday's frustration still fresh in his voice.

Maybe some of the Wailers' old followers couldn't hear it or didn't want to go where they were heading. But no one could doubt the explosion of creativity that was emerging from the band and Bob.

"At the 'Exodus' mix there was an incredible energy and excitement, because 'Exodus' was hot," remembers Chris Blackwell. "It just had that powerful, four/four beat, which there wasn't a lot of at that time. I'm not even sure whether it wasn't the first of what they call in Jamaica the running foot drum, like this disco kind of thing. We did a lot of echo, a lot of repeat, especially on the guitars, just to drive it. Then, the horn parts were great. There was a lot of excitement. And it was Bob's own exodus that was driving it.

"As we all know, some of the worst things that happen in life can be the things that galvanize you and change you, things that spark you off. The whole thing was, they wanted to kill him. It wasn't a joke. I think at that time he thought he might never go back to live in Jamaica," Blackwell concludes.

Almost three decades later, hearing *Exodus*'s songs gives me a jolt as fragments of the arrangement—the backing voices, say, or the horn arrangement, or a particularly slick piece of drumming by Carly—come rushing back, the way they were when the mixing process separated out their strand of DNA and shone a spotlight on their contribution. That is particularly true of "Exodus" itself, when on the long January night the elements of what came to be the title track were teased apart and welded together in new configurations. There's a lot to listen to, all good: the yin and yang of the mixed voices, led by Bob in full command; the plucked guitar,

Family Man's specialty, sounding rather like *Shaft*'s itchy wah-wah guitar; the horn section, again arranged by Family Man; Seeco's Rasta grounation drums, which peak two-thirds of the way into the song and then fade.

What Family Man refers to as "that straight four" is at the heart of the enormous success of "Exodus" and is fundamentally an idea of Karl Pitterson's. Specifically, the drum pattern change that Karl Pitterson suggested and Carly Barrett so promptly executed was a shift from the typical offbeat of reggae, which confused rockheads, to the straight, four-on-the-floor, forward propulsion of disco—sworn enemy of reggae and all roots music. Cunningly co-opting the essence of disco and its dominating beat, "Exodus" sweetly subverted it by letting loose its mechanical regularity among the shifting counterrhythms of the Caribbean.

" 'Exodus' is the first change in the drum pattern," says Ira Heaps, the veteran New York reggae producer and bass player. "It's obviously courting the black disco market, as Carly has an interesting pattern; there are some elements that Sly Dunbar popularized, like that original four on the floor; and half the flying cymbal pattern that Sly picked up from disco and brought to reggae. Carly's also made the bass drum pattern a bit more lively without really changing it. It's like, how do you keep the classic one-drop style but make it more danceable for more people? In classic reggae the hi-hat is all closed on the one-drop, but here the hi-hat is open. It must have been a bit unusual for Fams, but he is famous for taking out a beat, and that's still what he's doing here."

As all the musicians were bubbling with ideas, much was laid down that never made it on the record. "When I got the tracks to mix, every track was full. If you had all the faders up all the time, the tracks wouldn't breathe as they do now, because every bit was filled with arrangements—all of it good, incidentally," explains Chris Blackwell. "You could probably do mixes like that now and people would really like them, because they know the songs. But what I tended to do was minimize a bit, use things more sparingly. Use horns there, voices there, but not use all of it all the time."

Even more than "The Heathen," its predecessor on the record, "Exodus" plunged right into the commercial arena while being equally removed from regular pop preoccupations. The track had the album's most marked use of contemporary music technology. The treated chorus, the somewhat nasal delivery for example, that sounds like it's sung by an android, is not just the vocoder's first use on a reggae record, it's reputedly the audio effect's first recorded use in any genre, and further evidence of Tyrone's progressive contribution. The sound only became widely familiar years later, as employed by Laurie Anderson on "O Superman," before becoming a popular 1980s pop effect.

Being Bob's secretary, in the sense that he was the one Bob trusted to take down his endlessly evolving lyrics, Neville remembers the song's construction. "This was a song where Bob kinda start with the chorus, then did search [for the rest]. I remember Junior came over to Oakley Street and played some guitar while Bob was working it out." One line, however, was not strictly original. "We know where we're going" was the slogan from Manley's late 1976 campaign, the one that prompted the shooting.

"It's I play all that acoustic piano in the studio on the intro of 'Exodus,' because is me and Bob know what Exodus is all about, so me play the piano from the movie," Fams tells me, proceeding to sing the bold chords, illustrating the changes with waves of the hand that recall his musical director role. "People think it's Tyrone or Wire, but is I, Family Man Barrett, who arrange the horn section, too. My brother played the one-drop drum in the overdubbing in the studio, put in that straight four. . . ."

Others also noticed the subtle inclusion of the musical phrase from Ernest Gold's *Exodus* theme. Vin Gordon had been brought over with Glen da Costa to play horns, and in describing how many original arrangements they tried before settling on their own horn hook for "Exodus," Vin remembers, "The keyboard did the part that sounds like the *Exodus* film sound track, and we'd come in with our part after that."

Bob was definitely feeling experimental when recording this track. "He heard me singing like Satchmo one day and said, 'I want you to do that on "Exodus."' I was quite shocked that they actually allowed me to sing on Bob Marley's record," says Junior. "Then later on, Tyrone and myself did a lot more backing vocals, in place of Peter and Bunny, to get that kind of Wailers male sound."

"The effects on 'Exodus' are nothing like nowadays," comments Blackwell. "They're primitive, primeval, very early stuff. Generally, there was no such thing as dubbing, having repeat, echoes, and effects, nowhere else did that. Everybody else was trying to do a clean proper record. We did use some dub, but really just by widening it out, opening it up and spacing it."

So the ingredients waiting to be mixed were rather different from the typical reggae song, and its creation was propelled by the band's very open atmosphere. "Once the track was done, and there was a playback, that was it. It was almost like a one-hit," says Terry Barham. "We sort of climbed the big hill of getting it together and then . . . *boof!* . . . it seemed to be done. And a big cheer came up from the people listening in the control room. 'Cause before, when the band were playing it in the rehearsal room, it had sounded so great and you never really know whether you'll get it down. Now the song was trapped on tape." He laughs, remembering the triumph.

Family Man is hip to several levels of significance in "Exodus." He starts to sing: "Movement of Jah people . . . Many people will fight you down / When you see Jah light . . ." He pauses and says,

"You know, it's the same thing you see happening again, because society is not into the Rastafarian movement too tough. But we are coming from the Bible. They tell us about the Bible in church, but dem don't really act it, or try to present the image of the Nazarene heights." Family Man pauses and chuckles. "That's what the dreadlock is."

But Bob hinted at another level of the movement's meaning in an interview with Neil Spencer for the *New Musical Express* on April 23, 1977. Spencer asked him the meaning of the movement of Jah people:

> "Towards Africa, towards righteousness and towards man," and Bob's writing about it now "because it happen more in the last coupla months."
>
> He's less than specific about further details.
>
> "Me see these movements but me can't talk about it because the government no like it. If I talk about it, it look like a political power thing, so . . ."
>
> So this movement is happening in Jamaica?
>
> "Even in Jamaica, yeah it start in Jamaica, but it happen here too. It's just poor people, so y'don't hear about it, but it happen, man." He laughs quietly.

Neil Spencer and his readers were left wondering what the joke might be. Now it seems clear that the movement of which Bob spoke meant not just the repatriation to Africa already under way, with which he was actively involved, but also the reasonings about political possibilities that he was having with downtown dons such as Tek Life, Lips, and Claudie Massop regarding the possibility of smashing Jamaica's corrupt two-party system from within.

As Karl Pitterson says, " 'Exodus' is a serious song. Some people might say it's politically too serious." Indeed, with its exhilarating exploration of experiences that can be daunting even if they do make you grow, "Exodus" is a stirring call: not specifically to arms, but to a new way of living. It is a grand finale to the album' s first side.

6: "Jamming"

HIGH-KICKING INTO the album's second side with "Jamming" is an inspired move, as its jaunty tone inspires a twinkle that's light-years away from the dread portent of "Exodus."

" 'Jamming' was voiced at the Fallout Shelter on one of those late-night sessions at, like, five in the morning," remembers producer Karl Pitterson. Indeed, Bob's voice sounds well warmed up and supple, and his delicate drawl is suggestive, like a lazing late-night lover.

Reflecting on the song, Bob softly quoted, "Yeah, 'jamming in the name of the Lord . . .' " and added, to underline his spiritual seriousness, "You can be sure of that! Yeah, right straight from Yard," he concluded, lingering on his words and relishing their rootsical sound.

When "Jamming" started during the Wailers' live show, Bob would get a different little smile and do his special skip, the one that seemed as if he were juggling a soccer ball with his knees. He had plenty of time to practice the move, because as tour photographer Kate Simon says, " 'Jamming' was the song that Bob and the band played right through sound check on the whole tour."

The wordplay in the song is contagious, kicking around the idea of jamming: riffing in rehearsal while you grow music, jamming like the beboppers brewing new barrier-crashing sounds at Manhattan's Minton's Playhouse in the 1960s, jamming as in bodies fusing together in carnal and spiritual union, like the raucous press of bodies jammed together filling a Carnival street in West London or Toronto, or Brooklyn or Kingston.

Famously, Bob was always first on the bus, and on a leg of the *Exodus* tour that I traveled with Simon, we were both amused when we scrambled onto the bus after him, plonked ourselves down on the tartan seats, and caught him chuckling to himself, letting us in on his own personal X-rated version of the song with a lusty roll of the *r:* "Ramming, I wanna ram it with you." We all giggled.

The track's jaunty groove was to inspire Stevie Wonder's "Master Blaster." As bass player Ira Heaps analyzes it, "Carly's doing a one-drop four on the floor, the same style as 'Exodus,' but Fams is doing a straight-up reggae bass line coming in on the third beat, coming off the low five, and leaving a space. What's great is how Fams never leaves Bob's side; he follows Bob's melodic pattern on lines like 'Life is worth much more than gold,' " says Heaps.

Just that little bit faster than the record's early songs, the cheery propulsion of "Jamming" pulls off the very Bob coup of craftily insinuating serious thoughts, which suggest the invasion, while sounding simple as a nursery rhyme and catchy as bubblegum pop.

The brisk energy of an odd percussion sound at its start gives "Jamming" its spring, a cheeky rat-tat-tat kicking along the song's regular step. Chuckling, Dick Cuthell says, "No matter how loud you play 'Jamming,' you can turn it right down, but you can always hear this milk bottle that Seeco was playing." An infectious opener of the second side, 'Jamming' makes the healing begin.

" 'Jamming' is . . . a big rush," Chris Blackwell sums up, energized at its very memory. "It has that running foot drum, I think it was the first time the Wailers used it. At the time, everything was the disco sound, so all the records in the dance clubs like Studio 54 had that four/four beat. Jammin' . . . it's a party! Great! We're jamming, we're rocking. There it is; I love that expression. We're rocking. We're jamming," he repeats affectionately.

The breezy swing of "Jamming" was palpable all through the process of making it. Once the tracks had been laid down, it was time to sprinkle the I-Three's sugar on top. Marcia Griffiths scat-sings as she remembers, "Nobody else says or does it like Bob. He was just very, very different when it comes to the music. He knew some little things that only he could think of, that he would just put it in his song. At the end of 'Jamming,' when he says, 'I like—I hope you,' like he was gonna say 'I like,' or 'I hope you like jammin'.' But he just turned it around. Instead of just saying, 'I hope you like jamming,' he says, 'I like—I hope you . . . jamming . . .' That was just something he created. His phrasing is unique.

" 'Jamming' was really groovy because we would be dancin' behind the microphone, and Bob would come out too, to dance with us, and stay to listen back. We would come out dancing from behind the microphone, everyone was just dancing, dancing away. Because this song speaks for itself. *'Jammin'. Jammin'* in the name of the Lord.' " Marcia's emphasis makes it clear that, for her, the divine reference takes the song to another level. She is silent for a moment then concludes with relish, "I loved that song. *'Jammin'* right straight from Yard.' "

Similarly, while "Jamming" is a track of pure exhilaration on one level, it also mixes in many levels of personal and political comment.

Sitting in Denise Mills's garden in Ocho Rios, by an empty swimming pool crusted with green algae, Neville Garrick sprawls in a garden chair and softly quotes the song, " 'No bullet can stop us now / We neither beg nor we won't bow / Neither can be bought nor sold / We all defend the right / Jah Jah children must unite / Life is worth much more than gold' . . . all those 'Jamming' lyrics are coming from the attack on his person. Because Bob did never feel . . ." The enormousness of what he was trying to express causes Garrick to carefully search for words. "He felt sure that the youth of Jamaica did love him enough that some guy couldn't just come and pay them fe kill 'im. So 'im was very hurt behind that."

But the leap Bob makes in linking the immediate attack on himself and his family to the wider historical issues of slavery and colonialism with "Neither can be bought nor sold" really drives home the fact that years after slavery had supposedly come to an end, the ghetto people, his friends and attackers, were still being bought and sold to the highest bidder. The only difference in this case was that the purchasers were the political parties. The admonition that "life is worth much more than gold" is a much-needed rebuke to those lost souls, teenage gunmen who would boast of their hardness and how little regard they had for human life if it meant coming between them and their survival.

7: "Waiting in Vain"

"'WAITING IN VAIN' IS a nice tune, mon, from long time back," Bob told me. "It's for people who never dig the Wailers 'cos dem just couldn't relate. So what I do now is a tune like 'Waiting in Vain,' so dem might like it and wonder what a go on. A different light."

Leading the musicians into a take, Family Man's precise countdown, sounding slightly "well charged" (high), makes a spontaneous intro to "Waiting in Vain." Its swing is sensuous, with the intimate control of an expert lover.

Everyone present at the mix felt the song's sexual pull. Cindy Breakspeare, Bob's paramour and soon to be the mother of his child Damian, didn't visit the studio often, and certainly not when

Rita Marley would be there. But Cindy's stay in London to fulfill her Miss World duties overlapped with the whole making of *Exodus,* whereas Rita flew in and out for the time necessary to record the I-Three's backing vocals.

So Cindy was the only woman of Bob's in the studio the night "Waiting in Vain" was mixed—as far as she knew, anyway. Devoted to her though he was, Bob never pretended that his genuine commitment extended to absolute physical fidelity at all times.

"The studio was packed with people! All kind of girls!" says Breakspeare. "And I remember when I heard it, every hair on my arms just stood on end. And I thought to myself, 'Oh God, I hope he wrote this for me!' There was some girl there that I discovered later he'd had a fling with, and I remember thinking, 'She probably thought it was written for her!' " She laughs. "Oh, but hearing it for the very first time, it was so magical and beautiful. My God, if you weren't in love then, believe me, you were gonna be after. A lot of love songs came on this album. And he got shit for it, I know."

Actually singing the track proved challenging for Bob, as King Sounds remembers. "It was the night that Junior Marvin recorded his guitar solo. Bob sang 'Waiting in Vain' for about eight hours straight, right through the night, trying to get the right vibes on it. At the end, Tyrone came in with a girl called Linda that he was staying with in Trellick Towers [a modernist local landmark apartment building] and said, 'Bob, you're not gonna start singing this again? You want people to have to wait?' So Bob said, 'Okay, we'll leave.' That was the only thing I ever saw Bob get mad over. Then the next night, he came in and did it in one take."

Part of the song's charm comes from the protagonist, Bob, allowing himself to be so vulnerable. Like the courtly love of medieval troubadours, the woman, the love interest in this song, is seen as a higher ideal, almost untouchable. He is the supplicant, down on bended knee. The track's male obeisance and obedience to the goddess, or the ideal of the Rasta female, was a specific choice. When Marcia Griffiths arrived with Rita Marley to spend two weeks doing the backing vocals on the fairly well-finished tracks, "Waiting in Vain" was the first she sang on. Here, she laid down all the necessary backing voices for the track herself. Previously, when Judy Mowatt was pregnant Marcia had divided up the tracks with Rita. But on this tender ballad to Cindy Breakspeare, Rita's voice is absent. In the case of "Waiting in Vain," Marcia found that all her vocals were swapped for Bob's own multi-tracked voice. "I guess they wanted a mixture [on the record], with some male vocals as well," Marcia observes reasonably. "Nothing wrong with that."

When musician Ira Heaps checks one of the track's key hooks, an example of one of rock 'n' roll's most fundamental aspects, the blues-rock guitar solo, he smiles appreciatively. "That solo works on the straight pentatonic scale," he says, and nods.

He's referring to a specialty of Junior's, which shines on this track. The guitarist remembered the words of an old girlfriend's musician father, who was his mentor. "He told me, 'Always go with the singer. Pick out two notes the singer sings, and put them in your solo so there's a connection between him, the song, and your solo.' And I did, for example, on 'Waiting in Vain' I make it jazzy but melodic. That triplet at the end of the solo was quite a technical part, not easy for guitar players to copy. It was the most difficult part of the solo, but it was smooth, it was in time, and it was a climax."

Perhaps it was knowing how badly Bob wanted to build a bridge between Jamaica and America with music, how strong his need was to connect with Black America, in particular, but as soon as I heard the song, I felt it also suggested a yearning for radio success.

Skeptical at first, Chris Blackwell thinks about this for a moment, giving the track his own analysis—"Whoever you love, you can't depend on them returning it." He pauses, then continues, "Maybe Bob was summoning the AM radio in a bit more. You know something, you're a hundred percent right. It easily could be."

But Karl Pitterson chuckles at my wacky analysis. "That's a love song. That was obvious from the moment he started working on it." Lightly, Pitterson paraphrases the beseeching protagonist's feeling. "I know you got a lot of suitors, but . . ." He laughs knowingly. "A girl had Bob at that moment."

Cindy, most likely?

With a diplomatic caution born of years of not revealing his employer's intimate details, Karl replies, "Possibly Cindy, possibly." Returning to safer ground, he concludes firmly, " 'Waiting in Vain' really is a straight love song." Singing backup, Marcia Griffiths also noticed a shift in tone, pointing out, "The backing voices on 'Waiting in Vain' are a little more subtle and suggestive."

But with all the track's blithe appeal and seeming simplicity, there were some big hitches in its development. "I don't know why, but I always felt it was a better song than a record," says Chris Blackwell, shaking his head. "I personally sat with the faders at that desk listening to maybe a hundred and twenty different mixes of the song, so it was mixed to death in my head, but to this day, I still can't hear it [the way I'd like]. There's a change in it that just throws it off. It was such a great song, but somehow we didn't make a hit out of it, so maybe it never was mixed right. In my opinion, one never caught how to make that track feel in sync, and just smooth."

Years later, Blackwell can still easily slip into worrying about the track's perceived shortcomings. But Terry Barham remembers the same process rather differently. It's generally acknowledged that part of the charm of the Basing Street locale was the ease with which Blackwell, whose party it was to some extent, could drop in at unconventional hours to get a feel for how the project was growing, even before he settled in for the mix proper. So it was one night that Blackwell passed through at his customary hour, around two in the morning, when he knew the track would have taken some form. But although everyone had approved the track of "Waiting in Vain," Blackwell didn't feel the song had realized its potential. In groping their way through to the mix that eventually became a romantic classic, the *Exodus* team stumbled upon an instrumental innovation that would have an incalculable effect on the development of not only reggae but all popular music.

"First, he inspired a two-track mix that we cut up to try and rearrange the song, because it flowed wrongly," enumerates Terry Barham. "We tried to edit it, but because the rhythm wasn't steady, the edits showed and it wasn't very pleasant. But this time, the flow was good."

So the decision was made to rerecord the track, and in the absence of drummer Carlton Barrett that evening, a momentous move was made. "Waiting in Vain" became the first and only Wailers track to be recorded with one of Tyrone and Junior's new investments— a drum machine, one of the first rhythm machines, thus presaging the birth of digital dancehall by some ten years. "I can't remember exactly which drum style they picked, but they played with that drum machine to get the arrangement sorted, and then Carly came in and overdubbed his drums. Now the track was more even than before, but Carly had never had to overdub drums before, and it was hard for him, but after a few passes he got it right."

The drummer certainly wasn't too happy about it. "Carly was mad," remembers King Sounds. "He said, 'I hope this fucking machine isn't taking my place. Why will I come and play live if a machine comes to play for me?'"

His justified alarm aside, no more historic moment has happened in reggae: Carlton Barrett, quite possibly the master inventor of more drum styles than any other, was struggling to conform to the machine that would put many of his colleagues out of a job, more thoroughly than anyone could have believed possible, in under a decade.

8: "Turn Your Lights Down Low"

"TEN, TWELVE YEARS ME A SING. Am I always gonna sing about aggression and frustration and captivity and all dem t'ing? Well now, you think it's my pride to really keep on doing that? The thing is, that must end when it must end," said Bob firmly.

Even before *Exodus* came out, Bob knew that he'd probably get some flak for his more tender songs from critics invested in him being their idea of a revolutionary, as if singing about love and emotion meant going soft. Of course, without love and emotion, there wouldn't be much worth fighting for, and Bob understood that male-female balance very well.

"After the shooting," Bob began slowly, "me never want to . . . to just think about *shooting*. So me just ease up my mind and go in a different bag. What me stand for, me *always* stand for. Jah is my strength.

"How long must I sing the same song?" he continued, almost plaintively. "I must break it sometime and sing 'Turn [Your] Light[s] Down Low,' and deal with a *woman,* talk to some *lady,* y'know?" Bob laughed with delight at the prospect.

Between "Waiting in Vain" and its successor, "Turn Your Lights Down Low," *Exodus*'s two-track game of romantic love heats up. No longer questioning, Bob's tone is now intimate and confident, entitled, the voice of a man familiar with his lover's boudoir and body, or soon to be so. This time round, he knows how it all works, and the mystery has progressed from being that of the chase, pure and simple, to the thrill of discovering how close the physical packaging of two souls can get.

As Rabbi Larry Tabick explains, a central meaning of existence is the union of the genders, an intermingling that is encouraged to occur on a Friday night, welcoming the Sabbath. Thus human interaction echoes the union between people and their divine power. With this track, Bob beautifully blends his male and female aspects. His "Waiting in Vain" persona introduced a Bob who's not scared to plead, although he's obviously revving up for more direct action. Now, on "Turn Your Lights Down Low," he's back to being the alpha male, Dread at the controls, and guided by Jah.

" 'Turn Your Lights Down Low' was definitely written on my back step," insists Cindy Breakspeare. "You could rip Christ off the cross, but you couldn't take that one away from me. That was written outside my apartment at 356 Oakley Street. They can give me all the others they like but that one I will claim one hundred percent. He sat right back there on that step and wrote it. I know, because I was inside listening through the crack! But that's how Bob was. He wasn't gonna come inside and sit down and say, 'OK, I've written a song for you.' Bob was a read-between-the-lines kind of guy. He wasn't overt or show-offish that way, you know? And maybe, if you find yourself, a militant, wanting to express all these [other] feelings through song . . . I mean, let's not get overmushy here, but maybe he was afraid of that, too."

9: "Three Little Birds"

"JAMAICA REALLY A HEAVY LAND spiritually, regardless of what a go on," Bob said, referring to the "politricks," and went on to gleefully describe the joy he got from seeing three small winged creatures. "That really happened, that's where I get my inspiration," he insisted. I commented that it sounds like an uptempo nursery rhyme. Confidently, Bob replied, "The people that me deal with in my music, them know seh what I mean. People are gonna like that, people that don't even know about Rasta, and it will make them want to find out more."

Bob's longtime bred'ren Tony "Gilly" Gilbert was with Bob when he wrote the song. "It was just amazing how he put the words for 'Three Little Birds' together in a flow," Gilly recalls. "Bob got inspired by a lot of things around him, he observed life. I remember the three little birds. They were pretty birds, canaries, who would come by the windowsill at Hope Road."

In its blithe spirit, "Three Little Birds" is one of the bravest, most militant songs Bob ever did. It takes guts to unabashedly hymn the joy of being alive, with the purity of a child that some people never even experience, and others sense at any age. It's assisted by the track's feel—somewhere between folk music and a Baptist revival, with Seeco's tambourine, very prominent in the mix, working with Carly's drum fills.

That trio of songbirds, the I-Three, have always insisted that the song is about them. When the band left the stage after a show, they would stand in the wings listening to the waves of applause as the audience screamed for them to return. Marcia Griffiths recalls, "After the song was written, Bob would always refer to us as the Three Little Birds. After a show, there would be an encore, sometimes people even wanted us to go back onstage four times. Bob would still want to go back and he would say, 'What is my Three Little Birds saying?' If we consent to go on again, then he will go.

" 'Three Little Birds' was our song, officially for I-Three. It was more or less expressing how we all came together, when he says, 'Rise up this morning, smile with the rising sun.' We loved it. Even when we were recording it, we knew that it was our song. Everybody knew that he was referring to us when he said 'three little birds'—he never said four, or two. And then he would tell us that our lips are not for kissing, just for singing. We just laughed when he said that. Bob was an amazing man."

Heaps beams. "Now, this is the straight-up one-drop Marley style, with the straight-up reggae bass. Normally the skank is on the guitar and piano, but here it's the organ, which normally does the bubble, and the head [main theme] is on the synthesizer."

The end result was disarmingly simple, and a healer to soothe troubled minds. Says Chris Blackwell, "I always loved 'Three Little Birds,' I thought it was just so light, very poppy, and I thought Bob got away with it fine."

Terry Barham recognizes that along with "One Love," "Three Little Birds" was one of the true *Exodus* originals, those mysterious tracks dubbed "taken from Jamaican reels" that were first explored at *Rastaman Vibration* time. "I'm pretty sure," he affirms, "'cause I can remember most things and that song was already there when the London sessions began." He hums the melody. "You know that high synth sound? We didn't have anything in London that was capable of making it."

Apparently, simple as it seems, "Three Little Birds" conceals its mysteries.

"Something happened on 'Three Little Birds' after we'd already recorded it. It turned out that the main keyboard part"—and here Karl Pitterson scats it, then continues—"wasn't played by Tyrone Downey. Part of it got erased, so I had to go back and do it!" He laughs. "That song on the album is really calm, to the point that it seems like the three birds are actually landing on your doorstep, singing to you."

The song's uplift touched Marcia Griffiths, too. "Yes, the whole thing was really, really positive, from beginning to end. You know, every time you mention a track, I just know more and more that

Exodus is really a special album. Ordained by God, written by the hand of God himself."

10: "One Love/People Get Ready"

THE ORIGINAL WAILERS — Bob, Peter, and Bunny first recorded "One Love" on the Studio One label with Coxsone Dodd, in their rude-boy ska prime, on July 8, 1965. Thinking back on it, Bob mused, "[In those times] we were not really *trained* singers, y'know, we just *like singing* . . . learn harmony, like the sound."

Three decades plus after that original recording, "One Love" seems as if it's always been there, so ubiquitous has it become. Its structure feeds into the same longing that makes our sense of aesthetic harmony crave balance and proportion, creating universal standards of beauty that acknowledge, say, Michelangelo's *David,* or a stern Benin mask from antiquity, as kinds of perfection. So this one song has grown into an industry: commercials for Jamaica; singalongs at the end of benefit rock concerts; a slogan on mugs, T-shirts, and red, green, and gold crochet hats with long knitted dreadlocks attached; a catchall greeting almost as globally known as *ciao;* and a general code for healin' and feelin' good. From the bright splashes of Tyrone Downey's untreated piano intro, "One Love" has the verve of canvases by Jamaican intuitive Albert Artwell.

The track seems to skip, and the reason lies in part with the deft hands of Carlton Barrett. "Carly is accenting with the side sticks on the cymbals more than in the other songs; this is the one-drop with offbeat side sticks and hi-hat," observes Heaps.

" 'One Love' was a very spiritual song. We loved it from the beginning," says Marcia. "I didn't even know at the time that we were redoing it from the original Studio One version. All I knew was that it was a sweet melody and I was enjoyin' singin' it over and over, and enjoying the message."

"Early on when Bob was concerned about the early records he'd done for Coxsone, Scratch, and Danny Sims, those famous masters everyone releases because everybody claims them, I said I thought the best way to deal with it was to rerecord some of the old songs," explains Chris Blackwell. "So every record had three or four classic songs that he'd recorded before, like on *Exodus,* 'One Love/People Get Ready' had been recorded before. Bob always picked the songs, all I did was say to him that it was a good idea.

"The story with the double title was that the bridge part we had sounded to me exactly like a Curtis Mayfield tune. I said to him that credibility is absolutely everything, and we didn't want a situation where anybody could have a claim against a song of his. So why not just give Curtis Mayfield half? And Bob said, 'Yeah, good idea.' So that's how that particular version was done," Blackwell concludes.

Yet within the song's gentle glow a dark fire burns, as Bob unflinchingly confronts evil, and apocalypse too. Injecting blazing revelations into the heart of one of the happiest songs ever composed, is part of the genius of Bob Marley.

12

MOVEMENT TIME

THE WAILERS WERE ALREADY on the road promoting *Exodus* when I joined them in Germany. It's taken years to realize how that time was a bubble of happiness between the shock of the invasion and Bob's illness increasing. The family circle came under pressure after this tour, as success impinged on Bob's time with his roots-men, the Wailers.

Sounds, London, May 28, 1977

Kate Simon said to Bob, "You know, Bob, when you smile it's like seeing the sun come out."

She's right. It was like the sun emerging on the horizon when his head bobbed up behind Seeco's seat on the bus in Germany when they brought out the champagne to celebrate Seeco's birthday. The gnarled conga-player was grinning with shy pleasure, his girlfriend squirming with modest glee beside him, as the entire bus sang an affectionate, spirited HAPPY BIRTHDAY to him.

Neville says, "It's funny, everyone has birthdays on this trip . . ."

Family's sitting next to me, his usual blissed-out self, eye-

The punky reggae *Sounds* front cover by Kate Simon for the author's story (this image can also be found in Simon's book *Rebel Music*). On the *Exodus* tour bus in 1976, Bob's bandaged foot was still regarded as a slight injury. Alvin "Seeco" Patterson (l.) and Bob.
© *Kate Simon*

lashes curling tight over the swell of his cheek—and I comment on the—well, the *nicer* atmosphere on this bus.

"Yeah, mon," Fams sighs happily, "there always *is*."

The bus moves on through the night, bearing an extraordinary cargo of talent. Movement of Jah people.

When Bob, beaming, poured the champagne into our plastic glasses, a rare indulgence for the Rastas, it was even more of a celebration than either Kate or myself realized. It was a moment of triumph. The *Exodus* tour marked a dramatic upgrade for the Wailers on every level. Not only had Roger Mayer started to jazz up their instruments, but this was the first time they had enjoyed such typical rock band luxuries as comfortable buses and fleecy flight jackets embroidered with their names.

Indeed, after some fifteen years of struggle, *Exodus* was the first time that the Wailers were to enjoy the whole process of touring and promotion on a full budget, in an era when the music industry was growing, flexing its muscles, and feeling its strength.

Twenty-five years on, Family Man contemplates the rules of the music business as he's learned them since his childhood. He makes his pronouncement, stretching out the words with relish and concluding with a rich belly laugh. "Is not just making the album, you know. It's about the placing on the shelves, the marketing. . . ."

New Wailer Junior Marvin recalls a meeting at which the entire *Exodus* crew listened to the whole record. Amid an approving chorus, only Junior insisted that the midrange of the sound had been lost in favor of the bass.

Afterward, Bob took him aside and said he trusted Junior's ear. He funded an additional remix with the rock sensibility that Junior represented. The finely tuned cut was eagerly awaited.

But first, the product. Lister Hewan-Lowe was the promotions man for Island Records in New York, and the only black—and only Dread—person on staff. Marley was his assignment, and he'd been anticipating it for months.

Lister had a reggae radio show on a college station in New York and was a Wailers fan "from time," as Jamaicans say. Bob had been much on his mind since before the Smile Jamaica concert. "That whole shooting was so bizarre. Weeks before, I remember several visits to my office up at 444 Madison, up on the thirty-ninth floor, where close friends of his cadre would come and have private discussions with me, trying to twist my arm to convince him not to do the Smile Jamaica concert. They definitely thought it was a pretext for shooting, so I wasn't surprised when I heard what had happened. In fact, the thing that blew my mind about the shooting more than anything was that people survived."

When Lister got to hear the album, he embraced everything about it, and saw the virtues of the neo-disco drums on the track "Exodus." "I said, this is great, because the whole concept of Exodus is not strange to black or white Americans. This should really work. Bob's greatest triumph, his biggest breakthrough. Finally, things are changing, and Bob has the right kind of album, with the right kind of music. People claimed that musically, the *Exodus* album was perfect for the alleged 'black radio stations' in America."

This release had demanded particularly precise positioning. The excision of *Exodus* from *Kaya* required deft ears. Chris Blackwell was doing the division, and the tracks chosen were those that would represent two different parts of Bob Marley's psyche: *Exodus,* with the intrinsic friction it derives from contrasting and connecting heavy with light, and its more romantic successor and sister, *Kaya,* most of which was culled from the *Exodus* sessions.

One whole summer week, as Blackwell cruised in his old black Rolls-Royce up the M25 from his Oxfordshire retreat to the offices and studio in West London, he would listen to a cassette of the tracks over and over. He'd listen to it when the rest of the office was closed, with maybe Denise Mills or Suzette Newman hanging with him on the bright cushions in his glass-enclosed flower-filled office, behind a larger room in which a large round table surrounded by staff continued the company's egalitarian ideal. Blackwell immersed himself in every nuance of the sound and meaning of the wealth of tracks that resulted from the Hammersmith/Chiswick sessions, recorded over the busy winter of Bob and the Wailers' London exile.

"I wanted Side One to be super powerful, from 'Natural Mystic' fading up to the extreme energy of 'Exodus,' and Side Two to be more party, romantic, reflective, et cetera," said Blackwell. "I pretty much worked on it on my own, then ran it by Bob and Family Man, as Bob trusted Family Man's opinion very much."

It was a measure of Blackwell's fine ear that both men approved his selection.

And those skills were never more necessary. Despite its glamorous image, Island was experiencing a lull that could prove fatal if it extended. Although the label was associated with noteworthy bands, much of the label's cachet—and revenue—came from the distributed labels that had been given space to exist by Chris Blackwell's pioneering independent spirit. In order to accommodate these labels, including Chrysalis, Virgin, and E.G., Island had constructed a state-of-the-art pressing plant. It was a bold, if ultimately misguided, move by Blackwell and his then managing director, Dave Betteridge. Pressing was a key aspect of the record industry. All too often, Island and its associates had been squeezed out and forced to miss potential hits by pressing plants prioritizing bigger clients, major labels such as EMI and Polydor. Thus, to ensure the viability of its family labels and the growing independent sector, Island took the responsibility of maintaining control of the means of production.

However, this seemingly sound scheme didn't take into account the wholesale defection of the distributed labels, who were not invested in the idea of a consortium of independents and either took corporate deals or went out alone.

Then arts and marketing director Tim Clark, who now manages artists such as Robbie Williams, remembers, "We'd built up a big sales force which I had to let go. One of the worst things I've ever had to face, frankly. But it's a lesson you learned for the rest of your life. We'd got fat and started to think we were unbeatable and that we were going to be the best forever. Bob was one of the things that kept Island going through that period. He kept Island's reputation really high. And of course, following on from *Rastaman Vibration, Exodus* was the album. It was just huge, a massive, massive album. You heard 'Exodus,' the title track, everywhere. And so, if it hadn't been for Bob in many ways, we would have been in incredible trouble."

Of course, at the time of the album's release, there was no way of knowing for sure that *Exodus* would grow to be so successful. It took a lot of both planning and passion, beginning with the album sleeve.

One of the first decisions regarding *Exodus* was the sleeve, and perhaps predictably, the saga of its creation is pocked with ideas, conflicts, and a surprise resolution that turned out to be magically correct. Despite its success—the grafting of Amharic lettering onto the Latin letters of the title was simply subversive—the sleeve as we know it was a rush job pulled together by Neville Garrick after Bob rather sheepishly admitted that Cindy had insisted he didn't look good enough on the original sleeve photo: a fisheye lens effect that Neville intended to give the impression of each Wailer ensconced in a large translucent bubble, skimming between the towering water walls of the divided Red Sea. Alas, the boldness of the artist's vision was crushed yet again by the perceived aesthetic demands of the marketplace, and the fairground mirror distortion of Bob and company turned out to be as welcome as a barber at a Rasta grounation. Cindy Breakspeare didn't like the way Bob looked, and that was the end of that.

"Time was running out," recalls Neville Garrick tensely, though we're sitting, quite relaxed, by the empty swimming pool, its blue bottom dotted with fallen leaves. "But then I thought, this word, *exodus,* has so many interpretations, maybe the word's strong enough to stand enough by itself, just the word. . . ." His voice takes on a new rhythm. "Exodus . . . exodus. OK, very good—Ethiopia. We were getting a lot more information from Ethiopia than ever before, through Pepe Judah and the Twelve Tribes."

Thus inspired, Neville created the new sleeve. When he presented a copy to the crown prince, however, he was surprised to see Asfa-Wossen turn the sleeve round and round, examining it curiously from every angle. Garrick was then even more astonished to learn that an extraordinary act of synchronicity had occurred. His new, different, and unique graphics were actually just one letter short of spelling the word *Ethiopia* in Amharic lettering. Legend naturally had it that Yeshikassa planted that seed, though Garrick swears the lettering was simply his attempt at reimagining the Amharic alphabet.

So the *Exodus* package was ready for release, and all concerned would soon find out if the public was ready for the Wailers' bold leap of sound. Finally, the anticipated test pressings arrived.

"I'm sure the neighbors in St. Peter's Square must've got annoyed with us at some point, because it was a great spring day, every office window was open, and everybody was playing the 'white label' in their own offices. So it was probably coming out of the windows at various phases, all at one time," recalls press officer Brian Blevins. "But clearly, that was an amazing record, and the track 'Exodus' itself was so propulsive and kind of joyous and such a great dance song, too. It truly was a whole aura of excitement throughout the whole building."

Neville Garrick remembers, "Island went all out with the promotion. We had buses painted gold."

When I was reviewing *Exodus*, perhaps because I felt so involved with it, I tried extra hard to be objective. Frankly, I was never sure whether Bob ever read anything I wrote about him. The only time he ever commented on a piece of mine was the next time I saw him after this review was published. He kicked my critique right back at me. " 'Walking a dangerous tightrope,' ehhh, Viveen?" he teased, and his eyes twinkled because he knew we were both confident that Bob would never really go down.

Sounds, **London, May 21, 1977:** *Exodus* **album review**

From a purely marketing point of view, this is the one. With *Rastaman Vibration*'s appearance, there weren't many music fans on the planet unaware of Bob Marley's existence in his capacity as reggae's only international superstar and Rasta representative.

A heavy platform, and depressing when taken in conjunction with sales figures. The prognosis appeared to be that with all the talent, money, promotion in the world, reggae wasn't ever gonna SELL the way that rock sells.

If any album manages to break that barrier, *Exodus* should be it. Karl Pitterson's usual crisp, clean sound is calculated to be springy enough for rock fans while staying punchy enough to keep the roots fans just about satisfied. It's a dangerous tightrope, and Marley's treading it.

One of the most obvious things about the album is the way

it breaks down into a "hard" side (one) and a "soft" (two). The real heavyweights start at track three, side one—"Guiltiness." The album's finest hour, stately impassioned vocals ("these are the big fish that eat up the small fish, they would do anything to materialize their every wish . . .") while the track plus the I-Three's sound heart-rending, so poignantly severe singing about the fate of the downpressor that I'm reduced to jelly.

Then there's "Heathen," which steps so swinging, Bob's voice beseeching, thrillingly low on the irresistible rhythms of the chorus . . . Carly's drums tinkle the sound onward and upward, Family's bass unyielding as it dances between the notes. With a rhythm section solid as that, the Wailers have to remain superb. Then on through the sombre pared-down percussion of the title track, unswerving as it beckons Jah people to Africa. Marley's imperious as he whiplashes out the command to move . . . you'd have to be deaf to resist. So purposeful; it's all delivered with an authority that convinces. Majestic.

Side two is full of surprises. Superficially, it's a bunch of love songs, lines like "I don't want to wait in vain for your love" complete with crooning "ooh ooh girls." I pictured riots in Brixton when that came out. But as Marley explained to me, the message of Rasta is there for all those with ears to receive it. When you think he's talking about a girl playing hard to get, he's talking just as much about unheeding audiences of Babylon as he sings oh sooooo romantically, "it's your love that I'm waiting on, it's me love that you're running from . . ." See it deh?

Equally, the chirpy "simplicity" of the world contained in "Three Little Birds," a sweetly sprightly melody in which tame birds hop on Marley's windowsill to inform him, "don't worry 'bout a thing, 'cos every little thing's gonna be alright," could be construed as a manic attempt to reduce his revolutionary image to nil in three little words. Not (necessarily) so, Rasta! Checking it fully, the message is about positive Rastaman vibrations again, perfectly in keeping with the savage, somber exhortations of "Exodus."

Yet it's still true that side two, functioning on two levels as it does, is the least threatening side Marley's ever cut to white Western rock ears. Marley's answer to that was: (a) Why should he stay in the same place? Why sing "Burning and Looting" rehashes just to satisfy people's expectations? (b) It's only a return to the Wailers' roots (remember, the original Wailers cut a single of "What's New Pussycat," released on Island over here many moons ago), and (c) The advantage of being more accessible is that more people get to hear the message by buying the album, and there's no harm in that. . . .

As far as I'm concerned it's restricting and regressive to judge any album purely in terms of how closely it matches traditional "requirements" of its genre. If the emphasis has shifted from soul rebel street fighting man to natural mystic (the title of the mellow opening track, Marley's voice more silken and haunting than ever before) it's dumb to automatically register it as a Bad Thing.

Uncharitable people have been quick to view the new silver-voiced Marley as a cop-out, a hero in retreat, backpedaling furiously after the recent gunmen's attempt on his life. That's dumb, too.

Objectively, Marley's music has shifted into new gear, moved into a new space. OK, he sings with a new suppleness that you can describe as "soft," the way the lilting "So Much Things to Say" merges into the "Natty Dread"–style biblical blend of sorrow, tragedy and solemn pride on "Guiltiness" encapsulates the point—Marley's exhibiting a new degree of vocal control, capable of shifting emotions subtly but unmistakably as he sings one word.

While Marley's songwriting abilities remain as powerful as they are (and remember, there's an album's worth of fine material left in the can), while he continues to surround himself with musicians as excellent as the Barrett brothers, Dirty Harry and the rest, Bob Marley will continue to remain King of Reggae in the eyes of the world.

It was time to go forth and spread the word—and the reggae riddim. Album distribution was far from the science it became, or rather, the science to it was very human. In Island's case, it involved a few men (zero females) such as Trevor Wyatt shuttling round the country in vans, going into record shops and reggae market stalls.

"The Wailers were already an institution," says Wyatt. "Anytime I took any Wailers stuff out, Bob Marley in particular—it just flew. People wanted it like food. Things like the 'Smile Jamaica' single, even though it was around on import before, whenever I took it out it just flew, both versions. 'Jah Live' just flew. I knew *Exodus* was going to be big so I ordered a lot. 'Exodus' was the first single off the album, and, well, I'd say it flew. I'd get to somewhere like Brixton Market, and by the time I'd done the shops and got back to the van, the guys were coming over wanting more records. It was just insane, the amount of records we'd sell.

"Then after 'Exodus' was a hit, we came up with the disco mix of 'Jamming' with 'Punky Reggae Party' on the other side. For a minute, 'Punky Reggae Party' was the hit. But it was very plain that 'Jamming' was the side that everybody liked."

The infectious "Jamming" was to be a major factor in the global acceptance Marley was about to enjoy. "As Denise Mills told us, nothing would be the same from now on," says Neville Garrick. Now the Wailers' new celebrity was not just down to their reggae beat.

"When the news broke about Miss [World], Cindy Breakspeare, she mentioned that Bob Marley was her boyfriend in almost the first interview she did after winning. We suddenly got deluged with tabloid reporters from all over Europe. There were questions like, 'Is it true he smokes a pound of pot a day?' " recalls Brian Blevins, with some amusement. Marley's lover-man image, combined with his revolutionary stance, arcane spiritual beliefs, and novel hairstyle, made great media fodder.

After leaving the music weekly *Melody Maker,* Rob Partridge took over from Brian Blevins. His first job was to set up a photo shoot for the *Sun,* a mass circulation tabloid and not the sort of rag that usually featured Caribbean rebel music—a definite sign that the "straight" world had registered Bob on its radar.

"I remember Bob being incredibly twitchy and uncertain about it all, because he'd never done this before," Partridge recalls. Evidently there was still some ambiguity in the way Bob was perceived. In the *Sun* shoot he sat on the floor with his legs crossed, revealing an expanse of naked ankle, but the skin must have offended Island's art director, because he spray-painted sky blue socks onto the image, so Bob appeared more, if not better, dressed in future PR usages. And there would be more, many more, because, as Rob Partridge points out, "*Exodus* was still being promoted the following year, so you are talking about a campaign that stretched way beyond its natural launch date. It proves that we might have actually got to those people who actually didn't buy records, maybe two or three a year, max. Then you know that you've got yourself a huge hit record. Even in 1978, I remember Bob Marley doing *Top of the Pops.* Probably the only time he ever did that."

An appearance on the venerable British music program *Top of the Pops* was yet another sign of the Wailers' increasing acceptability, a stamp of approval from the pop-rock establishment, and marked his first British TV appearance since he, Peter, and Bunny had performed for the *Old Grey Whistle Test* three years previously. The current Wailers configuration had never been televised before.

A quaint *Top of the Pops* custom, enforced by the Musicians Union, was the prerecording of backing tracks, using British musicians where possible. However, in the case of the Wailers, a waiver was evidently made. Dick Cuthell, fresh off remixing "Jamming" and "Waiting in Vain," was assigned to produce the session with a representative of the Musicians Union present. "The guys weren't used to getting up early, and things were a bit grumpy. I'd got the whole studio wired for a live recording and the band just went from a bad sort of vibe to where they were steaming, it just kicked. It went so well that Bob said, 'I want you to be our engineer and use this for the record.' But of course, it was too late. Then at the actual *Top of the Pops,* the BBC people gawked at these guys as if they'd just beamed down from space."

No publicity hound, Bob was a reluctant interviewee. Once he rather plaintively asked, "Why must it always be me? You can't go and interview Family Man instead? Whenever I speak it always gets me in trouble." Or even when he didn't; Brian Blevins has never forgotten making complicated arrangements to send an influential journalist, Ray Coleman, editor of *Melody Maker,* to interview Bob at home. When he arrived, no one was there, and consequently, there was no *Melody Maker* story. "To break into his day to do press interviews or to get him into the office, it just really didn't work all that well."

Other factors also came into play. "Bob knew he had a manifest destiny," observes Partridge. "In every conversation, everything that Bob Marley approached, he felt that it was part of this wider plan. I always felt that Bob knew within himself that something greater was going on. We weren't just talking about an interview with whoever, but if it fitted into something bigger. If it didn't make sense, then Bob wouldn't do it."

Practically, Partridge decided to harness Bob's soccer obsession to work with, instead of against, his promotional duties, and a PR match was duly arranged: Wailers plus Island versus the media. The game took place on a brutally cold morning on one of the Wailers' regular pitches, in Battersea Park, with the landmark of the futurist power station looming behind them.

"Bob had all the skills necessary, he was a fantastic player. Trying to get the ball off him, off any of them, was just hopeless. They were so good, it was like playing Brazil," says Trevor Wyatt. "Because Bob was the person he was, the ball always came to him, and he was the midfield general, if you like. They did used to call him Skipper." Dick Cuthell agrees: "Everybody was focused on Bob and he was very competitive in his tackles. It was like David Beckham going to have a kick-about with a local team."

Everything was fine till the ball came from an unexpected angle, and Bob went down. He'd hurt a toe that had already been damaged in a game in Kingston.

"We had a couple of printers playing with us that were a bit sly on the tackle," says Wyatt. "But I don't remember him stopping for long, or making a fuss except for limping for a couple of minutes. It seemed minor; it's not like he went off to the hospital. And on that whole European tour, he wasn't struggling with the injury."

Indeed, Bob was the first to laugh at his bandaged foot, sticking it up on the backseat of the tour bus, or dropping it over an armrest. The little injury wasn't going to stop him from the biggest aspect of *Exodus*'s promotion, the road.

Just as the *Exodus* album was the first time the Wailers had in-struments of that caliber or such fine-tuning, it was also the first time the band was going out in such style. It was all a far cry from the drafty backstages in which the first edition of the Wailers en-dured a constant diet of fish and chips, just about the only thing they could find to eat that conformed to the Rasta dietary laws—the lifestyle that had made Bunny Wailer turn his back on touring permanently.

Now the band traveled with their old friend Gilly as the chef, and with an assistant. And since I'd been *Sounds'* girl on the spot covering the *livity* at 56 Hope Road right before the shooting, my editor sent me off again with Kate Simon to cover a couple of stops of the *Exodus* tour.

The general mood on tour was one of elation. I remember the bus swinging down the road from Island's Chiswick HQ and turn-ing a corner past Shepherds Bush Green. We drove past a hair-dresser's in a little Deco shopping arcade called Babylon, and everyone had a lot of fun with that. Quoting the song "Exodus," the cry went up—"We're leaving Babylon!" Over the years as a music journalist, I traveled with many bands on the road, but the Wailers did have a particular energy that may have come from the feeling that they'd been spared to do some important work. There's no doubt that they all felt it was more than a band, or a vehicle for making money; it really was a mission to spread a message of Rasta love and unity, hard as that may be for people to believe.

"I think it was the first real Bob Marley and the Wailers tour," recalls Wailers promoter Mick Cater, who fought to continue booking the band. "Don Taylor arrived as the manager and all of a sudden, the Wailers tour got taken away from us; he'd given it to William Morris and they were putting it out to tender."

Leading London promoter Harvey Goldsmith offered some dates, with the crowning gig being one night at the Hammersmith

Odeon, but Cater went all out and offered five nights at the Hammersmith Odeon. "They went, 'You're mad.' I said, 'OK, here's my money. Watch this.' We sold out in a minute.

"Because I'd been there from the very beginning, I was very finely tuned to what Bob was worth in terms of what we could do," continues Cater. "We had to do the tour in stages, because he didn't sell any records. The only albums that really, really sold, up until *Exodus,* were *Babylon by Bus* and the *Live at the Lyceum!* album. But in Europe, nothing. We did it all by touring."

On this tour, everything was upgraded. After years of racketing around playing with pickup equipment, the Wailers finally had their own arena rig. "Before that, they had picked up stuff locally and it was nuts," Mick specifies.

Supported by the band of venerable trombone player Rico (known as Don Drummond Jr.), it was a triumphant procession through Europe, and for the Wailers, it was like an initiation into the life of a big rock band on the road. Even the inevitable weed situations went smoothly, both the acquisition thereof and the dealing with customs (Seeco once forgot a little spliff behind his ear but got away with it). The unaccustomed comfort was welcome. The bus was outfitted with two daybeds at the rear, where Bob held court, lolling on the left-hand bed, which he'd seized as his personal throne.

The I-Three were adept at humanizing their sterile hotel rooms, draping red, green, and gold lion scarves over the lights. As they traveled, they picked up bulk supplies to take back to Jamaica, where the supermarket shelves were often bare of even the essentials, so their hotel rooms were full of large cardboard drums of goods.

The tour began in a slaughterhouse in Paris, which, considering the Rasta deemphasis on death, Bob initially wasn't too pleased about. The impassioned show marked a distinct change in Bob's audience—now the chic jet-set types were coming out in force, and according to the memoirs of Don Taylor, it was a given that famous females would be stalking the ever-popular Bob. Bianca Jagger and other luminaries thronged the gig, and various celebrities were miffed at not being allowed on the stage, a perk that tour manager Mick Cater reserved for Blackwell alone. No Rasta had ever experienced anything like the afterparty at the prototypical disco, Regine's. Uptown top ranking in a Eurocracy style, as a DJ might have said. A cynic might have commented that it was essence of Babylon—painted harlots, strumpets, and wild, wild women in spike heels—but everyone seemed to enjoy it anyway. These were the fruits of years of often grueling labors, and they tasted good. For a few days, I covered the tour for *Sounds,* and this article reminds me of how sweet it was.

Sounds, Munich, Germany, May 1977

"Isn't it a nice feeling . . . isn't it a nice day . . . isn't it a nice feeling . . ." Bob Marley croons, strumming on an acoustic guitar. He's glowing, planted on the neutral modern sofa, in this sunlit hotel room.

Outside the sliding plate-glass windows there's a balcony. Stand on the balcony and the river Isar rushes in a yellow froth far below, bubbling through spans of green leafy trees. We're in—where are we again? Oh yeah. Munich. The Hilton.

It's because, for example, Family Man never knows where the hell we are, that the Wailers travel in such a tight, closed unit. A real family on the road. It could be, and usually is, anywhere outside, but the Wailers' world is secure. A mobile Jamdown in a Babylon. European Dread.

Looking around this light, spacious living-room of the corner suite, some of the family are taking their ease. This Saturday a.m. is brilliant. There's a natural mystic flowing through the air, and everything happens crystal clear, because it's Saturday morning, and it's a day off the bus.

And everybody's either singing, beating time on a coffee table, or just aware of the sweet music dancing like sunlight through the room. You can hear the river bubble, the hissing wind through the trees, you can hear the distant sound of cars on the highway, and above it all you can hear Bob singing this tune, mellow as the river, fresh/free as the wind.

The melody swirls like incense in the air, interlocking everyone into a mood of peaceful i-nity, breathing in synchompatibility. The tennis on the colour TV is turned down low. The positive vibrations are turned up higher than high. Photographer Kate Simon says, "Now I'm gonna shoot some black and white," firmly switching cameras.

"Hey, sister," someone interrupts, "why dontcha shoot some black and black. No offence."

"That's cool," Kate says brightly, beaming like she's just scored the cover of the *National Geographic,* "I'll see what I can do." And shoots off another dozen pics while she speaks. And when that film's developed, there it'll be, black on black.

Roland Kirk called it blacknuss, playing just the black notes on the piano to make sweet rebel music, telling his brothers and sisters not to worry 'bout a thing, 'cos every little thing's gonna be alright.

Bob Marley and the Wailers call it Rastafari.

"WE KNOW WHERE WE'RE GOING, WE KNOW WHERE WE'RE FROM, WE LEAVIN' BABYLON" ("EXODUS")

I've been on the road with all kinds of bands, and so's Kate, but never on a tour quite as hermetically sealed as the Wailers'. Mick Cater, the man-on-the-road from Alec Leslie who set up the tour (very efficiently, I might add), had this to say:

"It's easy to arrange a Wailers tour. All they want is a room where they can be left alone to eat their ital [natural] food, and not be hassled. The only reason why they're staying in Hiltons and expensive hotels like that is because they're the only places with private kitchens."

The Wailers follow the Rastafarian way, they like everything to be natural.

And what's a more natural part of life than FOOD? Right! Where other bands hit the night-spots, the Wailers chow down.

The Wailers are the exact reverse of junk food junkies. You can't imagine Family queuing up at the Blue Boar for a plate of egg and chips, it just doesn't work that way. No, the Wailers have Gilly and Inez in i-fficial green/yellow tour jacket ON THE BUS to take care of their stomachs.

Gilly looks like a cross between a swashbuckling seafaring man and a giant doorman from the *Arabian Nights,* with scimitar and turban. He rolls as he walks, and he has a way of looming over you as he talks that can be almost alarming. At gigs, he positions himself by Tyrone's keyboards at the side of the stage, stepping solemnly in his imposing solar topee. Then he rushes to the kitchen and concocts those fabulous, indecipherable Jamaican brews. Standing sternly over the blender, he adds a splat of red, a smidgeon of brown, and whirrrrrrrs. Yumyumyum. What's this, Gilly?

"This life protoplasm, mon."

Seen. Not much answer to that, is there?

Like everybody connected with the Wailers, he's fiercely loyal and protective. Inez was almost reduced to tears when she arrived at the Heidelberg hotel and found NO KITCHEN. (Turns out they had space reserved in the main hotel cookery, so everything, of course, turned out to be ALRIGHT. Don't worry 'bout a thing.)

Neville Garrick, the Wailers' willowy art director, hovers on the blender, eyes glued to the Life Protoplasm. As soon as the first lot's done, he knocks a glass back, then says, "Where's the Skip?" and sprints solicitously off with the machine to ensure that Bob gets a generous dose of the life-giving juices.

A Brief Crosscut

Just 'cos you're a righteous man doesn't mean you're not human, too. Two contrasting encounters illuminate Marley's chemistry.

In Munich, Marley's manager, Don Taylor, presents me with my first ever ceremonial bowl of steaming hot Irish Moss (a JA beverage).

The city electric spreads out far down below, nothing but shadowy concrete hulks strung about with necklaces of sulphuric fluorescent light. Bob scans the *Telegraph,* then the *Express* (Jah only knows how *they* got here), and tosses them aside. Sighs, puts his feet in their broken-down Roman sandals (plus bandaged toe—some injury) on the chrome 'n' glass table.

What's new in the papers, Bob?

"Nothing, mon. Same thing every day."

He moves closer up the table.

"You like that?"

Sure I do, it's great. I can't begin to imagine what it is, but there's cinnamon and nutmeg, it's faintly acrid and faintly sweet . . . Bob's eyes are twinkling.

"That's good for ya . . . you know that?" His eyes twinkle. "Make your *pum-pum* wet."

Years later Kate Simon informed me, to my disappointment, that those jolly postshow feasts were not a regular occurrence and that after most shows, Wailers went their separate ways.

"Before they went onstage it was always really anticipatory and they were all really in an irie mood, looking forward and looking up, and smoking a ton of herb," she remembers. "Then after the show, it would be quite different. I noticed that Bob would be in a pretty quiet, contemplative mood. I remember him sitting with his head down in his hands, praying, backstage in Berlin after the show."

As in London, a special soccer match between Island, the media, and the Wailers was a highlight of the media schedule. This time, instead of the Battersea power station looming over the match, it was the Eiffel Tower, and once again Bob's Achilles' heel, his foot, took a blow.

"I was the first person who took him to a doctor," states Junior Marvin. "Me and him had this privacy thing, where he'd tell me certain things that he didn't want nobody else to know. He told me, 'I want you to take me to the doctor. I have to check a little man business. Don't tell Neville and them, me and you alone are going.' So we went alone, and the doctor gave him a full checkup. Then the doctor stumbled onto the toe and said, "By the way, it's better for you to amputate that toe. Maybe you'll lose your balance, because your big toe and your ear is what controls your balance, but you'll live." Then Bob still wants to play soccer with it. And when we played a match in Paris, this French journalist steps on Bob's foot with a spike, and it went right through the toe.' " Marvin shakes his head slowly, recalling the sad sequence of events.

"Of course, Bob's contract with Island is about to end, and everybody turns around and tells Bob that this doctor is part of a conspiracy," Marvin continues. "Who brought Junior into the band? Chris Blackwell. Whose contract is about to be up? Chris Blackwell's. And of course this is Don Taylor telling him all of this crap."

Regardless, the Wailers tour bus rolled on through Europe. The hostility of the police to the Wailers was palpable, I thought. Nonetheless, Berlin was treated to an unusual set, as before the show the Wailers had been introduced to a new breed of marijuana known as Thai sticks. Individually wrapped in thread, the slender fingers of weed arrived late in the day, shortly before the band was due to go on. They looked like the sort of delicate confection a caterer might use to decorate a tray, but packed such a punch that Bob, the perfectionist, didn't get onstage till ten o'clock and got the set list wrong.

"By the time they went on, Bob was out of his head," Mick Cater remembers. "The encore used to be 'Exodus,' then 'Get Up, Stand Up.' For some reason, he got it the wrong way around. Then he realized that it was all kind of weird, so he kicked back into the *Rastaman Vibration* tour set by starting off with 'Crazy Baldhead.' They played for about four hours. It was great. We didn't get him offstage until about two in the morning. What a night."

The stage shows were all triumphant, as the interaction between the players, who'd played together for most of a lifetime, was synced up like cartilage to bone. Bob had his signals to the band, like skipping back on the stage to skank between the Barrett brothers, controlling their pace. He knew how to subtly signal to the sound mixer, first Dave Harper, who used to roadie for Traffic, then Dennis Thompson, and to Neville Garrick, manning the lights. That familiar Bob gesture of covering half his face with his hand and knitting his brow as if mourning the plight of the world was often a sign to wrench the beat around.

Clutching a fine porcelain teacup in a wood-paneled tearoom in London's West End, Wailers' tour promoter, Mick Cater, recalls, "Europe was fine. There was no pressure. But coming into London, everybody got very twitchy. I don't remember where I heard it from, but I got the impression that something was gonna go down."

On the first night of the four London shows, it seemed as if a rerun of the Kingston invasion might indeed occur. Unusual precautions had been taken; it was Cater's first use of metal detectors. Cater sent a car for Bob and hooked up a walkie-talkie with his escort, Benjamin Foot, an early Wailers' road manager and son of Sir Hugh Foot, the former governor of Jamaica. Unusually for those pre-cell-phone days, they could keep in contact on the forty-five-minute trip from Harrington Gardens to north London. Despite, or because of, the heightened security, Foot remembers, Bob was in a great mood. He was quickly led to a room backstage that had been set up for his comfort with a guitar and a pinball machine. Throughout the day, expat Jamaicans had been trying to get in backstage. The order was strictly no uninvited guests. Bob was to be kept completely alone with the band.

But when the musicians arrived, one of the men squeezed in behind them and started spraying the backstage with bullets. Once again, Don Taylor flung himself in front of the bullets—but luckily, this time round it turned out to be a pellet gun.

Sounds, London, May 21, 1977

And I went in there feeling conscientious, like I really wanted to take notes. But believe me when I tell you, nothing seemed less important than notes. What was important was the naked emotion that vibrated the airwaves as the I-Three were chanting, "Don't give up the fight, don't give up the fight, don't give up the fight . . ."

Much of the Wailers' appeal/greatness is down to the fact that they are a real band, more so than any of their contemporaries. The core, solid as the pyramids, is Bob Marley and the

Barrett brothers, Carl[ton] on drums, Fams playing bass. Now Junior Marvin playing guitar adds his own positive vibe, lean, deep guitar playing, and unabashed showmanship as he drops to one knee in his tracks and snaaarls at the audience. He often turns to Tyrone playing keyboards and you can see the energy leap in an arch between them. Tyrone beams constantly.

Meanwhile, Family Man remains stolid, eyes downcast, playing with exquisite concentration and economy, his right hand hardly moves throughout the set. His movements elevate time and motion to poetry. When he walks offstage after the encore he shakes his bass in the air at the audience, a triumphant valediction salute. He knows he'd played like a real champ. The I-Three look serene in white, swaying, laughing amongst themselves, precise in their movements. They were enjoying the mock shooting to "I Shot the Sheriff" so much— their movements sang, kiss kiss, bang bang. . . .

The energy was feeding back on itself, escalating—when Bob danced up to Judy or clasped Rita around the neck, his emotion mixing in with theirs. Bob starts off not moving too much, slicing his rhythm guitar, but then his vocals are a cyclone, sweeping you into the air and away with tenderness when he sings "No Woman, No Cry."

When he sings, "Forget your sorrows and dance," your heart swells so much you're hardly aware that you're dancing, feet and soul.

During "Lively Up Yourself" Bob's movements were so free they made you sigh with pleasure at the fineness of living. Yes, ecstasy; the feeling is incredible tonight, with positive vibrations. One love blazed from his being. The encore was "Exodus, Movement of Jah People." It throbbed and burned forward, as natural and irresistible as the moon tugging the sea.

It's a natural, mystic flowing through the air. Let Jah be praised.

After the tour, everyone scattered. Neville and Bob went to Delaware to help Bob's mother pack up and move to Miami. Already, one Miami purchase arranged by Don Taylor had had to be put back on the market shortly after its purchase, as Bob decided it was too small, and a larger estate with a sweeping curved drive was bought in its place.

Seeing his mother settled in a warm place, with a garden big enough for her to grow the fresh produce that Bob enjoyed, was very significant for the singer. It was a relief to be able to leave Neville in his place before Bob went back to England, to go check on the American tour dates, and general accounts.

Denise Mills was charged with taking Bob to his doctor's appointment in Harley Street on July 7, 1977. That day was long marked for infamy, for in their numerological cogitations, akin to those of Kabbalistic rabbis, serious Rastas had long prophesied that the quadruple conjunction of the mystic number seven (the number of the Sabbath day of rest, and the number of years after which fields were supposed to lie fallow) would prove apocalyptic. A genuine feeling of trepidation about the date had been voiced by Culture on their track "Two Sevens Clash"; many Jamaicans didn't go out that day. Yet destiny works obliquely, and what seemed to pass like any normal day marked the end of one cycle of Bob Marley's *livity*.

Neville was helping Bob's mother settle into the new house in Miami when the call with the diagnosis of cancer came through from Bob. The news fell like an axe. Bob flew from London to Miami to see a doctor that Don Taylor had recommended.

"The doctor said if he cut off the toe, Bob could be on the road again in two months," recalls Junior, "but Bob said, 'You just want to cut off me toe so me can work again. That is the quick solution.' I think he read it that Blackwell and people must have wanted to get him back on the road again as quickly as possible since the album was really hitting. I didn't agree."

This American tour was of great significance to Bob. As far back as *Rastaman Vibration,* he'd written a wish-fulfilling couplet on "Roots Rock Reggae": "Bubbling on the Top 100 / Just like a mighty Dread." Bob wanted to help build a stronger bridge between black Americans and their fellow transplanted Africans in the Caribbean. Comments Garrick, "Black America being the most elusive market was something Bob worried and wondered about and tried to work on. He'd say, 'Dem call reggae jungle music. If I sweeten it with some R&B flavor, it will make them listen.' "

Lister Hewan-Lowe was focusing on black radio, which had traditionally been less receptive to Marley and reggae in general. "I'll never forget those experiences at stations like WBLS. They used to insult me and slam the door in my face when I came with reggae records." Hewan-Lowe's anger has not completely died. "But things changed with *Exodus.*

"The American tour was cancelled, though there was great pressure to see if it could still happen, just because this tour was extremely pivotal in Marley's career—really, really strategic. If everything worked as planned, with the setup and the momentum, Bob would have broken much bigger than U2; their project was set up the same way," continues Hewan-Lowe. "Bob really wanted to break America. He thought, as an artist, that he might have the white market, but look at the oppressed black people in America, twelve percent of the American population, and ninety percent of its prison population. He had to mobilize those people and get them involved in the 'Movement of Jah people.' That is where Bob Marley felt his legitimacy lay. Make the connection, bring them all together under one roof, and then you have the great exodus."

However, once the seriousness of Bob's condition was known, the American tour designed to break Bob in America was clearly out of the question.

"That's when Bob would have broken, because *Exodus* was a big turntable hit in America," states Neville Garrick. "After Frankie Crocker from New York's WBLS radio started playing it, everyone was on it. If we had toured America that year, if Bob didn't have the injury, he would have broken through, because it was just so successful. *Exodus* was definitely our breakthrough album."

So Bob found himself in Miami, and once again his family moved with him. Now he wasn't fleeing gunmen but trying to escape mortality. Reasoning about Rasta, I'd once pressed Bob on the Rasta disbelief in death, in an exchange published in *Melody Maker* in 1979 that got quite heated:

VG: How come you're aware of the danger of being assassinated if you don't believe in death?
BM: Hold on, now. You think you can go out there and lay down in front of the car and let it run over you? If I go outside and see the big bus coming and put my head underneath it, what do you think will happen?
VG: Your head will be crushed. And what will you be then?
BM: (shouts) DEAD! That is where people make a mistake. They say that the flesh doesn't value anything, but that's the biggest lie. But sister, I understand what you're saying. You're saying a man can be dead in his flesh, but his spirit lives. But I respect my flesh too, and I know my spirit . . .
VG: Oh I thought you meant death didn't exist at all.

BM: Yes, but you have to AVOID it! Death does not exist for me. God gave me this life and my estimation is, if he gives me this, why should he take it back? Only the Devil says that everybody has to die.

Now his faith was tested. "Bob told me directly that he did not understand why this doctor in London knew so much about him, so he also visited a doctor in Miami that also came up with the conclusion that he did have the melanoma cancer," says Neville Garrick.

Clearly, Bob was very disturbed by his experience with the doctor in London, as he also confided to Lister Hewan-Lowe that he didn't like the way the man seemed to be so familiar with his case. "Well, that's typical of Bob Marley, I think. He could be a little bit paranoid and superstitious. You can leave the country, but you can't take that instinct out of the person. He was convinced that he didn't have this cancer thing, and if he did have it, he could just beat it. Mentally, he was just like a bull," says Hewan-Lowe.

Bob's conspiracy theories were running riot, with good reason. It was hard to find a reliable doctor. Junior remembers it all too clearly. "This doctor grafts a piece of Bob's ass, puts it on his toe, and tells him, 'Go away, you're gonna be all right.' Doesn't check the rest of his body to see if the cancer's spread or not. But of course, the blood's already contaminated, so grafting the toe makes no difference at all."

Once again, Bob made a period that could have been a trial into something as positive as possible. Stella McLaughlan, who had run the night canteen at Basing Street Studios during the *Exodus* sessions, was now working with the Marleys in Miami, living at Mrs. Booker's house. She was around during Bob's stay, even once accompanying him to the hospital. "In that period, with Seeco and Neville there, Bob began to write a lot of the *Uprising* album. They would be up really late at night, just jamming." Diane Jobson asked Stella to look after the mounds of fan mail, and Stella suggested that they put out a newsletter instead. Bob thought it was a good idea, but he didn't like the name Bob Marley and the Wailers Fan Club. "Call it Movement of Jah People," he pronounced.

Right after the invasion, Skill Cole had left for Ethiopia, where they'd already repatriated a number of Jamaican Rastas to Sheshamane, the valley set aside for the black people of the West by Haile Selassie. Now he was eager for Bob to come and visit; it would be Bob's first visit to the African continent he'd worked toward for so long. Bob had promised to come when he felt better—but then the Peace Concert took precedence, so Skill had to wait. In keeping with the mood, the mellower *Kaya* album was released, and Cindy Breakspeare was pregnant with their son, Damian. He would grow up to reference "Exodus" on his song "Move" in 2005.

The Peace Concert was a group effort. Much had happened since Bob had sent Claudie a ticket to London, and the two bred'ren phoned Syd and Rita at Tommy Cowan's house, very excited at the prospect of peace. "Bob called Tommy's house and says, 'Listen, we're coming home. You have to organize something nice,' " recalls Syd Massop. "We started organizing the Peace Concert right there." Other prime movers included the band Inner Circle.

The idea of peace in the ghetto was accepted rather slowly in some quarters. Having been raised in London, Syd Massop found the ghetto's territorial concept so alien as to be incomprehensible.

"We started going around to the different communities, saying, 'Bob is coming home. We're gonna organize this thing. Everybody must get involved.' Of course, it spread like wildfire through the whole Kingston," says Syd. "We thought we'd better talk to some of the guys up at Concrete Jungle, the 'other side.' I can't fathom that I'm supposed to be a JLP person, in Claudie's party, so I'm not supposed to be running with some PNP friends. It's not in my concept."

So Syd and Rita Marley went to Concrete Jungle to look for an area leader named Tony Welch. But when Syd explained the Peace Concert idea, Welch replied, "Nobody say nothing to me. I'm gonna have to go talk to my leader." Then Syd explained this new way of thinking. "No, you don't have to get any leader involved. This is just about the people and the community."

But Welch and the others they approached all did check back with their bosses. "His leader obviously saw it as a good PR opportunity to go and meet Bob and come back with him. Because this was the whole image now, unity of both political party sides, coming together, to bring Bob home. None of them wanted to be left out," says Syd.

Tommy and Valerie Cowan organized buses to go round all the communities and bring people to the Peace Concert. Bob had charged Tommy with an even more delicate mission: to see if in the spirit of unity, his fellow former Wailers could be persuaded to reform for the night. "Because it was a coming together of political rivals. It was a coming together of different organizations of Rastafari. It was a coming together of the Wailers," Tommy explains.

Although Cowan had known all these musicians since his group, the Jamaicans, started out in the 1960s, at the same time as the Wailers, he felt that for such a special mission, it was better to move with Claudie. At Peter's house in Spanish Town, Claudie said to the tallest Wailer, "We want to do this concert and we want you to be part of it." "What kind of a concert is it?" asked Peter. "A peace concert," Claudie explained. Peter looked at him and said, "Claudie, the only peace you're gonna get in this country is six by six." "What do you mean by that?" asked Claudie. Laconically, Peter Tosh replied, "Six foot six [the dimensions of a grave] is called rest in peace."

Bunny received the invitation with the sort of tough calm he was adept at projecting, but made no comment.

Initially, the gathering of the Rasta tribes was met with equal caution. The Ethiopian Theocratic Council had already been very instrumental in arranging the peace. At Bob's behest, Tommy went to visit Prince Emmanuel of the strict sect, the Bobo Shantis. "He also had his reservations. He said, 'Tell Bob it's been four hundred years that we've been out of slavery, and you have to be very careful not to be trapped back into slavery. In other words, are the people really ready for this Peace Concert? Were the different factions of Rastafari, who were somewhat divided, ready to come together? Otherwise, this would set us back in the progress that we have made.' "

A meeting was held at Hope Road, gathering Rasta bred'ren from all over the island, who stayed for five days. Sadly, Diane Jobson remembers, no conclusions were reached. "Rasta don't deal with politricks," laughed the only woman present.

"We had the Twelve Tribes, of course. We had the Ethiopian Orthodox Church, which counts as a church and not as a Rasta group. But we had different factions of the Rasta bred'ren coming together," states Cowan. "The vision that Bob had for this was amazing. Bob was reading very much about what His Majesty was saying at the time, and one of the things we were looking at is that a country would not progress materially if it's not progressing equally spiritually. And that was what we were aiming to do. That's why a lot of people today don't know the real significance of Bob bringing the prime minister, Michael Manley, and Seaga together onstage. It was to bring them into a spiritual connection."

Thousands of people awaited Bob at the airport. But the triumphant return took an unusual twist. "The ghetto revolutionaries outmaneuver we, and we had to actually follow them," remembers Neville Garrick gleefully. In the recollections of Trench Town stalwart Michael Smith of Knowledge, however, the return played out rather differently.

Instead of going to Hope Road, Bob instead made them drive him straight to Trench Town. When he arrived at his old block on First Street, Bob sat in the car with his son Ziggy, waiting to be approached. When that didn't happen, he slowly got out of the car and walked over to the low wall under the big mango tree in whose shade they'd spent so many hours kicking conversation around like a soccer ball, smoking, harmonizing, and scrupulously dividing whatever small food they'd managed to rustle up. The hesitancy shown by his old Trench Town bred'ren was a big contrast to the exultation of his greeting at the airport. Bob understood very well that the members of the First Street posse were still smarting at the sense of exclusion they'd felt at Hope Road, and the feeling that politricks had divided childhood friends. But Bob's simple move reasserted the old communication. Suddenly everyone was talking, laughing, allowing themselves to show their relief and happiness at all being alive and reunited.

Having made peace with his old bred'ren, Bob drove on to reclaim Kingston. It seemed like no one slept that night. Fires burned in the narrow, winding zinc alleys, and Matches Lane rang with the grounation chants that normally sounded out in the wilds of the Wareika Hills. Peals of thunder split the sky. The very elements seemed to be acknowledging the Rasta hero's return.

13

THE ONE LOVE PEACE CONCERT

THE REHEARSALS FOR the One Love Peace Concert took place at Strawberry Hill. No plaque marks the spot. The Great House, where Lord Nelson strode and where in the 1950s Chris Blackwell and his mother would genteelly partake of tea in bone china cups and nibble on thin cucumber sandwiches, was destroyed by Hurricane Gilbert in 1988, and the whole property was redesigned into Caribbean chalets by the noted Jamaican architect Ann Hodges.

One morning twenty years later, driving down to Kingston from Strawberry Hill, I picked up a man hitchhiking at the bus stop. He said his name was Henry. A local Irish Town kid, now grown, he began to reminisce about being ten years old and hearing a heartbeat bass drifting out on the breezy night air, how he and his friends sneaked up to the old Great House from nearby Irish Town to listen in the moonlight to the Wailers play. No such music had ever happened up there before, and it hasn't since.

Henry described how they slipped across the great swath of lawn, moving closer and closer to the old Great House, when all of a sudden, they saw a light dancing in midair on the verandah, as if it were a pini-wallee (the patois name for firefly). Edging nearer,

At the climax of the Peace Concert. Bob clasps hands with political rivals, Michael Manley (PNP) (l.) and Edward Seaga (r.) (JLP). Surely a change was gonna come? 1978.
© *Adrian Boot/Bob Marley Music.*

they saw it was a spliff burning in Bob Marley's hand. The singer stood alone on the verandah, while the band jammed indoors, gazing down at the lights of Kingston glittering below, like a diamond necklace tossed onto black velvet. A sudden noise or something made Bob glance sharply, watchfully, in their direction and catch sight of the kids. They stared at him. He looked back, dead serious. Then Bob laughed, turned, and went back in to work. That smile was an invitation, and the youths stayed close to the house, listening and rocking, till the rehearsal ended in the early hours.

The mood could not have been more different from the last time the band and bred'ren and sist'ren had gathered at Strawberry Hill. In the enclosed world, suspended high above Kingston in the purer air, the ideas flowed freely as the former downtown enemies were united again, and the talk was of revolution. Master trombonist Vin Gordon remembers the idea being discussed: the possibility of creating a new political party, one that would embrace the spirit of Rasta, not fight it down. For the first time, the political representatives might be the elite of the people, chosen by the people, rather than of the ruling white minority who held themselves to be the elite by virtue of birth and wealth.

Yet there was always a tension between these street warriors and their quest for peace. Shortly before the show, Kate Simon and I went down to find Bucky Marshall in his downtown area. We found him relaxing, reclining regally across the hood of a 1960s American car in a dark, decaying street. In these near-derelict surroundings, Marshall's posse flanked him as if they were guarding a king, scowling suspiciously at Kate and myself. Though not as eloquent as Massop, Marshall spoke curtly and with decision about youths from both sides coming together to stop the bloodshed. Why did he think that local gunmen had decided to stop fighting right now? I asked him. "Because I shoot harder," Marshall replied, and for the first time, his stone-faced posse laughed.

Their unabashedly warrior response seems to confirm Laurie Gunst's assertion that guns for the JLP were smuggled into Jamaica in the crates for the Peace Concert's stage equipment.

The Peace Concert had a lot of work to do, but its ammunition was powerful. Not only a musical manifesto, it was also a showcase for the spectacular talent that caused reggae archivist Roger Steffens to call the 1970s reggae's golden age. A whole town sprang up outside the National Stadium to serve the thirty-two thousand people in attendance, with vendors to sell them everything from T-shirts to "festival" treats of sugar-sprinkled beignets. It seemed like everyone on the island who could walk, as well as some who couldn't, were all eagerly squeezing into the stadium to be part of what the DJs constantly reminded us over the sound system was a historic event. There was an almost euphoric feeling in the air at the possibility that a change might be coming.

"I went and met Bob over at sound check. He was very self-possessed. Not uncharacteristically self-possessed, but he was very serious," Kate Simon remembers. "He was really concentrating. Then as far as the concert goes, I remember that the crowd was really unruly and somewhat threatening. My watch was ripped off, and I'd never had any idea that the sleight of hand occurred."

The show was a wild ride. Racing about the stage, the band Inner Circle's singer, Jacob Miller, smoked a foot-long spliff, managed to snatch a policeman's cap, jammed it on his dreadlocks, and called Claudie Massop and Bucky Marshall onstage to show their unity. The audience adored their bad boy.

There had been rumors of an original Wailers reunion, but evidently the peace hadn't quite got that far yet. Peter Tosh hijacked the moment to deliver an unforgettable hour-long rant of incendiary oratory, making me glad I'd managed to save my cassette player from a sticksman (thief) I'd wrestled with right in front of the stage. Obviously that's particularly ironic at a peace concert, but the peace hadn't yet penetrated poor people's pockets and possibly never would. Uninhibited and wickedly sardonic, Peter disemboweled the establishment like a fire-and-brimstone preacher wreathed in ganja smoke. Lunging across the stage, Tosh's bass player, Robbie Shakespeare, brandished his instrument like a lance—the very same little Hofner that Paul McCartney used to play. Shakespeare's mentor, Family Man, had passed it on to his protégé.

Seeing Bob perform in Jamaica was always different from watching him perform anywhere else. Although he invariably enchanted every international audience, the immediacy with which Bob related to a Jamaican crowd, who understood his every nuance profoundly, was electric. The show was loaded with emotion, as thousands of Jamaicans rejoiced at seeing Bob back safe.

Wearing a hessian shirt that Syd Massop had made specially for the occasion, with a freehand map of Africa on the back, Bob whirled like a dervish. In a performance that seemed highly charged and personal, he sang an extraordinary extended version of "Jamming," slower than the record's. That night the tune had yet another edge, in addition to dancing and praising survival: jamming became the life force, the very breath and pulse of existence.

For just as it is written in Exodus 19:16, at the Peace Concert "there were thunders and lightning . . . and the voice of the trumpet exceeding loud; so that all the people in the camp trembled."

It seemed as if even the elements were in tune with Bob's will. Astonishing everyone, Marley summoned the two opposing political leaders, Manley and Seaga, onto the stage. As he did so, two flashes of lightning zapped the stage, so bright it seemed they must be planned, a lighting effect. "That lightning actually came from the heavens. It was bursting out. A whole total spiritual dance took place onstage. Nobody ever saw Bob dance the way he did that night. It was different than any other Bob Marley performance," recalls Tommy Cowan, still awed.

They truly were shots heard round the world, the iconic photos of Bob Marley concluding the Peace Concert by clasping the hands of the two opposing leaders, Seaga and Manley, aloft united over his head, as though he were mending a broken circuit. Seen in close-up on video, the gesture is even more powerful than it seemed among the crowd of thousands. Bob's expression is intent, transported, entranced. His intensity indicates that he is channeling all his resources, every ounce of energy in his weakening body, to transmit a laser beam of peace, welding together the two enemies whose hands he held, as if to seal and heal the waves of rage that had always divided Manley and Seaga in the past. Manley looked somewhat awkward and Seaga slightly shifty, but there they were, touching each other. Surely that primal connection was as valid as a vow.

14

BOB LIVES!

AT THAT CHARGED, TRIUMPHANT MOMENT when Bob Marley tried to unite the two political parties onstage at the Peace Concert, using his will as an electrical transformer to make their energy flow in the right direction, he had just three more years left in that physical form. I choose those words because, truly, Bob in many senses is still almost more alive than when he walked among us. On any street in any part of the world, people of every age wear his image—rivaling the faithful who wear medallions of Christ or a Star of David. When Bob wrote "Jah Live," incensed at people saying Haile Selassie had died, he was once again prophesying what would all too soon be his own reality. Bob lives.

After Bob Marley descended the stage from the Peace Concert, Jah Rastafari took his servant to the top of the mountain of global stardom and showed him the Promised Land. But like Moses, Bob would never really enter it, never savor its milk and honey.

"Look at that famous Peace Concert picture. Count the amount of survivors," insists Karl Pitterson, the Wailers' producer.

Karl is correct. Of the central protagonists, all are dead but Seaga, who at the time of this writing is elderly and frail.

Shortly after Peter Tosh's incendiary appearance at the Peace Concert, plainclothes cops pulled him in while he was smoking a

Bob is still among us, and his lion's roar keeps on growing stronger. The smile says "One Love" in his bedroom at Oakley Street, London.
© *Dennis Morris/Bob Marley Music. 1977.*

spliff outside a recording studio. They beat him so badly that when Bob was called to the station, it's said he wept to find his fellow Wailer lying semiconscious on the floor in his own blood. Tosh was shot dead in his home in Kingston in September 1987, allegedly by a friend he'd been helping, named Dennis Lobban.

Five months previously, Wailers drummer Carlton Barrett, Family Man's brother, had been shot dead in the street outside his house by his wife's lover.

Gunman-turned-peacemaker Bucky Marshall was shot dead soon after the Peace Concert in a dance hall in Brooklyn. Which of his many enemies was responsible has never been proved.

Claudie's widow, Syd Massop, remembers fretting over water shortages one morning in February 1980. Rushing out to a soccer match, Claudie teased her, "Don't worry, you smell sweet enough already." But as Claudie was coming home from the game, his car was pulled over by armed police. The forty-eight bullet holes located under his arms proved that Claudie strode confidently out to greet them, hands up to show he had nothing to hide and nothing to fear. After all, this was peacetime.

Simply put, peace had never been on everyone's agenda. For some people, peace doesn't pay, and the Rasta alternative that the Dreads were promoting threatened the existing power structure. "It don't look ordinary to me. A lot of us knew it was something . . . very unusual for all those people to be killed in that way," says Bob's close bred'ren, footballer Skill Cole. "They murdered the man Claudie. They murdered Peter Tosh. They kill all the rest of the guys who were front-runners, active. I think that society itself did not like the whole idea of the peace initiative, and hence, all of them have died mysteriously."

Reflecting on it all, Bob's Twelve Tribes bred'ren Michael Campbell sighs, "It would have been a people's movement." Mikey from Knowledge, Bob's Trench Town bred'ren, mourns, "But the peace didn't get the support." Considering how regularly so-called terrorists reinvent themselves as national statesmen, it's intriguing to imagine what might have become of Jamaica had the peace been encouraged. With the primary peacemakers gone, flawed as they may have been, one dimension of the dream died.

Yet rather than demotivating him, all these losses made Marley work even harder and be more determined to get his work done, as if he sensed forces closing in on him.

With its greater emphasis on love songs, the sparkling *Kaya* followed *Exodus*. Like Isaac Hayes on *Black Moses,* Bob wasn't scared to show that a tough man can—should—also be tender. A record of the *Exodus* tour came out, *Babylon by Bus* (1978), and then by the trilogy that rounded out his canon: *Survival* (1979), *Uprising* (1980), and the posthumous *Confrontation* (1983). Certainly, the recording of *Survival* and *Uprising* happened as Bob had always dreamed, with the sort of self-determination Marcus Garvey preached, in his own twenty-four-track studio at 56 Hope Road.

Assessing Bob's whole canon, his Rasta guru Mortimo Planno and Planno's disciple Nabbie say that *Exodus* is a transitional album in Bob's narrative, a gateway to the temple of his final earthly musical trinity. "Genesis can be translated as *Survival,* Exodus itself can be translated as *Uprising,* and Revelations as *Confrontation.* When you look at the Bible, the movement of Jah people is the journey to the fulfillment of the Book. Bob Marley's music is truly the message of the Rastaman."

Just as Bob said on *Rastaman Vibration,* that message is positive. Among Bob's commandments that his life teaches us are strength, struggle, endurance, and faith.

"Bob used to talk in great detail about having a studio where everything was made of gold," says Junior Marvin. The end of the Book of Exodus has page after page of precise detail about how to build the Tabernacle: "And he made thereunto four pillars of shittim wood, and overlaid them with gold; their hooks were of gold and he cast for them four sockets of silver" (Exodus 36:36). Indeed, Bob's final recordings were made under more control than he'd ever enjoyed before, in his own studio. After so many years of struggle, this state-of-the-art Tuff Gong studio was indeed Bob's Tabernacle, and its clean, contemporary design gleamed like precious metal in his eyes.

Riding on the success of *Exodus,* Bob was able to effect change in an immediate way, both in Jamaica and beyond. In Italy, where the Wailers had never been booked before, they played to more people than the Beatles in one concert. Bob was able to hire a private jet and put on a huge show for the Independence Day celebrations as Rhodesia finally became Zimbabwe in April 1980. Thousands of soldiers who had fought in the war there rushed the area and tried to get into the compound. As security struggled to control the forces with tear gas, Bob kept playing amid the anarchy, the last to leave the stage.

All around the world, reggae bands of every color have sprung up in his image. But for Bob Marley, undoubtedly one of his greatest satisfactions was finally managing to connect with the heart of America, as he had longed to do since listening to Curtis Mayfield and the Impressions on a transistor radio in a tenement yard in Trench Town.

"My intention is to bring reggae into the heart of America to help emancipate the minds of black people," Bob told his bred'ren Isaac Fergusson as he was going onstage to perform one of seven shows at Harlem's Apollo Theater in October 1979. Since the cancellation of the American *Exodus* tour because of his health concerns, Bob had longed to play Black America's classic venue. There were blocks-long lines of fans waiting outside the theater, and the Wailers tore it up. Bob was vigorous, happy, and energized, and as the audience responded with worship, Bob looked proud.

"After that show I went to Chris Blackwell's suite at the Essex House, Bob's New York crash pad, to find him furious angry and marching about the place cussing loudly. He was exploding with a couple of *baame claats* [Jamaican swear words] that shook the place," Isaac Fergusson recalls. "The singer of Inner Circle, Jacob Miller, had left Bob a nice portion of weed to enjoy after the concert, which his bred'ren had smoked up while he was out working."

Bob told Fergusson, "I know the responsibility and weight I carry talking for my people, but nobody will care about me until I *bow bow bow bow bow* with bullets." Here the singer gestured to indicate bullets penetrating his frame. Fergusson continues, "As fame engulfed Bob, with so many different strangers being brought into his life, it became harder to know who to trust and he became more suspicious—with good reason."

But Bob's ultimate enemy proved to be the cancer within his body. Only his determination to connect with black America enabled him to keep on moving. The next time he played New York, however, Bob was far more frail. Two nights at Madison Square Garden in September 1980 were carefully designed for maximum impact, as Bob would play with the Commodores. Isaac Fergusson was present to witness a remarkable musical moment.

Bob stepped forward to the edge of the stage, which seemed to surprise the other musicians. He plucked the first notes of "Redemption Song," his haunting acoustic testimony, recently released on the *Uprising* album. For what seemed a long time, Bob just surveyed the audience while they stared back at him. He seemed to be drinking in the sight of all these different sorts of Americans finally feeling what he'd been trying to express for all these years.

"In 'Redemption Song,' for the first time Bob really refers to himself by his Twelve Tribes name, Joseph, about whom the Bible says, 'For his hand was made strong by the hand of the Almighty,' " Fergusson says. "As he played the poignant melody, the crowd gave a mighty exhalation, as if Bob was breathing new life into them, and he smiled. There, on the stage at Madison Square Garden, Bob Marley manifested his identity and his destiny, and concluded one cycle of his mission to his flock."

That mission's progress was furthered when *Time* voted *Exodus* its Album of the Century in 1999. Marley's nominator was a Jamaican-born writer named Christopher John Farley, who recalls, "We took it seriously and everyone joined in the discussion. I actually sent *Exodus* out to as many people as I could, and that helped a lot. But in the end, the Wailers' win was the people's choice, and that's how Bob would have wanted it."

Many of Marley's hopes were never fulfilled. There is still no major organized alternative to the JLP and PNP, the parties that two well-connected cousins created in the 1930s. It was no secret that Bob's Island contract was up. He was about to sign a $10 million label-deal contract for Tuff Gong with Polygram Records. There were grand plans to create a sort of Jamaican Motown, involving every musician, and run with a different financial structure than the traditional music industry.

Before he left on that fateful American tour, Bob grounded with Mikey and the other Knowledge bred'ren down on First Street. Despite their protestations, Bob insisted he knew he would die soon. "Bwaoy, right after this tour done, I just want to build a rehearsal room and studio down in Trench Town," he said to Mikey, who somberly concludes, "That was the last thing he told me before the Boss Man went to the airport. But 'im never come back." A quarter of a century on, the open areas of Trench Town remain a lethal wasteland.

Bob never did get to cruise in his beloved silver BMW through the lush Jamaican landscape he treasured, or enjoy the tranquillity of his home at Nine Miles in total relaxation, enjoying the fruits of his labors. Nor did he repatriate to Ethiopia; the short time he spent there was made uncomfortable by the endless posters of Marx and Lenin. "Right now in Ethiopia they don't like any talk of

Selassie or Rasta. Because them bring off propaganda and want to change to a kind of Russian tradition. So I man say it's nice to go there but I don't really feel that the strength is there. Not until things change with the government and the people become the people again," he told Roz Reines in *The Face*.

Following Rasta advice, Bob chose not to have the toe amputation that conceivably could have saved him from cancer. During months of struggle, the failing warrior was baptized Berhane Selassie in the Ethiopian Orthodox Church. After treatment at the German clinic of a controversial physician, Dr. Josef Issels, Bob "flew away home" on May 11, 1981, to Miami. He just didn't make it to Jamaica.

In the true Rasta way, Bob refused to check for death. So it's ironic how Bob's funeral, which took over the entire island and was among the largest in the Western Hemisphere, became a measure of the man. The celebration of his life consolidated everything he'd achieved and suggested the extent of his incalculable impact on the world. From all corners of the earth, dignitaries, emissaries, and rock stars gathered, surprising one another and the media with Bob Marley's collective power.

As is true of all great men who pursue great ideals and who stay active all their lives, much about Robert Nesta Marley will always remain a mystery. But it's safe to say that reverberations of Marley's music will continue to "chant down Babylon." His profound body of work will always be manna in the wilderness to hungry minds and souls. New generations of sufferers and dreamers will still turn to Bob Marley's music for guidance, comfort, and inspiration, just as he turned to the Bible's Book of Exodus.

Bob's reply when I offered condolences on Claudie Massop's killing is a true testament: "I and I is Rasta and the struggle continues."

BIBLIOGRAPHY

UNLESS OTHERWISE ATTRIBUTED, all quotes in the book are from my own interviews, published in *Sounds, Melody Maker, New Musical Express,* and *Harpers & Queen,* or from the virtually innumerable interviews I conducted for this book over more than two years.

MAGAZINE ARTICLES

"Baroque Music Defined" (The Baroque Music Guide), www.baroque-music.org/bardefn.html.

"Classical Music Timeline" (WCPE), www.theclassicalstation.org.

Bhattacharji, Shobhana. "Triumphant Struggle," *Frontline,* vol. 15, no. 10. May 9–22, 1998.

Bradley, Lloyd. "Uprising!" *MOJO,* issue 136, March 2005.

Brazier, Chris. "Blacks Britannica," *Melody Maker,* September 9, 1978.

Campbell, Howard. "The Seaga Legacy: 'I consider West Kingston a diamond field,'" *The Jamaica Gleaner,* January 9, 2005.

Clarke, John Henry. "The American Antecedents of Marcus Garvey," www.africawithin.com/clarke/antecedents_of_garvey.htm.

Davis, Stephen. "Bob Marley: Sisterly Love." *Relix,* August 2004.

Dinham, Philip. "Making Change Happen in Real Jamaican Style . . . ," (September 1, 2002), www.jamaicans.com/articles/primecomments/0902_election1989.shtml.

Eder, Bruce. "Ernest Gold: Biography," *All Music Guide,* AMG.

Freedland, Michael. "Obituary: Elmer Bernstein," *Guardian Weekly*, Aug. 27–Sept. 2, 2004.

Fujiwara, Chris. "Otto Preminger," www.sensesofcinema.com/contents /directors/02/preminger.html.

Gayle, Carl. "Dread in-a Babylon," *Black Music*, September 1975.

———. "Getting My Share of Humiliation, Just Like the Blackheart Man," *Black Music*, October 1976.

Goldman, Vivien. "After the Flood: The Reggae Sunsplash '79," *Melody Maker*, July 14, 1979.

———. "Aswad: Hot with the Rods," *Sounds*, December 1976.

———. "Black Punks on 'Erb, Part 1," *Sounds*, October 16, 1976.

———. "Black Punks on 'Erb, Part 2," *Sounds*, October 23, 1976.

———. "Bob Marley: Movement of Jah People," *Sounds*, May 28, 1977.

———. "Can Reggae Stop War in Jamaica?" *Sounds*, April 29, 1978.

———. "Dread on Arrival: The Wailers' *Exodus* Tour," *Sounds*, May 28, 1977.

———. "Erban Culture: Culture," *Sounds*, March 18, 1978.

———. "Inner Circle: Reggae's Final Breakthrough," *Melody Maker*, February 24, 1979.

———. "Jah Punk, Pts 1 & 2: New Wave Digs Reggae, OK?" *Sounds*, September 3 & 10, 1977.

———. "Knocking Off the Opposition," *Melody Maker*, March 29, 1980.

———. "Lee Perry Has Found God, and His Name is Pipecock Jackson," *Melody Maker*, July 21, 1979.

———. "Marley, Treading a Dangerous Tightrope: A Review of *Exodus*," *Sounds*, May 21, 1977.

———. "Me Just Wanna Live, Y'Unnerstan?" *New Musical Express*, July 19, 1975.

———. "Peace Fighter Tapper Zukie," *Sounds*, April 8, 1978.

———. "Politics of Reggae: The One Love Peace Concert," *Harpers & Queen*, June 1978.

———. "Reggaematic Survival: Aswad," *Melody Maker*, November 11, 1978.

———. "Review: Bob Marley and the Wailers at Hammersmith Odeon, London," *Sounds*, May 21, 1977.

———. "So Much Things to Say," *Sounds*, June 11, 1977.

———. "The 3 Wise Is," *New Musical Express*, August 9, 1980.

———. "The Smoker You Drink, the Player You Get: Peter Tosh," *Sounds*, August 28, 1978.

———. "Uptown Ghetto Living," *Melody Maker*, August 11, 1979.

Goldman, Vivien, and Flip Fraser. "Rough Diamonds: The Mighty Diamonds," *Sounds*, August 21, 1976.

"Henry Burleigh, a Dedicated Gospel Performer!" (The African American Registry), www.aaregistry.com.

"Interview with Paul Robeson" (National Security Archives, George Washington University, 1998), www.gwu.edu/~nsarchiv/.

Kliers, Yael. "Roots—Ethiopian-Style," *The Jerusalem Report*, December 29, 2003.

Landau, Saul. "Behind the Violence in Jamaica" (ZNet Commentary), July 26, 2001, www.zmag.org/Zsustainers/Zdaily/2001-07/26landau.htm.

May, Chris. "Starting from Scratch, Lee Perry," *Black Music,* October 1977.

MOJO, issue 105. EMAP Metro Limited, August 2002.

MOJO: The Special Madness & the Ska Explosion Special Limited Edition, issue 16. EMAP Metro Limited.

MOJO: Trench Town London The World! issue 16, March 1995.

"*Moses und Aron,*" Opera News (Metropolitan Opera), www.metopera.org/synopses/moses.html.

Murrell, Nathaniel Samuel. "Tuning Hebrew Psalms to Reggae Rhythms: Rastas' Revolutionary Lamentations for Social Change," www.crosscurrents.org/murrell.htm.

"Music: Artist Profiles: Arnold Schoenberg" (BBC), www.bbc.co.uk/music/profiles/schoenberg.shtml.

Q/MOJO Bob Marley & Reggae Special Edition, vol. 1, issue 6, EMAP Metro Limited.

Reines, Roz. "Bob Marley's Fight to Live," *The Face,* January 1981.

Sobel, Dr. Ronald B. "Congregation of Emanu-El of the City of New York: A Brief History," www.emanuelnyc.org/history/history.html.

Sparacino, Micaele. "Program Notes: *Mosè in Egitto,*" Opera Camerata of Washington.

Spencer, Neil. "A Man for All Reasoning," *New Musical Express,* May 16, 1981.

Swafford, Jan. "Inventing America," *The Guardian,* September 26, 2003.

The Beat Bob Marley & the Wailers 20th Annual Collectors Edition, vol. 21, no. 3, 2002.

Van Biema, David. "The Legacy of Abraham," *Time*, vol. 160, no. 14, September 30, 2002.

Wendel, Dr. Thomas. "Antonin Dvořák," www.symphonysanjose.org/sym/season_Dvorak.asp.

Wignall, Mark. "Heather Robinson, an Honorable Politician," *The Jamaica Observer*, February 1, 2004.

———. "Vengeance Is Mine," *The Jamaica Observer*, May 8, 2005.

Williams, Richard. "Bob Marley: In the Studio with the Wailers," *Sounds*, June 23, 1973.

BOOKS

Barrett, Leonard E., Sr. *The Sun and the Drum: African Roots in Jamaican Folk Tradition* (Kingston, Jamaica: Sangster's Book Stores, in association with Heinemann, 1976).

Barrow, Steve, and Peter Dalton. *Reggae: The Rough Guide*. (London: Rough Guides Ltd., 1997).

Bedford, Henry F. *The Union Divides: Politics and Slavery, 1850–1861*. (New York: Macmillan Company, 1963).

Bizot, Jean-François. *Vaudou & Compagnies*. (Paris: Actuel/Editions de Panama, 2005).

Blake, Duane. *Shower Posse* (Rhode Island: Diamond Publishing, 2003).

Booker, Cedella. *Bob Marley: An Intimate Portrait by His Mother* (London: Penguin, 1997).

Boot, Adrian, and Chris Salewicz. *Bob Marley: Songs of Freedom* (New York: Viking Penguin, 1995).

Bradley, Lloyd. *Bass Culture: When Reggae Was King* (London: Penguin, 2000).

Brooks, Miguel F., trans., ed. *Kebra Nagast* (Kingston, Jamaica: LMH Publishing, 2001).

Budge, E. A. Wallis. *Egyptian Magic* (New York: Dover, 1971).

Campbell, Joseph. *The Hero with a Thousand Faces* (Princeton: Bollingen, 1972).

Chang, Kevin O'Brien, and Wayne Chen. *Reggae Routes: The Story of Jamaican Music* (Kingston, Jamaica: Ian Randle Publishers, 1998).

Cone, James H. *The Spirituals and the Blues* (New York: Seabury Press, 1972).

Cooper, Carolyn. *Sound Clash* (New York: Palgrave/Macmillan, 2004).

Davis, Stephen. *Bob Marley* (London: Plexus, 1993).

de Koningh, Michael, and Laurence Cane-Honeysett. *Young, Gifted & Black: The Story of Trojan Records* (London: Sanctuary Publishing, 2003).

de Las Casas, Bartolome. *The Devastation of the Indies,* Herma Briffault, trans. (Baltimore: Johns Hopkins University Press, 1992).

Dershowitz, Alan M. *The Genesis of Justice* (New York: Warner Books, 2000).

Duberman, Martin. *Paul Robeson* (New York: The New Press, 1989).

Eaton, George E. *Alexander Bustamante and Modern Jamaica* (Kingston, Jamaica: Kingston Publishers Limited, 1975).

Elias, Rabbi Joseph. *The Haggadah* (Brooklyn, N.Y.: Mesorah Publications, Ltd., 1995).

Emery, W. B. *Archaic Egypt* (London: Pelican, 1961).

Epstein, Dena J. *Sinful Tunes and Spirituals: Black Folk Music to the Civil War* (Urbana, Ill.: University of Illinois Press, 2003).

Epstein, Perle. *Kabbalah: The Way of the Jewish Mystic* (New York: Barnes & Noble Books, 1998).

Eson, Morris E. *Passover Haggadah for All Generations* (New York: Adraba, 2000).

Every Little Thing Gonna Be Alright: The Bob Marley Reader (Cambridge, Mass.: Da Capo Press, 2004).

Faulkner, William. *Go Down Moses* (New York: Vintage Books, 1973).

Frankel, Ellen. *The Five Books of Miriam: A Woman's Commentary on the Torah* (San Francisco: Harper San Francisco, 1996).

Freud, Sigmund. *Moses and Monotheism* (New York: Vintage Books, 1955).

Fryer, Peter. *Staying Power: The History of Black People in Britain* (London: Pluto Press, 1984).

Garvey, Marcus, and Amy Jacques Garvey. *The Philosophy and Opinions of Marcus Garvey, Or, Africa for the Africans* (Dover, Mass.: Majority Press, 1986).

Ginzberg, Louis. *Legends of the Bible* (Philadelphia: The Jewish Publication Society of America, 1992).

Goldman, Vivien, and Adrian Boot. *Bob Marley: Soul Rebel—Natural Mystic* (New York: St. Martin's Press, 1981).

Goldman, Vivien, and David Corio. *The Black Chord* (New York: Rizzoli, 2001).

Grossman, David. *The Second Book of Moses, Called Exodus: Authorized King James Version* (introduction). (New York: Grove Press, 1998).

Gunst, Laurie. *Born Fi' Dead* (New York: Henry Holt and Company, 1995).

Hammond, L. H. *In the Vanguard of a Race* (New York: Council of Women for Home Missions and Missionary Education Movement of the United States and Canada, 1922).

Himber, Charlotte. *Famous in Their Twenties* (New York: Association Press, 1942).

Hurston, Zora Neale. *Moses, Man of the Mountain* (Urbana, Ill.: University of Illinois Press, 1984).

Insight Guides: Jamaica (Hong Kong: APA Publications, 1995).

Kapuściński, Ryszard. *The Emperor* (New York: Vintage International, 1983).

Katz, David. *People Funny Boy: The Genius of Lee "Scratch" Perry* (London: Payback Press, 2001).

———. *Solid Foundation: An Oral History of Reggae* (New York: Bloomsbury USA, 2003).

Keneally, Thomas. *Moses the Lawgiver* (New York: Harper & Row, 1975).

Kessler, David. *The Falashas: The Forgotten Jews of Ethiopia* (London: George Allen & Unwin, 1982).

Kirsch, Jonathan. *Moses: A Life* (New York: Ballantine Books, 1998).

Lang, Paul Henry. *George Frideric Handel* (New York: Dover Publications, Inc., 1996).

———. "George Frideric Handel," *The Grove Concise Dictionary of Music* (Oxford/New York: Oxford University Press, 1988).

Laqueur, Walter. *Generation Exodus: The Fate of Young Jewish Refugees from Nazi Germany* (Hanover, N.H.: Brandeis University Press, 2001).

Lasar, Theodore. *The Lost Tribes of Israel Discovered* (New York: Earth Company, 1976).

Lee, Helene. *The First Rasta: Leonard Howell and the Rise of Rastafarianism* (Chicago: Lawrence Hill Books, 2003).

Leland, John. *Hip: The History* (New York: Ecco, 2004).

Mack, Douglas R. A. *From Babylon to Rastafari: Origin and History of the Rastafarian Movement* (Kingston, Jamaica: Research Associates School Times Publications, 1999).

Manuel, Peter, with Kenneth Bilby and Michael Largey. *Caribbean Currents: Caribbean Music from Rumba to Reggae* (Philadelphia: Temple University Press, 1995).

Marley, Rita. *No Woman No Cry—My Life with Bob Marley* (New York: Hyperion, 2004).

Matt, Daniel C. *The Essential Kabbalah* (New York: Quality Paperback Book Club, 1998).

Miles, Jack. *God: A Biography* (New York: Vintage, 1996).

Miller, Keith D. *Voice of Deliverance: The Language of Martin Luther King Jr. and Its Sources* (New York: The Free Press, 1992).

Morris, Dennis. *Bob Marley: A Rebel Life* (London: Plexus, 1999).

Murrell, Nathaniel Samuel, William David Spencer, and Adrian Anthony McFarlane, eds. *Chanting Down Babylon* (Kingston, Jamaica: Ian Randle Publishers, 1998).

Newman, Richard. *Go Down, Moses: Celebrating the African American Spiritual* (New York: Clarkson Potter, 1998).

Nicholson, Adam. *God's Secretaries: The Making of the King James Bible* (New York: Perennial, 2003).

Osborne, Richard. *Rossini* (Oxford/New York: Oxford University Press, 2002).

Plummer, John. *Movement of Jah People: The Growth of the Rastafarians* (Birmingham, England: Press Gang, 1978).

Robeson, Paul. *Here I Stand* (Boston: Beacon Press, 1988).

Robinson, Randall. *The Debt: What America Owes to Blacks* (New York: Dutton, 2000).

Salewicz, Chris. *Rude Boy* (London: Victor Gollancz, 2000).

Salewicz, Chris, and Adrian Boot. *Reggae Explosion: The Story of Jamaican Music* (New York: Harry N. Abrams, 2001).

Sarna, Nahum M. *Exploring Exodus: The Origins of Biblical Israel* (New York: Schocken Books, 1996).

Servadio, Gaia. *Rossini* (New York: Carroll & Graf, 2003).

Sewell, Tony. *Garvey's Children: The Legacy of Marcus Garvey* (Oxford, England: Macmillan Education, 1990).

Shawn, Arnold. *Arnold Schoenberg's Journey* (New York: Farrar, Straus & Giroux, 2002).

Sherlock, P., and Hazel Bennett. *The Story of the Jamaican People* (Kingston/Princeton: Ian Randle/Markus Wiener Publisher, 1998).

Simon, Kate. *Songs of Freedom* (London: Genesis, 2005).

Simpson, Anne Key. *Hard Trials: The Music and Life of Harry T. Burleigh* (Lanham, Md.: Scarecrow Press, 1990).

Sontag, Susan. *The Volcano Lover* (New York: Farrar, Straus & Giroux, 1992).

Steffens, Roger, and Leroy Jodie Pierson. *Bob Marley and the Wailers: The Definitive Discography* (Cambridge, Mass.: Rounder Books, 2005).

Stowe, Harriet Beecher. *Uncle Tom's Cabin* (New York: Random House, 1938).

Taylor, Don. *Marley and Me* (Kingston, Jamaica: LMH Publishing, 2001).

Thompson, Robert Farris. *Flash of the Spirit: African & Afro-American Art & Philosophy* (New York: Vintage, 1984).

Thurman, Howard. *Deep River and the Negro Spiritual Speaks of Life and Death* (Richmond, Ind.: Friends United Press, 1975).

Uris, Leon. *Exodus* (Garden City, N.Y.: Doubleday & Company, 1958).

White, Timothy. *Catch a Fire—The Life of Bob Marley* (New York: Henry Holt and Company, 1983).

Winkler, Anthony C. *Going Home to Teach* (Kingston, Jamaica: LMH Publishing, 1995).

Zimler, Richard. *The Last Kabbalist of Lisbon* (London: Arcadia Books, 1998).

LINER NOTES

Bond, Jeff. *Otto Preminger Presents* Exodus (Ernest Gold). Buddha Records, RCA LSO-1058.

Hicks, Anthony. *Israel in Egypt* (George Frideric Handel). King's College Choir, Cambridge, and the Brandenburg Consort, directed by Stephen Cleobury. Decca, 289-452-295-2.

Lazar, Moshe. *Moses und Aron* (Arnold Schoenberg). Royal Concertgebouw Orchestra, conducted by Pierre Boulez. Deutsche Grammophon, 449174-2.

Machart, Renaud. *Weihnachts Musik and Transcriptions* (Arnold Schoenberg). Arditti String Quartet, directed by Michel Béroff. Naïve, MO782160.

Pugliese, Giuseppe (M. Williams, trans.). *Mosè* (Gioachino Rossini). Orchestra e Coro del Teatro la Fenice, conducted by Gian Andrea Gwazzeni. Mondo Musica, MFOH10606.

ACKNOWLEDGMENTS

BLESSINGS

MY SPECIAL "SCHWISTA," the insightful photographer Janette Beckman: this book was born in our would-be endless chats at the late, lamented Jones Diner on Lafayette Street, Manhattan. Hail, Marsel. Cover photographer Kate Simon: my accomplice on so many of these adventures with Bob Marley and the Wailers. You shot what I saw, and more. Cheers to Rebecca Meek for seeing and manifesting my dream for the design. 'Nuff respect to all at Three Rivers Press, particularly Carrie Thornton, the best editor I've had in five books, and her eagle-eyed assistant, Brandi Bowles. My effervescent agent, William Clark, who really gets it. Emily Main saved me regularly with her clear transcribing and head. So thanks to these and more caring souls, named and un-named, for things ranging from just keeping the vibe alive to en-couragement, time, information, support both moral and very practical, and shelter on my *Exodus* quest.

My fellow Marley interviewers, biographers, and comrades: Chris Salewicz, Neil Spencer, Evet Hussey, Roz Reines, and Tim White in physical but not spiritual absentia. Likewise Denise Mills. My rigorous readers, critics, and think tank: Brian and Wayne Jobson; Tom Terrell; Stanley Meises; Naomi Gryn; Isaac Fergusson; Ras RoJAH Steffens; Colin Smikle; those fabulous Fictionaires, Evelyn McDonnell and Jana Martin; Michael Smith from the group Knowledge; and the Rasta historian Jah Blue, aka Norman Adams. His valuable book, *The Rastafari Movement in England: A Historical Report,* can be purchased by emailing: gwaworks@hotmail.com.

To all the Wailers family, particularly bassie Aston "Family Man" Barrett, Junior Marvin, Neville Garrick, Marcia Griffiths, Tony "Gilly" Gilbert, Karl Pitterson, Earl "Chinna" Smith, Vin Gordon, and Jennifer Miller.

The Island crew, old and new: Chris Blackwell, Suzette Newman, Brian Blevins, Rob and Tina Partridge, Tim Clark, Tom Hayes; the late Mary Blackwell, Charlie Comer, and Denise Mills; Cathy Snipper; and the folks at Strawberry Hill and Goldeneye: Miss Paulette, Clayton Hines, Jenny Wood, and Franklin. Universal's Bill Levenson and Stella McLaughlan.

The great Isaac Hayes and his assistant, Cheryl Riemer; Allan "Skill" Cole; Marni Nixon; Andrew and Martha Gold; Peter Bernstein; Lister Hewan-Lowe; Tommy Cowan; Ann, Samora, and Rico Hodges-Smikle; Sylvan Morris; Jim, Laura, James, Christina, Patrick Quinlan; Butch Morris; Bill and Gigi Laswell, Getty and Fifi Ghizaw; Maxine Walters; Clement "Sir Coxson" Dodd; Ziggi Golding; Jon Baker; Ernest Ranglin; Evet Hussey; Mitzi Evans; Towta Harvey; Vin Gordon; Dermot Hussey; Elena Oumano; Andrea Hutchence; Robert, Cohl, Stella, and Nora Katz; David and Lai Ngan Corio; Barbara Serlin; Don Letts; Tung Walsh; Dan Asher; Nigel Churchill; Brian Bacchus; Oberon Sinclair; Jon Carin and Scarlett; Robert Arbor; Mariane Pearl; Spencer; Noah, and Blaze Kidron-Style; Eve, Kevin, Paloma, and Olivier Tooley-Parkes; Monifah, Joel, Joel Jr., and Savannah Smith; Adriana Kaegi and Darman Lopez; Nina Ritter and Ron Burman; Lee Alexander; Sean O'Hagan; Bishop Richard Holloway; Rabbi Larry Tabick; Matisyahu, Aaron Bisman, and JDub Records; Ziggi Golding; Jon Baker; Nancy Burke; Andrea Hutchence; Nabbie Natural, Planno's devoted disciple; Ira Heaps and Malcolm Allen from Jammyland, Manhattan's home of reggae, virtual residence Jammyland.com; C. C. Smith & the Beat; Diane Jobson;

Perry Henzell; Dick Cuthell; Terry Barham; Pops; Delroy Washington; Jerry Dammers; Herbie Miller; Stephanie Black and her documentary, *Life and Debt;* Fifi and Getty Ghizaw; King Sounds; Michael Campbell; Plucky; Moses Bushiza, a true Exodus baby and inspiration; Andy, Lucilla, Chester, and Alfie Caine; Mick Brown; Caroline Coon; Leroy Anderson; Angus Gaye; Brinsley Forde; Jonh Ingham; Dave Fudger; Jon Savage; Dennis Bovell; Cimarons; Misty in Roots and Chris Bolton; John and Nora Lydon; Jeanette Lee-Sager, Geoff Travis and Rough Trade; Jumbo Vanrenen; Richard Branson; Weasel; Adrian Sherwood; Arri, Tessa, Viv Slit, and Phoebe Oliver; Moki and Neneh Cherry and all the party people; Andrea and Miquita Oliver, and Garfield Swaby; and a special African warrior, Ba. Carolyn Cooper at UWI; Touter, Ian, and Monty from Inner Circle (*Fatman Posse* rocks!); Ed Steinberg; Cat Coore from Third World; Michael Cogswell and the Louis Armstrong Foundation; Sticky; Cindy Breakspeare; Brian Bacchus; Dean Bowman, Jason Fine; and *Rolling Stone;* Lee "Scratch" and Mireille Perry David Katz; Caspar Llewellyn-Smith, Caryl Phillips, John Reider, Betsy Schmidt, and Barnard's Forum on Migration; Sue Steward; Dave and Kim Evans-Hucker; Nick "Manasseh" Raphael; Youth; Trevor Wyatt; Mick Cater; Dave Harper; the Clive Davis Department of Recorded Music at NYU's Tisch School of the Arts; Jim Anderson; Jason King; Jeff Tang; Katherine Flatt; and the rest. Do forgive me if I lost your name in that computer crash, and I do include you NYU interns, you know who you are. To my cousins Zachary Baker and James Russell; and big up to my Trench Town posse, the much Massive Dread, aka Denis James; his widow, Lona, and son Vivian; Jerry and the Village Drums of Freedom; Junior Widdecombe; & Mortimo Planno, who left us March 5, 2006.

And, of course, Hashem and Jah. In alphabetical order.

LIVICATION

THE DEATH OF BOTH my parents has somehow bracketed my experiences with Bob Marley, both in life and in the hectic mind contact one experiences while writing. My father died on the morning in July 1975 when I was due to pick up the Wailers from Heathrow Airport for their Lyceum show. En route to Bob Marley's 1981 funeral in Jamaica, the car I was in with Jamaican friends was attacked by a mob, and my father's cherished watch was stolen through the window while the car was rocked savagely from side to side. We were lucky to escape with our lives. After a decade of illness, my mother, a teenage refugee from Nazi Germany who'd landed in London, died on the day after I completed the first draft of this book in 2004. Irrational, perhaps, but I can only feel that last act of motherly timing enabled you to read this. Other ancestors to honor include my beloved aunts—my mother's sister, Hilde Sandler, and her cousin, Auntie Judy Bachrach, as well as the aunt I was named after but never knew, Chanya, a concert pianist who sheltered my father in Poland when he fled Nazi-era Berlin, but was taken to a concentration camp herself. She survived and moved to Israel, but no longer played professionally. So this song is also for her, and for Wilfred and Kimanee Barrett, the father and twenty-three-year-old son of Wailers cofounder and bass player Family Man, both killed in Kingston.

The solidarity that my sibs, Judith Goldenberg and Susan Godfrey, offered while I wrote this book, showing true sisterhood, is a tribute to our Exodus ancestors' struggle. Respect also to patriarch Jack Godfrey for all those amazing Seders, and Harvey Slippacoff; Louis Roseman; Michal Roseman, Miriam Levene, and their crews; Rachel, Mark, Max, Avigail, Rebecca, and Benjy; Aaron Gaby and my great great-nieces and nephews.

Sadly, however, though Bob Marley's sons work closely, there is little harmony among the Wailers' old extended family at the time of writing. Family Man Barrett tours with a Wailers lineup that includes guitarist Junior Marvin and horn player Glen Da Costa, and appearances by other Wailers regulars, such as guitar player Earl "Chinna" Smith and trombonist Vin Gordon, enabling a new generation to enjoy the real roots rhythms and be touched by Marley's canon played as only they can. However, the acrimony between the Wailers band and the Marley Estate has led to lawsuits that will commence next year. Although the situation currently resembles some of Bob Marley's more acerbic, cynical songs, like "The Heathen" or "Guiltiness," one can only hope that the communal spirit of Rasta and "One Love" will soon prevail.

After completing this book I traveled to Jamaica again; I can't count the times I've been there since 1976. Being in Trench Town again, Bob's old neighborhood that he hymned about so powerfully, I was saddened and angered by how, despite its restless energy, the area has declined. MTV and Jamaican TV were screening downtown Kingston on repeat with Damian Marley's stylish video for his conscious hit, "Welcome to Jamrock." It is the "Junior Gong's" signifier of some cold facts: ten men had just been shot dead in one weekend; and according to local estimates, over three-quarters of the local people are functionally illiterate. The frustration and feelings of inadequacy and rage that illiteracy can induce create a breeding-ground for violence. With few professional options, some hungry, angry man will always be convinced to take up the gun to feed his family.

Attempting to break the cycle is challenging. The Bob Marley Foundation does good work downtown, often on an unpublicized individual basis. A Canadian woman, Roslyn Ellison, has worked with the community to organize the Trench Town Reading Center, a modern library around the corner from where Bob was raised. My dear friend, Trench Town DJ Massive Dread, aka Dennis James, was killed by gunmen on January 22, 1995, for promoting this and other community efforts, like the Trench Town Culture Yard and Museum. Spearheaded by Jamaican architect Christopher Whyms-Stone, they have set up the Victory Basic School and renovated Marley's old Government Yard, with help from the German embassy and others, as a community center for tourists and locals alike. The plan is to provide Internet access downtown and acquire a library vehicle to visit both JLP and PNP areas, thus bypassing the brutal duality of interparty violence to inspire a new, more empowered generation. But all involved undergo threats and harassment. One prime Culture Yard mover I'd met there two years previously, the spiritual artist Jah Stone, has been forced to leave the area.

The violent confrontations described in this book between gunmen from the opposing political parties still occur constantly; but now the gunmen, still effectively controlled by larger political forces, are armed for real war and crazier because of cocaine. The Reading Center and Culture Yard crews represent the true Movement of Jah People Spirit. They intend to break the cycle in the only way possible—by educating the youth, creating possibilities beyond the tired old PNP/JLP duels. It's a rare gunman who doesn't want to see his child have a better life, and Bob Marley's dream of peace in the ghetto can still happen. A portion of the proceeds of this book will go toward that dream.

If you wish to contribute independently, please send all donations to the chairman of the Trench Town Reading Center, Roslyn Ellison, at:

www.trenchtownreadingcentre.com

or

For further information on the Trench Town Culture Yard, contact project manager Christopher Whyms-Stone at:

www.trenchtowncultureyard.com or stonec@kasnet.com.

Claudie Massop's widow, Syd, has established a developmental training school called Port Antonio Design & Training, which also deserves support. Their contact: portantoniodesigns@yahoo.com. Finally, my sincere apologies in advance for any accidental omissions or errors in this book. Please feel free to contact me with additional information at www.viviengoldman.com

One love
Vivien Goldman, LES, NYC 2006

INDEX

About the Author:

Vivien Goldman wrote Bob Marley's first biography, *Bob Marley, Soul Rebel—Natural Mystic* (1981) and *The Black Chord* (1999), connecting music in the African diaspora. This is her fifth book. A writer, broadcaster, and musician, Goldman has devoted much of her work to Afro-Caribbean and global perspectives. Her journalism has appeared in the *New York Times, Interview, Rolling Stone, Spin,* the *Daily Telegraph,* and *The Beat,* among others. Currently, Goldman is an adjunct professor at the Clive Davis Department of Recorded Music at NYU's Tisch School of the Arts, teaching courses on reggae and punk music. A Londoner, Goldman lives on Manhattan's Lower East Side.

Printed in the United States
by Baker & Taylor Publisher Services